THE G
LONDON
— BY —
BUS & TUBE

Judy Allen

ROBERT NICHOLSON PUBLICATIONS
in association with
London Transport

A Nicholson Guide

First published in 1987 by Robert Nicholson Publications
16 Golden Square London W1R 4BN in association with
London Transport 55 Broadway SW1H 0BD

© Text and illustrations, **Robert Nicholson Publications 1987**
© Central London maps and London Underground map,
London Regional Transport 1987

Design by Bob Vickers
Line drawings by Matthew Doyle

The author would like to thank the editor, Jacqueline Krendel, for her
encouragement and assistance during the compilation of this guide. Thanks are also
due to Graham Woodall and his team at London Transport for the prompt and
invaluable supply of information on all aspects of travelling in London.

Typeset by Rowland Phototypesetting Ltd,
Bury St Edmunds, Suffolk.
Printed in Great Britain by Scotprint Ltd, Musselburgh.

ISBN 0 948576 08 1

Contents

Using this guide

This new Nicholson guide has been specially designed to enable both the Londoner and the visitor to get the best out of London by using public transport. The introduction deals practically with all aspects of transport in the capital, including an easy-to-use listing of the principal bus routes servicing Central London.

The A–Z gazetteer features more than 500 places, sights and attractions clearly presented in alphabetical order. Wherever possible, gazetteer entries are map referenced to the Central London maps at the back of the book (e.g. **Houses of Parliament 3P4**). At the end of every entry, the nearest Underground station is given, as well as the numbers of the buses which stop at or near the place described. In some cases, British Rail stations and Green Line coach numbers are supplied where these services provide an alternative or better means of arriving at a particular destination. Stations on the forthcoming Docklands Light Railway are also given where applicable.

The final section of the guide is devoted to 10 sightseeing days in London. Each day has its own theme (e.g. Royal London) with an itinerary which can be followed in its entirety or dipped into for suggestions on how to spend a few hours or more. All the places included in the days out section are fully described with transport details in the gazetteer.

With comprehensive information, street and transport maps, this guide can genuinely claim to get you there. But, London is a fast-paced city. Its services and facilities can often change at short notice. So to avoid disappointment, it is always recommended to telephone in advance before embarking on a special journey and to check all travel details with London Transport's 24-hour information service.

Symbols and abbreviations used in the guide:

⊖	Nearest Underground station	*L*	Lunch
▦	Buses stopping at or nearby	*D*	Dinner
⇌	Nearest British Rail station		

The word *Charge* denotes an entrance fee.

How to use London Transport

The public transport system in and around London is very extensive. For some journeys, bus is best – and certainly it is preferable for those who want to enjoy the view. For some journeys the Underground is best – and certainly it is faster. In South London, where the Underground system is more limited, British Rail Southern Region fills the gaps. For long journeys, a combination of two, or even of all three, modes of transport may be necessary. London Transport (LT) is ready to advise on any and all possible journeys within the whole Greater London area.

If the timing of a journey is crucial, it is wise to bear in mind that the advertised departure and arrival times, in particular of buses, are ideals which cannot always be achieved. Wet roads, rush hour traffic jams, and road works all conspire to delay overland transport.

LT has come a long way since the days of horse-drawn trams – a visit to the London Transport Museum in Covent Garden shows just how far. This fascinating and extensive collection of buses, trams, trolleybuses and tube trains appeals to all ages, especially as visitors are encouraged to try out some of the controls themselves.

London Transport Information

Twenty-four hour information

For any information on travel in Greater London – routes, fares, times – telephone 01-222 1234 at any time of the day or night.

Travel Information Centres

These Centres give detailed information on any aspect of travelling in and around London; offer free bus and Underground maps and other travel literature; sell London Explorer and other special tickets; and take bookings for guided tours on which special discounts are often available. They are at:

Charing Cross Station *Open Mon–Sun 08.15–18.00.*
Euston Station *Open Mon–Thur & Sat 07.15–18.00; Fri 07.15 –19.30; Sun 08.15–18.00.*
King's Cross Station *Open Mon–Thur, Sat & Sun 08.15 –18.00; Fri 08.15–19.30.*

Oxford Circus Station *Open Mon–Wed, Fri & Sat 08.15–18.00; Thur 08.15–21.30; closed Sun.*
Piccadilly Circus Station *Open Mon–Sun 08.15–21.30.*
St James's Park Station *Open Mon–Fri 08.15–17.00; closed Sat & Sun.*
Victoria Station *Open Mon–Sun 08.15–21.30.*
Heathrow Terminals 1,2,3, Station *Open Mon–Sat 07.15–21.00; Sun 08.15–21.30.*
Heathrow Terminal 1, Arrivals *Open Mon–Sat 07.30–21.30; Sun 08.30–21.30.*
Heathrow Terminal 2, Arrivals *Open Mon–Sat 08.00–17.00; Sun 08.15–18.00.*
Heathrow Terminal 3, Arrivals *Open Mon–Sat 06.45–13.00; Sun 08.15–15.00.*
Heathrow Terminal 4, Arrivals *Open Mon–Sat 06.45–21.00; Sun 08.15–21.30.*
West Croydon Bus Station *Open Mon–Sat 08.00–19.00; closed Sun.*

Underground Stations
Underground stations in Central London also carry a stock of free bus and Underground maps.

London Buses

The first London omnibus, drawn by three horses, travelled from the Yorkshire Stingo pub in Paddington to The Bank of England on 4th July 1829. Today there are approximately 5,000 motor-driven buses, organised into 350 routes, covering 1,700 miles of road.

The red double-decker London bus is a well-known feature of the London scene, although there are a few red single-deckers too. Buses of different colours may be found on some LT routes – look for the familiar bar and circle symbol on the front of the bus to tell you if your LT ticket is valid.

Routes

An extensive network of routes covers London and outlying areas and links with British Rail stations and the London Underground system to ensure that any part of Greater London is accessible from any other part.

Bus Stops

There are two different types of bus stop, each with its own symbol; the compulsory stop 🚍 at which every bus will stop, and the request stop ⊖ at which the bus will only stop if you hold out your hand in good time; if the bus is full it won't stop at all. If you are on the bus and wish to get off at a request stop, you must ring the bell, again, in good time.

Most bus stops in Central London are named. The name is written on the bus stop sign and in some cases on the shelter as well.

All bus stops in Central London, and many in outlying areas, carry information on routes and on planned times of buses, including last buses. Many also carry a map of the immediate vicinity. If you are in a one-way traffic system, this map will clearly show where you may pick up the bus on its return trip.

Queueing

It is customary to queue (better known to Americans as making a line) at bus stops – and a lot of bad feeling can be generated by anyone who slips on to a bus ahead of the queue!

Paying

On one-person operated buses, the driver will take the fare as you enter. These buses are entered from the front.

On buses which have both driver and conductor, the conductor will come to you to take the fare. These buses are usually entered from the back.

Smoking

There is no smoking at all on single-decker buses, on the lower deck of double-decker buses, or at the front of the top deck. Smoking is permitted on the rear seats of the top deck only.

Luggage

Luggage is taken on board at the discretion of the driver or conductor – and the same applies to dogs.

Night Buses

Night buses – which have the prefix N added to their route numbers on bus maps and time-tables – now serve all major points in Central London and very many outlying areas too. They take over where last daytime buses leave off between *23.00* and *24.00*, continue until first buses start out, and tend to be speedier than day buses because there is so little traffic. All major night bus routes pass through Trafalgar Square.

Note that it is wise to hold out your hand for a night bus, even at a compulsory stop, in case the driver doesn't see you in the dark.

Red Arrows

The one-man operated single-decker Red Arrow buses are principally railway station links, shopper and commuter buses. There
are five of them:
the 500 links Victoria Station with Oxford Circus and operates
from *Mon–Sat, but not evenings*;
the 501 links Waterloo, Holborn and London Bridge and operates
from *Mon–Fri, but not evenings*;
the 502 links Waterloo, Fleet Street and Liverpool Street and
operates *from Mon–Fri, but not evenings*;
the 507 links Victoria with Waterloo and operates from *Mon–Sun
and evenings*;
the 513 links Waterloo and London Bridge and operates from
Mon–Fri during peak hours only.

Minibuses

London Transport have recently introduced some Minibus routes
using small, single-decker buses operating at frequent intervals.
The two that are currently in operation are the C1 and C2 on
which standard bus fares apply and all LT tickets are valid.

London Underground

The London Underground system, the first in the world, was
opened in 1863 with the Metropolitan line, which then consisted
of seven stations between Paddington and Farringdon. It now
serves 248 Underground stations, as well as a further 20 or so
British Rail stations.

London Underground stations can be easily recognised by
the distinctive symbol ⊖. The Underground, often called 'the
tube' by Londoners, is the fastest method of getting from A to B
in London because it avoids the traffic.

Routes

An extensive network of routes travels under Central London and
on to the outlying areas. The system also links with British Rail
stations. A complete Underground map, on which the different
routes are colour-coded, is prominently displayed in every Underground station. See p. 144 of this guide.

Paying

There is a ticket office in every station. In many there are also automatic ticket machines which can give change. It is essential to have a ticket before boarding the train.

Turnstiles

In some stations you pass through an automatic turnstile in order to reach the trains. Feed the ticket in to the turnstile, pass through, and remember to pick up the ticket the other side. Tickets are always handed in or shown to a collector on the way out.

Escalators

Stand on the right; keep moving on the left. Dogs and small children must be carried.

Smoking

No smoking is allowed on Underground trains at any time, nor is smoking permitted anywhere in stations which are underground.

Luggage

There is no restriction on reasonably-sized luggage, and dogs travel free.

Weekends and evenings

The following central area Underground stations are closed at weekends or in the evenings due to lack of demand:
Aldwych *open Mon–Fri peak hours only; closed evenings and Sat & Sun.*
Barbican *closed Sun.*
Cannon Street *closed evenings and Sat & Sun.*
Chancery Lane *closed Sun.*
Kensington Olympia *closed Sun.*
Mornington Crescent *closed Sat & Sun.*
Shoreditch *open Mon–Fri peak hours only and Sun mornings; closed all Sat and evenings.*
Temple *closed Sun.*
West Brompton *closed Sat & Sun.*

Last Underground trains

Last trains leave Central London between *24.00 & 24.30 Mon –Sat* and between *23.30 & 24.30 Sun.*

Airport Connections

Heathrow

Airbuses

There are two airbuses, each with plenty of luggage space, which connect the individual terminals at Heathrow with Central London.

The **A1** travels between Victoria Station and Heathrow, calling at Hyde Park Corner, Cromwell Road (Forum Hotel) and Cromwell Road (junction with Earl's Court Road). The A1 *operates every day from early morning to mid evening* at approximately 20-minute or 30-minute intervals. Total journey time is 50–75 minutes.

The **A2** travels between Euston Station and Heathrow, calling at Russell Square, Southampton Row, Marble Arch, Bayswater Road (Albion Street, Lancaster Gate and Queensway), Notting Hill Gate and Holland Park (Kensington Hilton). The A2 *operates every day from early morning to mid evening* at approximately 30-minute intervals. Total journey time is 65–80 minutes.

Night bus **N97** provides an all-night link between Central London and Heathrow *every night*.

Underground link

There is an Underground link between Central London and Heathrow on the Piccadilly line, with a train running every 5–10 minutes. You can travel direct from the following stations: Baron's Court, Earl's Court, Gloucester Road, Green Park, Hammersmith, Holborn, Hyde Park Corner, King's Cross, Knightsbridge, Leicester Square, Piccadilly Circus, Russell Square and South Kensington. The journey from Central London takes approximately 45 minutes. The Piccadilly line links up with other lines on the London Underground system. It is possible to get to Heathrow from any station on the Piccadilly line but there might not always be a through train, so you may have to change at Hammersmith or Acton Town.

Gatwick

British Rail runs the Gatwick Express from Victoria Station. There are *four trains an hour from 06.00 to 24.00*, and *one train an hour from 24.00 to 06.00*. Buy a through ticket, via Victoria, from any underground station. Journey time from Victoria is 30 minutes.

Zones

To ensure that fares are fair, London has been divided into zones. There are three bus zones. The Central Zone covers the West End and the City. Its boundaries are Kensington to the west, Shoreditch to the east, Elephant and Castle to the south, and Baker Street and King's Cross to the north. The Inner Zone is a ring about three miles wide which encircles the Central Zone. The Outer Zone extends from the edges of the Inner Zone right to the boundaries of the Greater London area, and sometimes slightly beyond. In the case of the Underground system, the Outer Zone is further subdivided into three zones, making five in all.

Special Tickets

LT issues certain special tickets, which can save both time and money.

London Explorer

The most useful ticket for the visitor is the London Explorer, which can cover one, three, four or seven days according to need. It is valid on bus, Underground train and Airbus. The ticket includes discount vouchers for a number of London attractions. Personal photographs are not needed to acquire the London Explorer pass.

One Day Bus Passes

These are available for Outer and Inner Zones only.

Weekly, Monthly and Annual Bus Passes

These can be purchased to cover one, two or three zones. You need a small passport-sized photograph.

Travelcards

These may be purchased to cover one or any combination of two or more zones, and are valid on bus and Underground. You need a small passport-sized photograph. There is also a one-day Off-Peak Travelcard which *cannot be used before 09.30 Mon–Fri*, but can be used at *any time on Sat & Sun*.

Capitalcards

These can be purchased to cover two or more zones and are valid on bus, Underground and British Rail. You need a passport-sized photograph. There is also a one-day Capitalcard which *cannot be used before 09.30 Mon–Fri*, but can be used at *any time on Sat & Sun*.

Child Bus Passes and Travelcards

These offer the same facilities as the adult passes, but a passport-sized photograph and proof of age must be presented to a London Post Office or London Buses garage which will issue a Child-Rate Photocard, which in turn must be presented when buying the Child Bus Pass or Travelcard.

Where to buy Special Tickets

The London Explorer passes are available from the LT Travel Information Centres. Explorers, other special tickets and passes are also available from Underground stations. Bus-only passes may also be bought from some newsagents or from bus garages.

Sightseeing Bus Tours

The Original London Transport Sightseeing Tour is the only one to use traditional red London buses with the open platform at the back. All tours are accompanied by a qualified guide.

Boarding points

Board the bus in the Haymarket, or at Speaker's Corner, at Baker Street Station or at Victoria Underground Station. *Tours run daily*, at roughly hourly intervals, *between 10.00 and 17.00*, and take about 1½ hours.

Paying

Pay as you board the tour, or book in advance at one of the LT Travel Information Centres where you get a discount and can ask for a special discount ticket which allows entry to Madame Tussaud's ahead of the queues.

Touristlink T2

This is an unguided bus tour service calling at all London's principal sights. You pay only once and can get off and get on again all day. *Operates summer months only.*

Sights to See

The tours take in all the main sights of London, including Picca-
dilly Circus, the National Gallery, Nelson's Column, Horse
Guards, the Houses of Parliament, Lambeth Palace, St Clement
Danes, the Mansion House, HMS Belfast, the Tower of London,
St Paul's Cathedral, Westminster Abbey, Buckingham Palace,
the Royal Albert Hall and Marble Arch.

Sightseeing Coach Tours

Day and half-day tours run all year, although there are fewer in the
winter months than during the summer season. Each coach
carries a well-informed tour guide. Lunch is usually included, and
the price is always inclusive of any admission charges. A few
tours combine bus and river boat for best effect.

Boarding point

All coaches depart from Wilton Road Coach Station in Victoria.
Courtesy coaches are provided from the main hotel areas of
London to connect with the tours which start in Wilton Road.

Booking

Booking in advance is wise. Go to any of the LT Travel Information
Centres; to Wilton Road Coach Station or any National Express
agent; to any major London hotel; to the London Visitor and
Convention Bureau at Victoria Station; to Selfridges or Harrods.
Or book by post from Travel Information London Transport, 55
Broadway, London SW1H 0BD. Any of the above will supply free
leaflets with full details of available tours. For further information
telephone 01-222 3456.

Sights to See

There are various London tours from full-day tours to speciality
tours, including 'London and the River by Night', and 'Greenwich
and the Thames Barrier'. There are also many tours and excur-
sions going further afield including tours to Richmond and Hampton Court; Royal Windsor; Chartwell and Hever Castle; Oxford
and Stratford-upon-Avon; Stonehenge and Bath; Canterbury and
Leeds Castle, and Warwick Castle. Ask for details at any LT Travel
Information Centre.

Lost Property

With luck and honesty, anything left on a bus or Underground train should turn up at the Lost Property Office, 200 Baker Street, NW1; *open 09.30–14.00 Mon–Fri.* Personal callers and postal enquiries only. There is also a 24-hour recorded information service on 01-486 2496.

Docklands Light Railway

The latest addition to LT is this elevated light railway, to be opened in summer 1987, to service the old docklands area with its rapidly expanding new business and accommodation developments.

Green Line Coaches

The single-decker one-person operated Green Line coaches are not run by LT but provide useful links with points outside Greater London. Information about these services can be obtained by telephoning 01-668 7261.

British Rail

British Rail is best known for the Inter-City trains which link major towns and cities all over the country. However, it also runs many suburban lines. In South London, the Southern Region suburban trains provide a useful alternative and indeed, a vital supplement to bus and Underground travel – especially as the London Underground has a rather limited service south of the River Thames.

London Transport 24-hour information service
For any information on travel in Greater London – routes, fares, times – telephone 01-222 1234 at any time of the day or night.

Guide to Central London Bus Routes

Below is a guide to the principal Central London bus routes included in this book, showing the main places they serve.

All routes operate in both directions so you can use the information here to tell you which direction the bus should be travelling to get you where you want to go. For example, if you are at Aldwych and want to take bus 6 to Little Venice, you know you want to get on one travelling towards Kensal Rise. The names printed in capital letters (eg BAKER STREET) are terminal points.

Details of other buses not included in this list (and rush hour variations) are given on the bus stops they serve or you can call in at any LT Travel Information Centre or telephone 01-222 1234.

1
Mon Sun
MARYLEBONE*, Baker St*, OXFORD CIRCUS and Oxford St, Charing Cross Rd, Leicester Sq, Trafalgar Sq, Strand, Aldwych, Waterloo, Surrey Docks, GREENWICH. (*No service to these points evenings or Sat & Sun.)

2B
Mon–Sun
BAKER STREET STATION, Oxford St, Marble Arch, Park Lane, Hyde Park Corner, Victoria, Vauxhall, Brixton, CRYSTAL PALACE.

3
Mon–Sun
OXFORD CIRCUS, Regent St, Piccadilly Circus, Trafalgar Sq, Whitehall, Westminster, Lambeth Bridge, Brixton, CRYSTAL PALACE.

4
Mon–Sat
WATERLOO, Aldwych, Fleet St, St Paul's, Barbican, Islington, Finsbury Park, ARCHWAY.

6
Mon–Sun
KENSAL RISE, Little Venice, Edgware Rd, Marble Arch, Oxford St, Piccadilly Circus, Trafalgar Sq, Strand, Aldwych, Fleet St, St Paul's, Bank, Liverpool St, HACKNEY WICK.

7
Mon–Sun
TOTTENHAM COURT ROAD STATION (Mon–Fri only), OXFORD CIRCUS and Oxford St, Marble Arch, Paddington, Ladbroke Grove, ACTON (and to Kew and RICHMOND on Sun).

8
Mon–Sun
WILLESDEN, Kilburn, Maida Vale, Edgware Rd, Marble Arch, Oxford St, Bloomsbury, Holborn, St Paul's, Bank, Liverpool St, Shoreditch, Bethnal Green, OLD FORD.

9
Mon–Sun
LIVERPOOL STREET STATION, Bank, St Paul's, Fleet St, Aldwych, Strand, Trafalgar Sq, Piccadilly, Hyde Park Corner, Knightsbridge, Kensington, Hammersmith, MORTLAKE.

10
Mon–Sun
VICTORIA*, Lambeth Bridge*, Elephant & Castle*, LONDON BRIDGE, Monument, Aldgate, Whitechapel, Mile End, Stratford, WANSTEAD. (*No evening service to these points.)

11
Mon–Sun
LIVERPOOL STREET STATION, Bank, St Paul's, Fleet St, Aldwych, Strand, Trafalgar Sq, Whitehall, Westminster, Victoria, Sloane Sq, Chelsea, Fulham, HAMMERSMITH (and to SHEPHERD'S BUSH Mon–Sat except evenings).

12
Mon–Sun
EAST ACTON, Shepherd's Bush, Notting Hill, Bayswater Rd, Marble Arch, Oxford St, Regent St, Piccadilly Circus, Trafalgar Sq, Whitehall, Westminster, Elephant & Castle, Camberwell, Peckham, DULWICH/PENGE.

13
Mon–Sun
ALDWYCH*, Strand*, Trafalgar Sq*, Piccadilly Circus*, Regent St*, OXFORD CIRCUS and Oxford St, Marylebone/Baker St, St John's Wood, Swiss Cottage, Golders Green, NORTH FINCHLEY. (*No service to these points on Sun.)

14
Mon–Sun
EUSTON*, Tottenham Court Rd/Gower St, Charing Cross Rd, Shaftesbury Av, Piccadilly, Hyde Park Corner, Knightsbridge, South Kensington, Fulham, PUTNEY HEATH. (*Runs on to/from King's Cross and TURNPIKE LANE on Sun.)

14A
Mon–Sat
PICCADILLY CIRCUS, Shaftesbury Av, Charing Cross Rd, Tottenham Court Rd/Gower St, Euston, King's Cross, Holloway, HORNSEY RISE/TURNPIKE LANE.

15
Mon–Sun
LADBROKE GROVE, Paddington, Edgware Rd, Marble Arch, Oxford St, Regent St, Piccadilly Circus, Trafalgar Sq, Strand, Aldwych, Fleet St, St Paul's, Monument, Tower, Aldgate, Stepney, Poplar, EAST HAM.

15A
Mon–Fri
As **15** but from St Paul's runs via Bank instead of Monument and Tower.

16
Mon–Sun
VICTORIA, Hyde Park Corner, Park Lane, Marble Arch, Edgware Rd, Maida Vale, Kilburn, Cricklewood, NEASDEN.

16A
Mon–Sat
OXFORD CIRCUS and Oxford St, Marble Arch, Edgware Rd, Maida Vale, Kilburn, Cricklewood, BRENT CROSS (not evenings).

17
Mon–Sat
LONDON BRIDGE*, Southwark Bridge*, St Paul's*, Holborn, Gray's Inn Rd, King's Cross, Holloway, Archway, NORTH FINCHLEY. (*No service to these points evenings or Sat.)

18
Mon–Sun
KING'S CROSS*, Euston*, BAKER ST, Marylebone Rd, Paddington, Kensal Green, Harlesden, Wembley, SUDBURY. (*No service to these points evenings; no service at King's Cross on Sun.)

19
Mon–Sun
FINSBURY PARK, Islington, Rosebery Av, Holborn, Bloomsbury, Charing Cross Rd, Shaftesbury Av, Piccadilly, Hyde Park Corner, Knightsbridge, Sloane Sq, Chelsea, Battersea, Clapham Junction, TOOTING.

22
Mon–Sun
HOMERTON, Liverpool St, Bank, St Paul's, Holborn, Bloomsbury, Charing Cross Rd, Shaftesbury Av, Piccadilly, Hyde Park Corner, Knightsbridge, Sloane Sq, Chelsea, Parsons Green, PUTNEY COMMON.

24
Mon–Sun
PIMLICO, Victoria, Westminster, Whitehall, Trafalgar Sq, Leicester Sq, Charing Cross Rd, Tottenham Court Rd/Gower St, Camden Town, HAMPSTEAD HEATH.

25
Mon–Sun
VICTORIA, Hyde Park Corner, Piccadilly*, Bond St*, Oxford St, Bloomsbury, Holborn, St Paul's, Bank, Leadenhall St, Aldgate, Whitechapel, Mile End, Stratford, ILFORD. (*Evening service runs instead via Park Lane and Marble Arch.)

27
Mon–Sun
ARCHWAY, Camden Town, Marylebone Rd, Baker St Station, Paddington, Notting Hill, Kensington, Hammersmith, Chiswick, Kew, RICHMOND.

28
Mon–Sun
GOLDERS GREEN, West Hampstead, Kilburn, Notting Hill, Kensington, Fulham, WANDSWORTH.

29
Mon–Sun
VICTORIA, Westminster, Whitehall, Trafalgar Sq, Leicester Sq, Charing Cross Rd, Tottenham Court Rd/Gower St, Camden Town, Holloway, Finsbury Park, WOOD GREEN/ENFIELD.

30
Mon–Sun
HACKNEY WICK, Islington, King's Cross, Euston, Marylebone Rd, Baker St, Oxford St, Marble Arch, Park Lane, Hyde Park Corner, Knightsbridge, South Kensington, Earl's Court, WEST BROMPTON.

31
Mon–Sun
CHELSEA, Earl's Court, Kensington, Notting Hill, Kilburn, Swiss Cottage, CAMDEN TOWN.

35
Mon–Sun
CLAPTON, Shoreditch, Liverpool St, Gracechurch St, Monument, London Bridge, Elephant & Castle, Camberwell, Brixton, CLAPHAM JUNCTION.

36
Mon–Sun
QUEEN'S PARK, Paddington, Edgware Rd, Marble Arch, Park Lane, Hyde Park Corner, Victoria, Vauxhall, Peckham, Lewisham, HITHER GREEN.

38
Mon–Sun
VICTORIA, Hyde Park Corner, Piccadilly, Shaftesbury Av, Bloomsbury, Holborn, Islington, LEYTON.

39
Mon–Sat
VICTORIA, Cheyne Walk, Battersea, Clapham Junction, PUTNEY.

43
Mon–Sat
LONDON BRIDGE, Monument, Bank, Moorgate, Islington, Holloway, Archway, Muswell Hill, FRIERN BARNET.

44
Mon–Sun
LONDON BRIDGE, St George's Circus, Lambeth Palace, Vauxhall, Battersea Park, Wandsworth, MITCHAM.

45
Mon–Sun
KING'S CROSS, Gray's Inn Rd, Holborn, Ludgate Circus, Blackfriars, Elephant & Castle, Camberwell, Clapham, Battersea, Chelsea, SOUTH KENSINGTON.

47
Mon–Sun
SHOREDITCH, Liverpool St, Gracechurch St, Monument, London Bridge, Tooley St (HMS Belfast), Tower Bridge (southside), Rotherhithe, Surrey Docks, Lewisham, Catford, DOWNHAM.

49
Mon–Sun
SHEPHERD'S BUSH, Holland Park, Kensington, Gloucester Rd, South Kensington, Chelsea, Battersea, Clapham Junction, STREATHAM.

52/52A
Mon–Sun
VICTORIA, Hyde Park Corner, Knightsbridge, Kensington, Notting Hill, Ladbroke Grove, WESTBOURNE PARK (52A), Willesden, MILL HILL (52).

53
Mon–Sun
OXFORD CIRCUS, Regent St, Piccadilly Circus, Trafalgar Sq, Whitehall, Westminster, Elephant & Castle, New Cross, Blackheath, Woolwich, PLUMSTEAD.

55
Mon–Sun
VICTORIA, Hyde Park Corner, Piccadilly, Shaftesbury Av, Charing Cross Rd, Bloomsbury, Clerkenwell, Shoreditch, Hackney, Leyton, WHIPPS CROSS.

63
Mon–Sun
KING'S CROSS, Farringdon, Ludgate Circus, Blackfriars, Elephant & Castle, Peckham, Honor Oak, CRYSTAL PALACE.

68
Mon–Sun
EUSTON*, Russell Sq, Holborn, Kingsway, Aldwych, Waterloo, Elephant & Castle, Camberwell, Norwood, CROYDON. (*Runs on to Camden Town and Chalk Farm on Sun.)

70
Mon–Fri
VICTORIA, Westminster Bridge, Waterloo, Southwark St, London Bridge, Tooley St (HMS Belfast), Tower Bridge (southside), Rotherhithe, PECKHAM.

73
Mon–Sun
HAMMERSMITH, Kensington, Knightsbridge, Hyde Park Corner, Park Lane, Marble Arch, Oxford St, Tottenham Court Rd/Gower St, Euston, King's Cross, Islington, STOKE NEWINGTON.

74
Mon–Sun
CAMDEN TOWN, The Zoo, Regent's Park, Baker St/Marylebone Rd, Oxford St, Marble Arch, Park Lane, Hyde Park Corner, Knightsbridge, South Kensington, Cromwell Rd, Earl's Court, West Brompton, Fulham, Putney, ROEHAMPTON.

76
Mon–Sat
WATERLOO, Blackfriars, Ludgate Circus, St Paul's, Bank, Moorgate, Hoxton, Tottenham, NORTHUMBERLAND PARK.

77/77A
Mon–Sun
KING'S CROSS, Euston, Russell Sq, Holborn, Kingsway, Aldwych, Strand, Trafalgar Sq, Whitehall, Westminster, Millbank, Vauxhall, Clapham Junction, WANDSWORTH/TOOTING.

78
Mon–Sun
SHOREDITCH, Liverpool St, Aldgate, Tower Bridge, Elephant & Castle, Peckham, DULWICH.

82
Mon–Sun
VICTORIA, Hyde Park Corner, Park Lane, Oxford St, Marylebone/Baker St, St John's Wood, Swiss Cottage, Golders Green, NORTH FINCHLEY.

88
Mon–Sun
ACTON GREEN, Shepherd's Bush, Notting Hill, Bayswater Rd, Marble Arch, Oxford St, Regent St, Piccadilly Circus, Trafalgar Sq, Whitehall, Westminster, Vauxhall, Clapham, TOOTING/MITCHAM.

113
Mon–Sun
OXFORD CIRCUS and Oxford St, Marylebone/Baker St, St John's Wood, Swiss Cottage, Hendon, Mill Hill, EDGWARE.

137
Mon–Sun
ARCHWAY*, Camden Town*, Gt Portland St*, OXFORD CIRCUS and Oxford St, Marble Arch, Park Lane, Hyde Park Corner, Knightsbridge, Sloane Sq, Battersea Park, Clapham Common, Streatham, CRYSTAL PALACE. (*No service to these points evenings or Sun.)

141
Mon–Sun
WOOD GREEN, Newington Green, MOORGATE, Barbican*, St Paul's*, Ludgate Circus*, Blackfriars*, Elephant & Castle*, Camberwell*, New Cross*, Catford*, GROVE PARK*. (*No service to these points on Sun.)

159
Mon–Sun
WEST HAMPSTEAD, Abbey Rd, St John's Wood, Baker St/Marylebone, Oxford St, Regent St, Piccadilly Circus, Trafalgar Sq, Whitehall, Westminster, Lambeth Bridge, Kennington, Brixton, THORNTON HEATH.

168
Mon–Sat
WATERLOO, Aldwych, Kingsway, Holborn, Russell Sq, Euston, Camden Town, Chalk Farm, HAMPSTEAD HEATH.

170
Mon–Fri
ALDWYCH, Strand, Trafalgar Sq, Whitehall, Westminster, Vauxhall, Battersea Park, Wandsworth, ROEHAMPTON.

171
Mon–Sun
ISLINGTON*, Rosebery Av*, Holborn*, Kingsway*, ALDWYCH, Waterloo, Elephant & Castle, Camberwell, Peckham, New Cross, FOREST HILL. (*No service to these places Sat or Sun – see **171A**.)

171A
Mon–Sun
TOTTENHAM, Islington, Rosebery Av, Gray's Inn Rd, High Holborn, Fetter Lane, Fleet St, Aldwych, WATERLOO.

177
Mon–Sun
WATERLOO, Elephant & Castle, New Cross, Greenwich, Woolwich, PLUMSTEAD/ABBEY WOOD.

188
Mon–Sun
EUSTON, Russell Sq, Holborn, Kingsway, Aldwych, Waterloo, Tower Bridge (southside), Surrey Docks, GREENWICH.

199
Mon–Sat
TRAFALGAR SQUARE, Strand, Aldwych, Waterloo, Elephant & Castle, Surrey Docks, Lewisham, BROMLEY.

500
Mon–Sat
VICTORIA, Marble Arch, OXFORD ST (Red Arrow service – not evenings).

501
Mon–Fri
WATERLOO, Kingsway, Holborn, St Paul's, Bank, LONDON BRIDGE (Red Arrow service – not evenings).

502
Mon–Fri
WATERLOO, Aldwych, Fleet St, St Paul's, London Wall (returning via Bank), LIVERPOOL ST (Red Arrow service – not evenings).

507
Mon–Sun
VICTORIA, Lambeth Bridge, WATERLOO (Red Arrow service – also evenings).

C1
Mon–Sat
WESTMINSTER, Victoria, Belgravia, Sloane Sq, Knightsbridge, South Kensington, KENSINGTON HIGH ST. (Minibus service.)

C2
Mon–Sun
REGENT STREET, Oxford Circus, Portland Pl, Regent's Park (for Zoo), Camden Town, PARLIAMENT HILL FIELDS. (Minibus service.)

London Transport 24-hour information service
For any information on travel in Greater London – routes, fares, times – telephone 01-222 1234 at any time of the day or night.

A

Abbey Road Studios
3 Abbey Rd NW8. 01-286 1161. The studios where the Beatles recorded their earliest LPs are not open to the public, but anyone may use the zebra crossing made famous on the sleeve of the 'Abbey Road' album.
θ St John's Wood (then walk via Grove End Rd)
🚌46, 159

Achilles Statue   3O1
Hyde Park Corner W2. Set up in 1822 in honour of the Duke of Wellington and commissioned by the Ladies of England who were somewhat shaken to discover they had funded London's first nude statue. The sculptor was Sir Richard Westmacott; the material – 33 tons of bronze from captured French guns, some taken at Waterloo.
θ Hyde Park Corner
🚌2B, 9, 14, 14A, 16, 19, 22, 25, 30, 36, 38, 52, 52A, 55, 73, 74, 82, 137, 500

Admiralty Arch   3N4
The Mall SW1. Sir Aston Webb's massive triple arch of 1910 – a memorial to Queen Victoria – bestrides the eastern end of the Mall.
θ Charing Cross
🚌1, 3, 6, 9, 11, 12, 13, 15, 15A, 24, 29, 53, 77, 77A, 88, 109, 159, 170, 176, 199

Albany   3N3
Piccadilly W1. Privately owned apartments, with several famous residents often of a literary or political persuasion. A patrician Georgian mansion built by Sir William Chambers in 1770.
θ Piccadilly Circus
🚌3, 6, 9, 12, 13, 14, 14A, 15, 15A, 19, 22, 38, 53, 55, 88, 159

The Albert   3P4
52 Victoria St SW1. 01-222 5577. Grand, imposing Victorian pub with original gas lights and engraved glass windows. Excellent restaurant serving traditional English roasts and full English breakfasts too, *at 08.00*. New Scotland Yard's

local, and popular with MPs (there's a division bell in the restaurant). *Pub open normal licensing hours Mon –Sun. Restaurant open LD Mon– Sun.*
θ St James's Park
🚌10, 11, 24, 29, 70, 507, C1

Albert Bridge   51Y
SW3. Fairytale cantilever and suspension bridge built by R. W. Ordish in 1873 with a toll hut at each end and signs asking troops to break step when crossing to reduce the strain. Still threatened by the weight of modern traffic despite the addition of a central support.
θ Sloane Square (then bus 19, 22, then walk), South Kensington (then bus 45, 49)
🚌39 (direct), or 11, 22 to King's Road then walk, or 19, 45, 49 to Cheyne Walk

Albert Memorial   2H4
Kensington Gdns SW7. The ultimate mid-Victorian memorial, built in lavishly Gothic style by Sir George Gilbert Scott in 1863–72. The figure of the Prince, cast in bronze by Joseph Durham, is shown studying the catalogue to the Great Exhibition. The steps and podium seethe with the works of various sculptors, representing the continents, the arts and industry.
θ South Kensington, High Street Kensington
🚌9, 33, 49, 52, 52A, 73, C1

Albery Theatre   3N4
St Martins La WC2. 01-836 3878. Formerly the New Theatre. Architecturally appealing and once the home of the Old Vic Company. One of the Wyndham theatres (others are Criterion, Donmar Warehouse, Piccadilly and Wyndham's) and theatre tours are available.
θ Leicester Square
🚌1, 24, 20, 170

Aldwych Theatre   3M5
Aldwych WC2. 01-836 6404. The Royal Shakespeare Company was based here until it moved to the

Barbican Arts Centre in 1982. Now under new management and offering a varied programme.
⊖ Covent Garden
🚌1, 4, 5, 6, 9, 11, 13, 15, 15A, 68, 77, 77A, 168, 170, 171, 171A, 176, 188, 199, 501, 502

Alexandra Park & Palace
N22. 01-883 0809. Two hundred sloping, tree-planted acres, eight of which were occupied by the Palace until it was abbreviated by fire in 1981. There is a new pavilion, with some sporting facilities, miniature golf, regular weekend band concerts, children's concerts and itinerant fairs. *Open 24 hrs.*
⊖ Finsbury Park (then bus W3)
🚌W3
⇌ Alexandra Palace (then bus W3)

**All Hallows by the   4T5
Tower**
Byward St EC3. 01-481 2928. Founded in 675, rebuilt during the 11th, 13th and 15th centuries and restored after Second World War bomb damage. Has London's best collection of memorial brasses, an upstairs refectory which serves light lunches on week days, and a Roman mosaic floor, cAD122, in the crypt. *Open Mon–Sun. Crypt museum open daily by arrangement with verger. Charge.*
⊖ Tower Hill
🚌15, 42, 56, 78, 278

All Hallows by the Wall   4S5
83 London Wall EC2. 01-588 3388. 13thC church on and beside the medieval City wall, rebuilt 1765–7 by the younger Dance. The huge pulpit is reached by way of the vestry, itself just over the wall and, strictly speaking, outside the City. *Open Mon–Sun. Free.*
⊖ Liverpool Street
🚌9, 11, 21, 43, 76, 133, 141, 502, Sun only 279A

Ambassadors Theatre   3M4
West St WC2. 01-836 1171. Cosy, intimate theatre where 'The Mousetrap', now at the St Martin's, began its phenomenally long run.
⊖ Leicester Square
🚌1, 14, 14A, 19, 22, 24, 29, 38, 55, 176

Anchor   4T3
Bankside SE1. 01-407 1577. The original pub on this site, whose clientele was a hideous mix of smugglers, press gangs and warders from The Clink prison, was destroyed in the Fire of London. This building is 18thC with exposed beams, open fires, rough walls, five small bars and three restaurants. The antique bric-a-brac includes a first edition of Dr Johnson's Dictionary. *Open Mon–Sun. Restaurant closed L Sat.*
⊖ Mansion House (then cross Southwark Bridge), London Bridge (then walk via Cathedral and Clink St)
🚌10, 17, 21, 35, 43, 44, 47, 48, 70, 133, 149, 501, P3

Annabel's   3N2
44 Berkeley Sq W1. 01-629 2350. Exclusive and expensive nightclub, richly furnished with Royalty, aristocrats and stars. Short but distinguished menu; rarely short of asparagus or truffles. Very hard to join although a member may find it easier to arrange temporary membership for an overseas friend than full membership for a resident.
⊖ Green Park
🚌9, 14, 19, 22, 38, 55 to Green Park Station

**Antiquarius Antique   5X1
Market**
135–141 King's Rd SW3. 01-351 5353. Covered complex of small purpose-built stalls where it is a

pleasure to get lost amongst the fine and applied arts, silver, jewellery, Edwardian silk blouses, Victorian dolls' houses, furniture and bric-a-brac. *Open 10.00–18.00 Mon–Sat.*
⊖ Sloane Square (then bus)
🚌 11, 19, 22, 45, 49

Apsley House *3O2*
149 Piccadilly W1. 01-499 5676. An Adam house, altered in the early 19thC by Wyatt (who added the portico and the Bath stone facing), which was known as No I London when it was the home of the first Duke of Wellington. Now administered by the Victoria and Albert Museum and a perfect setting for the Iron Duke's silver, plate, porcelain and priceless paintings – including works by Velasquez, Rubens and Murillo. *Open 10.00–18.00 Tue–Thur & Sat; 14.30–18.00 Sun. Closed Mon, Fri & Nat Hols.* Charge.
⊖ Hyde Park Corner
🚌 2B, 9, 14, 14A, 16, 19, 22, 25, 30, 36, 38, 52, 52A, 55, 73, 74, 82, 137, 500

Aquascutum *3N3*
100 Regent St W1. 01-734 6090. Established in 1851, this smart department store on three floors has a large selection of quality men's and women's clothes and accessories. Noted for its own-label high fashions and fashion classics – rainwear, knitwear, tweeds, coats, suits, jackets, town and country casuals. By appointment to HM The Queen Mother who purchases her

weatherproof coats here. *Open 09.00–17.30 Mon–Wed, Fri & Sat; 09.00–19.00 Thur. Closed Sun.*
⊖ Piccadilly Circus
🚌 3, 6, 9, 12, 13, 14, 14A, 15, 15A, 19, 22, 38, 53, 55, 88, 159

Army & Navy Stores *3P3*
105 Victoria St SW1. 01-834 1234. Suppliers to the services in the 1890s. Now a generously stocked department store with self-service restaurants on the 1st and 2nd floors and a coffee and croissant bar on the ground floor. *Open 09.00 –17.30 Mon–Thur; 09.00–18.00 Fri & Sat.*
⊖ St James's Park
🚌 10, 11, 24, 29, 70, 507, C1

Artillery Museum
The Rotunda, Repository Rd, Woolwich Common SE18. 01-856 5533. The Rotunda is a Nash-designed architectural 'tent', which originally stood in St James's Park. The guns and muskets contained within it date from the 14thC to the present day. *Open 12.00–17.00 Mon–Fri; 13.00–17.00 Sat & Sun. Closes 16.00 Nov–Mar.* Charge.
🚌 53, 54, 75
≋ Woolwich Arsenal

Arts Theatre Club *3M4*
6 Gt Newport St WC2. 01-836 2132. Opened in 1927 as a club theatre to circumvent the Lord Chamberlain's censorious restrictions. Nowadays the Arts Club itself is separate from the two theatres, one small and one a studio, which offer a variety of plays. In the afternoons the Unicorn Theatre puts on children's plays for schools with public matinees on Saturday and Sunday. Restaurant and bar open before performances.
⊖ Leicester Square
🚌 1, 24, 29, 176

Asprey's *3N2*
165 New Bond St W1. 01-493 6767. A shop whose name is associated with glamour, quality and high prices. Contains glittering displays of antique and modern jewellery, the work of goldsmiths and silversmiths, upmarket luggage and other luxury gifts. *Open 09.00– 17.30 Mon–Fri; 09.00–13.00 Sat.*
⊖ Green Park
🚌 25

B

Baden-Powell House *2J4*
Queens Gate SW7. 01-584 7030.
The headquarters of the Scout
movement, guarded by Donald Pot-
ter's granite statue of its founder,
General Lord Baden-Powell. Inside
is a permanent exhibition on the
history of the movement and on the
life of B-P himself. *Open Mon–Sun
07.00–23.00. Closed Xmas.*
⊖ South Kensington, Gloucester
Road
🚌 49, 74, C1

Ball Court *4T5*
Next to 39 Cornhill EC3. Straight out
of Dickens. Within the Court the
18thC Simpson's Chophouse
opens on weekday lunchtimes to
serve olde English food – including
their speciality of stewed cheese.
⊖ Bank
🚌 15A, 25

Bank of England *4S4*
Threadneedle St EC2. 01-601 4444.
The old lady of Threadneedle Street
is the guardian of the nation's gold.
Security naturally precludes casual
visitors, but the messengers and
doormen – in their pink coats, red
waistcoats and top hats – are often
colourfully visible. The outer walls
are still the ones designed by Sir
John Soane, the Bank's architect
from 1788–1833. Visits, by appointment only, must be booked well in
advance.
⊖ Bank
🚌 6, 8, 9, 11, 15A, 21, 25, 43, 76,
133, 149, 501

Bankside *4T3*
Southwark SE1. Southwark's
waterfront, notorious in the 16thC
for its taverns and whorehouses,
bear-baiting rings and playhouses,
has been rebuilt and landscaped
into an attractive riverside walkway,
dominated by Sir Giles C. Scott's
monumental electric power station.
Here are: the Bankside Gallery with
its changing exhibitions of the work
of contemporary British painters;
the Bear Gardens Museum and Art
Centre which echoes the area in its

Elizabethan hey-day; Rose Alley
where the Rose Theatre stood; and
a plaque in Park Street marking the
site of Shakespeare's Globe. There
are fine views across the river to the
City and St Paul's – Wren is said to
have lodged in 49 Park Street and
from his windows he could watch
the Cathedral rise.
⊖ Blackfriars
🚌 45, 59, 63, 70, 76, 141, 149

Banqueting House *3O4*
Whitehall SW1. 01-930 4179.
Splendid survivor of the royal
Palace of Whitehall, principal London residence of the Court during
the reign of Henry VIII. The present
hall, built in 1625 by Inigo Jones,
was the first Palladian building to be
completed in England. Inside, the
ceilings were painted for Charles I
by Peter Paul Rubens. Outside a
tablet marks the window through
which the King stepped to his ex-
ecution. *Open 10.00–17.00 Tue–
Sat; 14.00–17.00 Sun. Closed Mon
(except Nat Hols) and when in use
for Government functions.* Charge.
⊖ Charing Cross
🚌 3, 11, 12, 24, 29, 53, 77, 77A,
88, 109, 159, 170

Barbican Arts Centre *4R4*
Barbican EC2. Admin: 01-638 4141.
Recorded information on events:
01-628 9760. Box office: 01-628
8795. Credit card bookings: 01-638
8891. This walled city within the
City, notorious for the size and com-
plexity of its design, is the country's
largest arts centre, with a wealth of
facilities. The Barbican Theatre,
reached from levels 3–6, is the
home of The Royal Shakespeare
Company who also use the small
studio theatre, The Pit, on level 1.
The Barbican Hall on levels 5 and 6
is the home of the London Symphony Orchestra, and also offers a
wide range of musical experiences
from guest performers. There is an
art gallery and an open-air sculpture
court reached from level 8; a cinema on level 1 (and two more on
level 9 which are usually used for

conferences); a library on level 7, its collection biased towards the arts; a restaurant on level 7; an open-air cafe beside an artificial lake with real ducks on level 5; and bars and snack bars on levels 1, 3, 5 and 6. Also within the complex are the City Business School, The Guildhall School of Music and Drama, St Giles Cripplegate church where Cromwell was married and Milton is buried. In addition, there are an Exhibition Halls reached via a walkway on level 8, and numerous residential apartments. *Open Mon–Sun.*
⊖ Barbican (closed Sun), Moorgate
🚍 4, 9, 11, 21, 43, 76, 133, 141, 214, 271, 502, Sun only 279A

Barnum's Carnival   **2J1**
Novelties
67 Hammersmith Rd W14. 01-602 1211. A cornucopia of plastic creepy-crawlies, party hats, monster masks, and all the equipment for expressing intemperate joy – hooters, bleepers, rattles and streamers. *Open 09.15–17.00 Mon–Fri; 10.00–16.00 Sat.*
⊖ Kensington Olympia
🚍 9, 27, 28, 33, 73, 91

Baron of Beef   **4S4**
Gutter La, off Gresham St EC2. 01-606 6961. Very traditional, vastly popular City restaurant with an all-English ambience. Chief speciality is the roast beef and Yorkshire pudding from the trolley. Lobster, sole, salmon, roast duck, beefsteak and oyster pie are also tempting. Delicious summer pudding served all year round. A fine wine list catering for the connoisseur and everyman. Essential to reserve for lunch. *Open l D Mon–Fri to 21.00. Party bookings evenings & Sat.*
⊖ St Paul's
🚍 4, 8, 22, 25, 141, 501, 502

Battersea Arts Centre
Old Town Hall, Lavender Hill SW11. Admin: 01-223 6557/8/9. Box office: 01-223 8413. An active centre running a variety of day and evening classes and workshops with the emphasis on dance and music, although there is also a fully equipped pottery and photographic workshop. The Centre houses an art gallery with changing exhibitions of local work, a small cinema and a theatre which accommodates a mix of visiting fringe productions, dance, mime and music. An interesting bookshop, a pleasant licensed cafe, a regular Sunday craft market and five or six annual arts festivals on a variety of themes complete its range of facilities and activities. *Open 10.00–23.00 Wed –Sat; 10.00–22.30 Sun. Bookshop open 11.30–20.00 Wed–Sun. Closed Mon & Tue (except box office and cafe, 12.00–14.30).*
⊖ Vauxhall (then bus 44, 170),
South Kensington (then bus 45, 49)
🚍 19, 35, 37, 39, 44, 45, 49, 170

Battersea Park   **5Y2**
SW11. 01-228 2798. The marshy area, known as Battersea Fields, where the Duke of Wellington and the Earl of Winchelsea once fought a duel, has been stabilised with earth displaced by the building of Victoria Docks. It is now a most attractive 200-acre park with a curvaceous boating lake where waterfowl live, a deer enclosure, a small children's zoo (01-228 9957) with penguins, pygmy goats and pony rides, playing fields, a running track and tennis courts. Sculpture by Henry Moore. Brass and jazz bands play here on summer Sunday afternoons, and the three best known of the many lively events held within it are the Easter Parade, the Historic Vehicles Rally in May, and the South London Carnival in August. *Open dawn–dusk. Free.*
⊖ Sloane Square (then bus 137)
🚍 19, 39, 44, 45, 49, 137, 170
🚄 Battersea Park

Battle of Britain Museum
Grahame Park Way NW9. 01-205 2266. A separate section of the main RAF museum containing a permanent memorial to the men, women and machines involved in the great air battle of 1940. British, German and Italian aircraft – Spitfire, Hurricane, Gladiator, Defiant, Blenheim, Messerschmidt, Heinkel, Junkers, Fiat. Also a replica of the No 11 group operations room at RAF Uxbridge. Equipment, models, documents, relics and works of art. *Open 10.00 –18.00 Mon–Sat; 14.00–18.00 Sun. Closed Xmas & Good Fri.* Charge.
⊖ Colindale
🚍 226

Bear Gardens Museum &   **4T4**
Arts Centre
Bear Gardens SE1. 01-261 1353.
Elizabethan Bankside was a riotous
assemblage of theatres, bear-
baiting gardens, inns and brothels
and the intriguing exhibitions in this
small museum offer a convincing
evocation of this lively if murky
past. There are models of the Globe
and other theatres, a diorama of the
ice fairs, and occasional seasons of
suitable live entertainment in the
small replica of a 16thC playhouse.
*Open 10.00–17.30 Tue–Sat; 14.00
–18.00 Sun.* Charge.
⊖ Mansion House (then walk over
Southwark Bridge)
🚌 17, 44, 70, 149

Belfast, HMS   **4U5**
Symons Wharf, Vine La SE1. 01-
407 6434. The largest cruiser ever
built for the Royal Navy is most
suitably reached by means of a regular ferry from Tower Pier, or else
by gangway from Symons Wharf on
the South Bank. She is now a
permanent museum and her
bridge, engine rooms, gun turrets,
decks, galley and sick bay may all be
explored. *Open 11.00–17.50 Mon
–Sun. Closes 16.30 in winter.*
Charge.
⊖ London Bridge, Tower Hill (then
ferry)
🚌 15, 42, 47, 56, 70, 78, 188, 278

Berwick Street Market   **3M3**
Soho W1. General market in the
heart of Soho. The fruit and veget-
ables are particularly good quality,
and prices reasonable, especially at
the southern end of the street.
Open 09.00–18.00 Mon–Sat.
⊖ Piccadilly Circus
🚌 1, 7, 8, 14, 14A, 19, 22, 25, 38,
55, 73

Bethnal Green Museum of
Childhood
Cambridge Heath Rd E2. 01-980
2415. An appealing outpost of the
Victoria and Albert Museum with
much material for those interested
in the social history of childhood.
Also fascinating for those eager to
peer into dozens of minutely equipped dolls' houses, to compare the
facial expressions of Victorian with
modern Teddy bears, and to marvel
at miniature trains, mechanical
toys, puppets, theatres and kaleido-

scopes. Regular workshops and
activities are arranged for young
visitors. *Open 10.00–18.00 Mon–
Thur & Sat; 14.30–18.00 Sun.
Closed Fri.* Free.
⊖ Bethnal Green
🚌 8, 106, 253
⇌ Cambridge Heath

Billingsgate   **4T5**
Lower Thames St EC3. The famous
fish market moved to a new site in
the West India docks in 1982, leaving Horace Jones' building of 1875
deserted and in the grip of perma-
frost from all the ice used over the
years to keep the fish eyes bright
and the scales gleaming. Offices,
shops, restaurants and a riverside
terrace are planned for later in the
decade.
⊖ Monument
🚌 10, 15, 21, 35, 40, 43, 47, 48,
133, 501

Billingsgate Wholesale Fish
Market
North Quay, West India Docks Rd,
Isle of Dogs. 01-987 1118. Lon-
don's principal fish market, moved
from its age-old location in the City,
flourishes as ever. Can be wet
underfoot and pungent of aroma.
*Open from 05.30 Tue–Sat. Closed
Sun & Mon.*
⊖ Mile End (then bus D1)
Docklands Railway: Poplar
🚌 D1

The Blackfriar   **4T3**
174 Queen Victoria St EC4. 01-236
5650. Wedge-shaped building in
the shadows of Blackfriars railway
bridge, with arguably one of the
richest and strangest pub interiors
in London. The main bar is an Art
Nouveau temple of marble with
bronze bas-reliefs of friars. The inner bar has an arched mosaic ceiling, red marble columns and more
friars, accompanied by demons,
fairies and alabaster animals. *Open
Mon–Fri. Closes by 22.00 & all Sat
& Sun.*
⊖ Blackfriars
🚌 45, 59, 63, 76, 141

Blackheath
SE3. 01-858 1692. 275 acres of
open grassland, used for general
recreation and adjoining the attractive Blackheath Village with its old
pubs and good bookshop. Ideal for

kite-flying and watching the sunset. Good views in all directions, especially from Point Hill in the northwest. Occasionally welcomes a circus or funfair. *Open 24 hours.*
🚌 53, 54, 75, 89, 108
🚆 Blackheath, Maze Hill

Blooms Restaurant   **4S6**
90 Whitechapel High St E1. 01-247 6001/377 1120. Bustling Kosher Jewish restaurant dishing up immensely generous portions of kreplech (dumpling) soup, salt beef, gefilte fish and lockshen pudding. Or, try a take-away salt beef sandwich from the counter inside the door. Licensed. *Open LD Sun–Thur, L only Fri. Closed D Fri, all Sat & Jewish Hols.*
🚇 Aldgate East
🚌 5, 10, 15, 15A, 22A, 25, 40, 67, 225, 253

Bloomsbury   **3L4**
WC1. An area of 18thC terraces and calm leafy squares whose title still conjures up a literary and elegantly Bohemian flavour. Between the wars Virginia Woolf, Vanessa Bell and Lytton Strachey amongst others formed 'the Bloomsbury set' in the shadow of the British Museum with, at its heart, the domed reading room where so many influential writers have researched and written – and still do. The Russells, Dukes of Bedford, once owned the area and their various names, including Tavistock and Woburn, still seem to claim it.
🚇 Holborn, Russell Square, Tottenham Court Road
🚌 1, 7, 8, 14, 14A, 19, 22, 24, 25, 29, 38, 55, 68, 73, 77, 77A, 134, 168, 176, 188

The Body Shop   **3M3**
32 Gt Marlborough St W1. 01-437 5137. Principal shop in a chain of distinctive green shops selling natural skin products, soaps, bath oils and pot pourris. Inside everything smells as good as it looks. Many branches, some selling pop jewellery, simple toys, gift baskets filled with own-brand toiletries and all kinds of knick-knacks. *Open 10.00–18.00 Mon–Sat, to 19.00 Thur. Closed Sun.*
🚇 Oxford Circus
🚌 3, 6, 12, 13, 15, 15A, 53, 88, 159, C2

Bomber Command Museum
Grahame Park Way NW9. 01-205 2266. An off-shoot of the RAF Museum, and within the same complex, with a range of aircraft from World War I to an Avro-Vulcan of the post-war era. Here also are the only Halifax and the only Wellington left in the world, a B17 Flying Fortress and a B25 Mitchell of the USAF. *Open 10.00–17.00 Mon–Sat; 14.00–17.00 Sun. Charge.*
🚇 Colindale
🚌 226

Bond Street, Old & New   **3M2**
W1. Fashionable and expensive shopping street for good clothes, furs, Persian rugs, jewellery, pictures and prints. On the second floor of the Time-Life building at 153 is a little-noticed frieze by Henry Moore – Time-Life Screen.
🚇 Green Park (for Old Bond Street)
🚌 9, 14, 14A, 19, 22, 25, 38, 55 (for Old Bond Street)
🚇 Bond Street (for New Bond Street)
🚌 1, 6, 7, 8, 12, 13, 15, 15A, 16A, 25, 73, 88, 113, 137, 159, 500 (for New Bond Street)

W. & F. C. Bonham & Sons 2H6

Montpelier Galleries, Montpelier St SW7. 01-584 9161. Fine art auctioneers dealing in oils and watercolours, prints, books, clocks, silver, porcelain, furniture, jewellery, furs and Oriental works of art. Enquire about the occasional evening 'theme' auctions – dog paintings to coincide with Crufts, for example. *Open 09.00–17.30 Mon–Fri. Closed Sat & Sun.*
Θ Knightsbridge
🚌9, 14, 19, 22, 30, 52, 52A, 73, 74, 137, C1

Bonham's Chelsea Galleries

65–69 Lots Rd SW10. 01-352 0466. Sales of contemporary Edwardian and Victorian furniture and carpets on Tuesday at *10.00.* Also Beginners Collectors Sales every other Friday, handling the middle price ranges of prints, ceramics and books. *Open 09.00–17.30 Mon–Fri. Closed Sat & Sun.*
Θ Sloane Square (then bus 11, 22)
🚌11, 22

Brass Rubbing Centre 3N3

St James's Church, Piccadilly W1. 01-437 6023. Here are replicas of 70 British and European brasses, instructions on how to take a rubbing and the necessary materials. A small monumental animal comes cheaper than a large crusading knight. *Open 10.00–18.00 Mon–Sat; 12.00–18.00 Sun.* Charge.
Θ Piccadilly Circus
🚌3, 6, 9, 12, 13, 14, 15, 15A, 19, 22, 38, 53, 55, 88, 159

British Piano & Musical Museum

368 High St, Brentford, Middx. 01-560 8108. The finest collection of reproducing piano systems and reproducing pipe organs in Europe, all under one roof in a 100-year-old church. Also orchestrions, orchestrelles, player pianos, music boxes and a giant Wurlitzer. The 90-minute guided tour includes performances by most of them. There are evening concerts, too, send s.a.e. for details. *Open Apr–Oct 14.00–17.00 Sat & Sun. Closed weekdays, Nat Hols & winter.* Donation welcome.
Θ South Ealing (then bus 65), Gunnersbury (then bus 237, 267)
🚌65, 237, 267, E1, E2
≥ Kew Bridge

British Museum 3L4

Gt Russell St WC1. 01-636 1555. The imposing building by Sir Robert Smirke, which went up in 1823–47, houses one of the largest and greatest collections in the world. Its treasures are so rich and varied that no one should even attempt to see them all in a single visit. Here are Babylonian, Greek, Etruscan, Roman, British, Oriental and Asian antiquities – prehistoric, medieval and later. Here are prints, drawings, maps, coins, medals, sarcophagi, papyri, jewellery, vases, domestic utensils and royal accoutrements. Among the most dramatic and famous of the many priceless exhibits are the Elgin marbles, the Egyptian mummies, the mighty Assyrian bulls and lions, the Rosetta Stone, Magna Carta and the Sutton Hoo Ship Burial. There are tours of the circular domed reading room on the hour from 11.00–16.00 and regular lectures, film shows, gallery talks and special exhibitions. Good cafeteria, too. *Open 10.00–17.00 Mon–Sat; 14.30–18.00 Sun.* Free.
Θ Tottenham Court Road, Russell Square
🚌1, 7, 8, 14, 14A, 19, 22, 24, 25, 29, 38, 55, 68, 73, 77, 77A, 134, 168, 176, 188

British Rail Collector's 1C5
Corner

Cobourg St NW1. 01-387 9400 extn 2537. If driven by an urge to possess an obsolete British Railways name plate, a hand lamp, signal, station clock or railman's hat, this is

the place to go. It's a little hard to find but the enthusiasts manage. *Open 09.00–17.00 Mon–Fri; 09.00 –16.30 Sat. Closed Sun & lunchtimes. (Times subject to alteration without notice.)*
⊖ Euston
🚌 14, 14A, 18, 30, 68, 73, 77, 77A, 168, 188

British Travel Centre *3N3*
Rex House, 4–12 Lower Regent St SW1. Personal callers only. New home of the British Tourist Authority Information Centre, incorporating the American Express Travel Service Office, British Rail ticket office and a bureau de change. Details on where to go throughout the UK. Book a room, coach trip or theatre ticket, buy plane or train tickets, hire cars – all under one roof. Also exhibitions, videos, travel bookshop and gifts. *Open 09.00– 18.30 Mon–Sat; 10.00–16.00 Sun.*
⊖ Piccadilly Circus
🚌 3, 6, 9, 12, 13, 14, 14A, 15, 15A, 19, 22, 38, 53, 55, 88, 159

Brixton Market
Atlantic Rd SW9, and all around. Large and exuberant general market with a strong West Indian flavour, further enlivened by the loud reggae reverberating around the railway arches. *Open 08.00– 18.00 Mon–Sat. Closed Wed afternoon & Sun.*
⊖ Brixton
🚌 2, 2B, 3, 35, 37, 45, 50, 109, 133, 159, 196, P4

Brixton Windmill
Blenheim Gdns, Brixton Hill SW9. 01-673 5398. An early 19thC tower mill which is in use until 1934. It was closed for some years, and is currently being re-furbished in order to grind corn once more. (Opening times and charge yet to be decided – enquire.)
⊖ Brixton (then bus)
🚌 50, 59, 95, 109, 133, 159

Broadcasting Gallery *2H6*
70 Brompton Rd SW3. 01-584 7011. Run by the Independent Broadcasting Authority, the gallery covers the story of independent radio and television. The 90-minute guided tour shows how programmes are made, how advertising works, explains technological in-

novations and the relevance of cable and satellite TV. There are also cameras ancient and modern and an example of one of the earliest studios. *Open by appointment Mon–Fri. Book for tours at 10.00, 11.00, 14.00 or 15.00. No children under 16. Free.*
⊖ Knightsbridge
🚌 9, 14, 19, 22, 30, 52, 52A, 73, 137, C1

Broadcasting House *3L2*
Langham Pl W1. 01-580 4468. The HQ of the BBC, compared by some to a beached ocean liner. Much drama is now based at the Maida Vale Studios because the vibrations from the Bakerloo line, which pass underneath here, threaten to get in on the act.
⊖ Oxford Circus
🚌 1, 3, 6, 7, 8, 12, 13, 15, 15A, 16A, 25, 53, 73, 88, 113, 137, 159, 500, C1

Brompton Cemetery *2K3*
Old Brompton Rd or Fulham Rd SW6. Spreading Victorian necropolis crowded with ornate tombs and ranks of tall gravestones. The stands of Chelsea football ground loom over the wall in a nice juxtaposition of the quick and the dead. The domed chapel is no longer open but its flanking WCs are as well. *Open 08.00–dusk Mon–Sun. Free.*
⊖ West Brompton (Mon–Fri), Earl's Court (Sat & Sun)
🚌 30, 31, 74

Brompton Oratory   *2H6*
Brompton Rd SW7. Actually 'the church of the London Oratory'; the Oratorians are a community of priests who follow the teachings of the Florentine St Philip Neri and were introduced to Britain by Frederick William Faber and by Cardinal Newman whose marble statue stands outside the priests' house next door. The church is Italianate Roman Catholic, with a baroque marbled interior, designed by Herbert Cribble in 1878. Some of the fine statues come from the Cathedral of Siena. *Open daylight hours – please respect services.* Donation welcome.
⊖ South Kensington
🚌 14, 30, 74, C1

Buckingham Palace   *3O3*
SW1. The Sovereign's London residence. Built in 1705 as the Duke of Buckingham's house, remodelled into a palace by Nash in 1830, refaced by Sir Aston Webb in 1913. Its 40 acres of grounds are the setting for prestigious summer garden parties – by invitation only. The military pomp and pageantry of the changing of the guard starts daily at *11.30* (alternate days in winter). The Royal Standard flies to proclaim the royal presence.
⊖ Green Park, Victoria, Hyde Park Corner
🚌 2, 2B, 9, 10, 11, 14, 14A, 16, 19, 22, 24, 25, 29, 30, 36, 36B, 38, 39, 52, 52A, 55, 70, 73, 74, 82, 137, 185, 500, 507, C1

Burberry's   *3N4*
18 Haymarket SW1. 01-930 3343. Shop famous for classic raincoats, cut in English style, for men and women. Also stocks suits and accessories such as hats and scarves. *Open 09.00–17.30 Mon –Sat; until 19.00 Thur.*
⊖ Piccadilly Circus
🚌 3, 6, 9, 12, 13, 14, 15, 15A, 19, 22, 38, 53, 55, 88, 159

Burberry's   *3M3*
165 Regent St W1. 01-734 4060. Classic clothes and accessories. *Open 09.00–17.30 Mon–Sat; until 19.00 Thur.*
⊖ Oxford Circus
🚌 3, 6, 12, 13, 15, 15A, 53, 88, 159

Burlington Arcade   *3N3*
Off Piccadilly W1. Charming and elegant Regency shopping arcade, with original windows, mostly full of jewellery and cashmere. You may not run, sing or whistle here, and there is a uniformed beadle to see that you don't and to lock the gates when the shops close. *Open 08.30–17.30 Mon–Sat. Closed Sun.*
⊖ Piccadilly Circus
🚌 3, 6, 9, 12, 13, 14, 14A, 15, 15A, 19, 22, 38, 53, 55, 88, 159

Bush Theatre
Bush Hotel, Shepherd's Bush Green W12. 01-740 0501. Well-known fringe theatre, its curtainless stage and raked seating occupying the floor above the busy pub. Originally established to attract the non-theatre-going public, its new productions now often transfer to the West End. *Performances Tue–Sat.*
⊖ Shepherd's Bush
🚌 11, 12, 49, 72, 88, 105, 207, 220, 255, 283, 295

Cabinet War Rooms 3O4

Clive Steps, King Charles St SW1. 01-930 6961. The secret war-time HQ of Churchill's Cabinet has been opened to the public. The six-acre labyrinth of corridors and rooms underneath the heart of government Whitehall are fully equipped with genuine war-time furniture and fittings. *Open 10.00–17.50 Tue–Sun. Closed Mon & Nat Hols.* Charge.
⊖ Charing Cross, Westminster
🚌3, 11, 12, 24, 29, 53, 77, 77A, 88, 109, 159, 170

Café Royal 3N3

68 Regent St W1. Grill Room 01-439 6320. The lush, plush, extravagant rococo Grill Room is unchanged since the days when Rex Whistler, Oscar Wilde and Aubrey Beardsley ate beneath the painted ceiling and reflected in the massive mirrors. Long and ambitious menu featuring elaborate French and English dishes. Formal service and a remarkable wine cellar. *Open LD Mon–Sun.*
⊖ Piccadilly Circus
🚌3, 6, 12, 13, 15, 15A, 53, 88, 159

Camden Lock 1A3

Where Chalk Farm Rd crosses Regent's Canal, NW1. The lock itself is pretty – attractive canalside walks go in either direction and art and craft shops surround a cobbled courtyard. At weekends an itinerant market flourishes with stalls crammed with antiques, junk and bric-a-brac. The market has a food stand by the entrance – and here too is Dingwalls lively music club.
⊖ Camden Town, Chalk Farm
🚌24, 31, 68

Camden Passage

Islington High St N1. Puts Islington on the tourist map. A narrow paved street lined with small antique shops, both general and specialist, with unexpected arcades opening off it filled with yet more treasures. There are silver, lace, furniture, prints, fob watches, snuff and snuff boxes, porcelain, militaria, maps, jewellery and more. Market stalls reinforce the shops on Wednesday morning and all Saturday, and on Thursday and Friday second-hand book stalls take over. There are some good restaurants here, too. *Open 09.00–18.00 Mon–Sat. Market stalls 08.00–16.00 Wed & Sat; 09.00–17.00 Thur & Fri.*
⊖ Angel
🚌4, 19, 30, 38, 43, 73, 171, 171A, 214, 271, 279, Sun only 263A, 279A

Canonbury Tower

Canonbury Pl N1. 01-226 5111. Just round the corner from one of London's most beautiful squares is this 16thC building with a romantic history of an elopement, a father's wrath and the timely intervention of Queen Elizabeth I. It is the HQ of the successful Tavistock Amateur Theatre Company, whose members will show you around the fine

oak-panelled rooms after the Saturday evening performance. Appointments may be made for parties at other times.
⊖ Highbury and Islington
🚌 4, 19, 30, 38, 43, 73, 171, 171A, 271, 277, 279, Sun only 263A, 279A

Cannon Cinema (1, 2, 3, 4)   **1D1**
Edgware Rd W2. 01-723 5901. Current releases.
⊖ Edgware Road
🚌 6, 7, 8, 15, 15A, 16, 16A, 18, 27, 36, 176

Cannon Cinema (1, 2)   **3M4**
135 Shaftesbury Av W1. 01-836 8861. Current releases.
⊖ Leicester Square
🚌 1, 14, 14A, 19, 22, 24, 29, 38, 55, 176

Cannon Cinema,   **3L1**
Baker Street
Station Approach, Marylebone Rd NW1. 01-935 9772. Modern cinema with two screens adjacent to Baker Street tube station. New releases, long runs and adult movies. *Late shows Fri & Sat.*
⊖ Baker Street
🚌 1, 2B, 13, 18, 27, 30, 74, 82, 113, 159, 176

Cannon Cinema,   **3N4**
Haymarket
Haymarket SW1. 01-839 1527. Three screens showing long-running British and American releases and new releases. *Late shows Fri & Sat.*
⊖ Piccadilly Circus
🚌 3, 6, 9, 12, 13, 14, 14A, 15, 15A, 19, 22, 38, 53, 55, 88, 159, T1

Cannon Cinema,   **3M3**
Oxford Street
Oxford St W1. 01-636 0310. Five screens showing general releases. *Late shows Fri & Sat.*
⊖ Oxford Circus, Tottenham Court Road
🚌 3, 6, 7, 8, 12, 13, 15, 15A, 25, 53, 88, 113, 159, 500, C2

Cannon Cinema,   **3N4**
Panton Street
Panton St SW1. 01-930 0631. Four small cinemas under one roof showing very new releases.
⊖ Piccadilly Circus
🚌 3, 6, 9, 12, 13, 14, 14A, 15, 15A, 19, 22, 38, 53, 55, 88, 159

Cannon Premiere Cinema   **3N4**
Swiss Centre, Leicester Sq WC2. 01-439 4470. New releases in this complex of four cinemas. *Late shows Fri & Sat.*
⊖ Leicester Square, Piccadilly Circus
🚌 1, 3, 6, 9, 12, 13, 14, 14A, 15, 15A, 19, 22, 24, 29, 38, 53, 55, 88, 159, 176

Cannon Royal Cinema   **3N4**
35–37 Charing Cross Rd WC2. 01-930 6915. Long-running British and American releases. *Late shows Fri & Sat.*
⊖ Leicester Square
🚌 1, 24, 29, 176

Cannon Street Station   **4T4**
Cannon St EC4. Information on 01-928 5100. Rebuilt in 1965, with office accommodation above, the station serves the south-east London suburbs, Kent and East Sussex. *Station closed Sat & Sun.*
⊖ Cannon Street (Mon–Fri only)
🚌 15, 17, 149
≠ Cannon Street (Mon–Fri only)

Carlyle's House   **5Y1**
24 Cheyne Row SW3. 01-352 7087. Thomas Carlyle, formidable 'sage of Chelsea' and author of – among other works – 'The History of the French Revolution', lived here with his wife Jane from 1834 until their respective deaths. The interior of their modest 18thC house has been so successfully preserved that there is an eerie sense of his immanence. His desk, books, manuscripts and letters are in the skylit attic study, built as a haven from distracting sounds but a failure, since it had the curious effect of magnifying them. *Open 11.00–17.00 Wed–Sat; 14.00–17.00 Sun. Closed Mon, Tue & Nov–Mar.* Charge.
⊖ South Kensington (then bus 45, 49)
🚌 39 (direct), or 11, 22 to King's Road, or 19, 45, 49 to Cheyne Walk

Carnaby Street   **3M3**
W1. A paved pedestrian precinct of boutiques and Indian emporia, thrumming with taped light rock. Still haunted by the ghost of the Swinging Sixties. This is no longer where it's at, but it is where it's been.

⊖ Oxford Circus
🚌 1, 3, 6, 7, 8, 12, 13, 15, 15A, 16A, 25, 53, 73, 88, 113, 137, 159, 500, C2

The Cenotaph   *3O4*
Whitehall SW1. Sir Edwin Lutyen's movingly simple memorial to the dead of two World Wars. The annual Service of Remembrance takes place here in November.
⊖ Westminster
🚌 3, 11, 12, 24, 29, 53, 77, 77A, 88, 109, 159, 170, C1

Charing Cross Hotel   *3N5*
Strand WC2. 01-839 7282. The Betjeman Carvery is open for lunch and dinner every day. Help yourself to traditional British beef, lamb and pork with all that goes with them – Yorkshire pudding and roast potatoes for example. *Open LD Mon – Sun.*
⊖ Charing Cross, Embankment
🚌 1, 3, 6, 9, 11, 12, 13, 15, 15A, 24, 29, 53, 77, 77A, 88, 109, 159, 170, 176, 199
➤ Charing Cross

Charing Cross Station   *3N5*
Strand WC2. Information on 01-928 5100. Built in 1864 to serve the south-east London suburbs and Kent. The cross itself, in the station forecourt, is a replica of the last of the 'Eleanor crosses', set up by Edward I to mark the resting places of his Queen's cortege as it journeyed from Nottingham to Westminster Abbey.

⊖ Charing Cross, Embankment
🚌 1, 3, 6, 9, 11, 12, 13, 15, 15A, 24, 29, 53, 77, 77A, 88, 109, 159, 170, 176, 199
➤ Charing Cross

Charlton House
Charlton Rd SE7. 01-856 3951. Perfect small red brick Jacobean manor house, built 1607–12, with fine ceilings and staircase and some bizarre chimney pieces. Now occupied by an active Community Centre whose staff will conduct a tour when circumstances permit – lunchtime is usually best. Telephone manager for appointment.
🚌 53, 54, 75
➤ Charlton

Chartered Insurance   *4S4*
Institute Museum
20 Aldermanbury EC2. 01-606 3835. In the days before the Fire Brigade the insurance companies did the job – but each would only douse flames on a building bearing its own fire mark. Here you may inspect these marks and the fire-fighting equipment used on the property they protected. *Open 09.15 – 17.00 Mon – Fri. Closed Sat, Sun & Nat Hols.* Free.
⊖ Bank
🚌 8, 22, 25, 501, 502

Chelsea Barracks   *5X3*
Chelsea Bridge Rd SW3. Sleek early 60s building which is one of the homes of the Coldstream, Grenadier, Scots and Welsh Guards. Some weekdays they parade at *10.20* and leave at *10.55* to relieve the Guard at Buckingham Palace. On other days and at weekends they leave from Wellington Barracks at *11.00.* The National Tourist Information Centre, (telephone 01-730 3488), has details of their movements.
⊖ Sloane Square
🚌 11, 39, 137

Chelsea Bridge   *5Y3*
SW3. Seven hundred feet of handsome suspension bridge linking Chelsea with Battersea Park. It was rebuilt in the 1930s, 60 years after Albert Bridge, and is regularly repainted to enliven its distinctive structure.
⊖ Sloane Square (then bus 137)
🚌 137

Chelsea Old Church, All Saints
5Y1

Chelsea Embankment SW3. The modern brick exterior comes as a shock – the church was bombed in 1941 and restored in the 50s – but inside it is rich in evocative memorials; the 17thC Sara Colville rises in her shroud, Lord and Lady Dacre are commemorated in baroque splendour, there are wall plaques to Henry James and William de Morgan. The chapel, which was built by Sir Thomas Moore in 1528, incorporates a 14thC archway.
θ South Kensington (then bus 45, 49)
🚌 19, 39, 45, 49

Chelsea Old Town Hall
5X1

King's Rd SW3. 01-352 1856. The venue for the Chelsea Antiques Fair in March and September and the Chelsea Arts Society and Craftsmen's Fair in October. Also houses the Registrar's offices, an indoor swimming pool and sports centre, and the local library. The attractive building was put up in the 1880s by John Brydon, its Ionic façade added in 1908 by Leonard Stokes.
θ Sloane Square (then bus)
🚌 11, 19, 22, 49

Chelsea Physic Garden
5Y2

Royal Hospital Rd SW3. 01-352 5646. This is the second oldest Botanical Garden in the UK – only the one at Oxford is older. It was founded by the Society of Apothecaries in 1673. Plants are grown for research and teaching purposes and seeds exchanged on a worldwide scale – the seeds which grew into the cottonfields of the Southern US originated here. *Open 14.00 –17.00 Wed & Sun or by appointment*. Charge.
θ Sloane Square
🚌 39

Chelsea Royal Hospital
5X2

Royal Hospital Rd SW3. 01-730 0161. Unique retirement home founded by Charles II for aged and infirm soldiers – the 'Chelsea Pensioners' – whose scarlet frock coats and black tricorns dazzle visitors. The building of 1682 is by Wren, the stables and small museum of 1814 –17 are by Sir John Soane. The pleasant grounds hold the famous massed blooms of the Chelsea Flower Show each May. *Open 10.00–12.00 & 14.15–16.00 Mon –Fri; 14.00–16.00 Sun. Closed Sat.* Free.
θ Sloane Square
🚌 11, 39, 137

Cheshire Cheese, Ye Olde
4S2

145 Fleet St EC4. 01-353 6170. Rambling, low ceiling'd and atmospheric old inn with three smallish bars and three small restaurants, all with oak tables and sawdusted floors. The 14thC crypt of Whitefriars Monastery, still intact beneath the cellar bar, is hired out for parties. Famous for good, rich game puddings in autumn and winter. *Open Mon–Fri. Closes 21.00 & all Sat & Sun.*
θ Blackfriars
🚌 4, 6, 9, 11, 15, 15A, 171A, 502

Chessington World of Adventures

Leatherhead Rd, Chessington, Surrey. 03737 27227. Sixty-five acres of zoo on the outskirts of London. Spectacular family rides set in specially designed areas – The Mystic East, Calamity Canyon, The Fifth Dimension. A monorail travels overhead giving a marvellous view of the children's zoo, the bird garden and the polar bear plunge. *Open 10.00–17.00 Mon–Sun. Closed Xmas day.* Charge.
θ Richmond (then bus 71)
🚌 71, Green Line 714
≈ Chessington South

Cheyne Walk
5Y1

SW3. This picturesque riverside road with its appealing Georgian houses and ferocious modern traffic is part of the heart of old Chelsea. Great names keep its magic alive. George Eliot died at No 4, Rossetti and Swinburne lived at No 16, Whistler worked his way through 21, 96 and 101, Mrs Gaskell was born at 93 and Turner spent his later years at 119.
θ South Kensington (then bus 45, 49)
🚌 19, 39, 45, 49

Chiswick House

Burlington La W4. 01-995 0508. A lovely Palladian villa, designed in 1725–9 by the third Earl of Burlington as a gallery where fine pictures were hung and artists and writers

entertained. The attractive grounds with canals, orangery and Italian garden, and the almost baroque splendour of the interior, were all designed by William Kent, who used perspective painting to great effect on the inside of the dome of the central salon, making it appear higher than it actually is. Pleasant garden cafeteria. *Open 09.30– 13.00 & 14.00–18.30 Tue–Sun. Closed Mon all year, Tue & 16.00 Oct–Mar.* Charge.
⊖ Hammersmith (then bus 290)
🚌 290, E3
⇌ Chiswick

Chiswick Mall
W4. Lovely 17th and 18thC riverside houses between Strand-on-the-Green near Kew Bridge and Hammersmith Bridge. An extremely pleasant walk punctuated by excellent old riverside hostelries.
⊖ Hammersmith (then bus 290)
🚌 290

Christie, Manson & Woods *3N3*
8 King St, St James's SW1. 01-839 9060. Internationally famous and fully comprehensive fine art auctioneers in whose premises works of art and large sums of money have changed hands since 1766. Sales generally begin at *11.00* and continue after lunch. *Open 09.00 10.45 Mon–Fri. Closed Sat & Sun.*
⊖ Green Park
🚌 9, 14, 14A, 19, 22, 38, 55

Christie's South Kensington *2J5*
58 Old Brompton Rd SW7. 01-581 2231. A slightly down-market younger brother of the St James's branch, dealing in toys, cars, jewellery, wine and furs. *Open 09.00 –17.00 Mon–Fri. Closed Sat & Sun.*
⊖ South Kensington
🚌 14, 30, 45, 49

Clarence House *3O3*
Stable Yard SW1. Built by Nash in 1825 for the Duke of Clarence who later became William IV, and now the London residence of Queen Elizabeth the Queen Mother. When she is at home a lone piper plays in the garden at *09.00* each day.
⊖ Green Park, St James's Park
🚌 9, 14, 14A, 19, 22, 25, 38, 55

Claridges Hotel *3M2*
Brook St W1. 01-629 8860. Quiet luxury and traditional comfort.

There is a 30s atmosphere in the restaurant with its haute cuisine and distinguished wine list, a good Smörgasbord in the Causerie, and a touch of class in the comfortable lounge where liveried footmen serve sandwiches and pastries until *17.30* when they change their livery and take orders for cocktails.
⊖ Bond Street
🚌 25

Cleopatra's Needle *3N5*
Victoria Embankment SW1. One of a pair of obelisks from an Egyptian tomb, c1450 BC, a gift from Egypt, set up here in 1877 and nothing to do with the lady herself. Two 'time capsule' jars beneath the pedestal contain some things the Victorians felt would interest future archaeologists – including a box of hairpins and Bradshaw's Railway Timetable.
⊖ Embankment, Temple (not Sun)
🚌 1, 3, 6, 9, 11, 12, 13, 15, 15A, 24, 29, 53, 77, 77A, 88, 109, 159, 170, 176, 199, T1 to Trafalgar Square

Cockney Pride *3N3*
6 Jermyn St SW1. 01-930 5339. Nostalgic reconstruction of a Victorian cockney pub, where real ale

is served with the bangers and mash. Live and lively Cockney bands play in the big bar every night. *Open Mon–Sun.*

ⓔ Piccadilly Circus

▆▆▆3, 6, 9, 12, 13, 14, 14A, 15, 15A, 19, 22, 38, 53, 55, 88, 159

Cockpit Theatre   1D1

Gateforth St NW8. 01-262 7907. A purpose-built youth arts workshop, with an adaptable studio theatre, where avant-garde drama and music are offered by visiting companies, both professional and amateur. The organisers sometimes set up musical and dramatic events in unexpected parts of town – Clapham Common for example. Bar and light snacks in the foyer. *Open   09.00–22.30   Mon–Sun. Closed two weeks at Xmas, two weeks in Jul.*

ⓔ Marylebone, Edgware Road

▆▆▆159

Coliseum   3N4

St Martin's La WC2. 01-836 3161. The English National Opera has been based since the 1960s in this splendidly lavish theatre designed by Oswald Stoll in 1904, with the first revolving stage in Britain and a majestic arched and columned interior. International ballet companies perform for limited seasons when the ENO is on its summer tours.

ⓔ Leicester Square, Charing Cross

▆▆▆1, 3, 6, 9, 11, 12, 13, 15, 15A, 24, 29, 53, 77, 77A, 88, 109, 159, 170, 176, 199

Comedy Theatre   3N4

Panton St SW1. 01-930 2578. Small proscenium arch theatre originally built for comic opera, now offering the normal West End mix of comedy and drama.

ⓔ Piccadilly Circus

▆▆▆3, 6, 9, 12, 13, 14, 15, 15A, 19, 22, 38, 53, 55, 88, 159

Commonwealth Institute   2H2

230 Kensington High St W8. 01-603 4535. Behind a forest of flagpoles stands what appears to be a glass and concrete tent. Inside are three levels of exhibition galleries illustrating the cultural and economic life not only of the Commonwealth but of the continents of Asia and Africa as well. There is a library and

resource centre, an adaptable theatre-cum-cinema, an art gallery, a book and gift shop, coffee bar and restaurant – and frequent lively carnivals or festivals. *Open 10.00– 17.30 Mon–Sat; 14.00–17.30 Sun. Closed Nat Hols. Free.*

ⓔ High Street Kensington

▆▆▆9, 27, 28, 31, 33, 49, 73, C1

Connaught Hotel   3N2

Carlos Pl W1. 01-499 7070. Dignified and distinguished, its panelled dining room and à la carte Grill still enjoy an unrivalled reputation for excellent English and French cuisine.

ⓔ Bond Street

▆▆▆25

Courtauld Institute   3L4
Galleries

Woburn Sq WC1. 01-580 1015. Rich and rare paintings, including works by Botticelli, Rubens, Rembrandt, Tiepolo, Goya, the French Impressionists and Post-Impressionists. The collection is made up of Samuel Courtauld's bequest, the collection of Lord Lee of Fareham, the Roger Fry bequest of 19thC and 20thC British and French paintings, the Witt Collection of Old Master Drawings and the Gambier-Parry bequest of early Italian paintings. *Open 10.00–17.00 Mon–Sat; 14.30–18.00 Sun. Closed Nat Hols. Charge.*

ⓔ Russell Square, Goodge Street

▆▆▆68, 77, 77A, 168, 188

Covent Garden   3N4

WC2. Originally designed by Inigo Jones (with his St Paul's church) as a residential square in the 1630s. The market buildings, including the Floral Hall by E. M. Barry, were added in the mid 19thC. In the early 1970s the wholesale fruit and veg market moved to Nine Elms and in came small shops for clothes, herbs, books and chocolates and stalls for arts and crafts, and all the wonders of the London Transport Museum. The area is now London's nearest equivalent to the Left Bank in Paris. There are health foods, crêpes, hamburgers and full meals, often at outside tables. The Punch and Judy pub is near the site of the first puppet show. The Crusting Pipe is a good wine bar. Chic restaurants vie for the custom of well-

and also of books. Coffee bar for light refreshment. *Open 14.00– 17.00 Tue–Sat; 14.00–17.00 Sun. Closed Mon.* Free.
⊖ Piccadilly Circus, Charing Cross
🚌 1, 3, 6, 9, 11, 12, 13, 14, 14A, 15, 15A, 19, 22, 24, 29, 38, 53, 55, 77, 77A, 88, 159, 170, 176, 199

Craftsman Potters Shop   3M3
Marshall St W1. 01-437 7605. Beautiful and interesting pottery, hand-made by craftsmen, and also books, tools and information about relevant exhibitions. *Open 10.00– 17.30 Mon–Fri; 10.30–17.00 Sat. Closed Sun.*
⊖ Tottenham Court Road
🚌 1, 7, 8, 14, 14A, 19, 22, 24, 29, 38, 55, 73, 134, 176

Cranks Restaurant   3M3
8 Marshall St W1. 01-437 9431. Stone-ground excellence at this earliest of London's health food restaurants. Light piney decor, soft baroque background music, juices, infusions, vegetable dishes, salads and sticky cakes. *Open LD Mon –Sat. Closed Sun.*
⊖ Oxford Circus, Piccadilly Circus
🚌 3, 6, 9, 12, 13, 15, 15A, 53, 88, 159, 176

hooled visitors and business diners, while street entertainers compete for more transient attention. Attractive and fun – if a bit precious and overpriced.
⊖ Covent Garden
🚌 1, 6, 9, 11, 13, 15, 15A, 77, 77A, 170, 176, 199 (all go to the Strand)

Covent Garden General   3M4
Stores
111 Long Acre WC2. 01-240 0331. Modish household effects and attractive gifts – lots of basketry, china and enamelled tinware. Also a healthy salad bar which opens one hour after the shop opens and closes one hour before the shop. *Open Mon–Sat 10.00–24.00; Sun 12.00–19.00.*
⊖ Covent Garden
🚌 1, 6, 9, 11, 13, 15, 15A, 77, 77A, 170, 176, 199 (all go to the Strand)

Crafts Council Gallery   3N4
12 Waterloo Pl SW1. 01-930 4811. The Crafts Council is concerned with craft conservation and education and administers various grants and loan schemes to encourage new work. The Gallery shows changing exhibitions and is a source of information, not least by way of the well-stocked colour slide index,

Criterion Theatre   3N3
Piccadilly Circus W1. 01-930 3216. A listed building and London's only underground theatre in the strictly physical sense. You even go down to the Upper Circle, through a lobby still decorated with original Victorian tiles. One of the Wyndham theatres (others are Albery, Donmar Warehouse, Piccadilly and Wyndham's) and theatre tours are available.
⊖ Piccadilly Circus
🚌 3, 6, 9, 12, 13, 14, 15, 15A, 19, 22, 38, 53, 55, 88, 159

Crosby Hall   5Y1
Cheyne Walk SW3. 01-352 9663. Incorporates the magnificent 15thC dining hall of the City mansion of Sir John Crosby. It was transplanted piecemeal to its site in 1910. Serves as a residence for The British Federation of University Women. Telephone for appointment to view. Free.
⊖ South Kensington (then bus 45, 49)
🚌 19, 39, 45, 49

Crystal Palace
SE19. 01-778 7148. Paxton's won-drous glass building known as the Crystal Palace, the centrepiece of The Great Exhibition of 1851, was removed here from its original site in Hyde Park and burnt to the ground in 1936. The 70-acre hillside park, with its wide views, has a National Youth and Sports Centre with an Olympic-size swimming pool and a fine modern sports sta-dium, as well as an artificial ski slope. The boating and fishing lake has four islands which are inhabited by 20 large replicas of prehistoric reptiles, including a wistful iguana-don, designed by Richard Owen in 1854, and there are real live animals of a small and strokable kind in the children's zoo. Bands play in sum-mer. *Open 08.00–½ hour before dusk.*
⊖ Brixton (then bus 2B, 3)
🚌 2B, 3, 63, 108B, 122, 137, 157, 227, 249
🚊 Crystal Palace

Cuming Musem
Newington District Library, Wal-worth Rd SE17. 01-703 3324. The quaint and personal collection of Richard Cuming and his son, begun in 1872, to which has been added items of local interest disinterred from beneath Southwark during archaeological digs and the sinking of new foundations. Among the treasures are charms to cure rheumatism, an ex-dancing bear and some 12thC carvings from Southwark Cathedral. *Open 10.00 –17.30 Tue–Sat; 14.00–17.00 Sun. Closed Mon & Nat Hols.* Free.
⊖ Elephant and Castle
🚌 12, 35, 40, 45, 68, 171, 176, 184, 185A

Curzon Cinema Mayfair   *3N2*
Curzon St W1. 01-499 3737. De-liciously comfortable surroundings in which to watch quality new re-leases. Good coffee on sale in the foyer. It's wise to book.
⊖ Hyde Park Corner
🚌 2B, 9, 14, 14A, 16, 19, 22, 25, 30, 36, 38, 52, 52A, 55, 73, 74, 82, 137, 500

Curzon Cinema West End   *3M4*
93 Shaftesbury Av WC2. 01-439 4805. New West End releases.
⊖ Leicester Square
🚌 1, 14, 14A, 19, 22, 24, 29, 38, 55, 176

Cutty Sark
King William Walk SE10. 01-858 3445. One of the great sailing tea clippers, built in 1869, now stands in dry dock waiting for visitors to admire her accommodation and rig-ging. Next to her is Gipsy Moth IV in which Sir Francis Chichester sailed around the world in 1966. *Both ships open 11.00–18.00 Mon–Sat; 14.30–18.00 Sun. Closed 17.00 Oct–Mar.* Charge.
⊖ Surrey Docks (then bus 1, 188)
Docklands Railway: Island Gardens (then by foot tunnel)
🚌 1, 177, 180, 188, 286
🚊 Greenwich

Daily Mail   **4T2**
Northcliffe House, Carmelite St EC4. 01-353 6000. Six-month waiting list for a tour of the newspaper offices. Minimum age 14, groups of 12. *From 21.00–23.15 Tue & Wed.* Contact General Production Manager.
⊖ Blackfriars, Chancery Lane (not Sun)
🚌 4, 6, 9, 11, 15, 15A, 17, 45, 46, 63, 141, 171A, 502, 513

Daily Mirror   **4S2**
Holborn Circus EC1. 01-353 0246. Three-month waiting list for a tour of the newspaper's offices. Minimum age 16, groups of 12. *From 21.00–23.15 Tue & Wed.* Contact Production Department.
⊖ Chancery Lane (not Sun), Farringdon
🚌 8, 17, 22, 25, 45, 46, 171A, 221, 243, 259, 501

Davenport's Joke Shop   **3L4**
51 Gt Russell St WC1. 01-405 8524. An antidote to the splendid and dignified antiquities in The British Museum opposite – sneezing powder, masks, tricks, jokes and also some of the more elaborate and expensive deceptions used by professional conjurors. *Open 09.30–17.30 Mon–Fri. Closed Sat & Sun.*
⊖ Tottenham Court Road
🚌 1, 7, 8, 14, 19, 22, 24, 25, 29, 38, 55, 73, 134, 176

David Shilling Hats   **1D3**
36 Marylebone High St W1. 01-487 3179. The most eccentric of David Shilling's designs are modelled annually by his mother at Royal Ascot; indeed the three of them, mother, son and hat, have become a national institution. He will make you a simple little number in a few hours – an extravaganza takes a bit longer. Appointment wise if you want the man himself. *Open 09.00–18.00 Mon–Fri. Closed Sat & Sun.*
⊖ Baker Street, Bond Street, Regent's Park (then walk)
🚌 137, C2 (to Portland Place) 1, 2, 2B, 13, 30, 74, 82, 113, 159 (to Paddington Street) 18, 27, 30, 176 (to Marylebone High Street)

Debenham's   **3M2**
344–8 Oxford St W1. 01-580 3000. One of the major department stores. Here are fashionable clothes at reasonable prices and also well-stocked departments for lingerie, hosiery, cosmetics and kitchenware. There is a cafeteria on the second floor and a self-service restaurant in the basement. The recent, extensive refurbishment includes a new atrium as its centre-piece. *Open 09.30–18.00 Mon & Tue, Fri & Sat; 10.00–18.00 Wed; 09.30–20.00 Thur. Closed Sun.*
⊖ Bond Street
🚌 1, 6, 7, 8, 12, 13, 15, 15A, 16A, 25, 73, 88, 113, 137, 159, 500

Design Centre   **3N4**
28 Haymarket SW1. 01-839 8000. The Design Council is an arbiter of taste and quality, awarding its distinctive triangular marks of approval to British goods which come up to its high standards. Here are changing exhibitions of the newest of the approved and a card index to direct you to retail outlets. Many of the smaller items – glass, kitchenware, stationery and cards – are for sale. Pleasant little coffee bar. *Open 10.00–18.00 Mon & Tue; 10.00–20.00 Wed–Sat; 13.00–18.00 Sun.* Free.
⊖ Piccadilly Circus
🚌 3, 6, 9, 12, 13, 14, 15, 15A, 19, 22, 38, 53, 55, 88, 159

Diamond Centre   **3M2**
10 Hanover St W1. 01-629 5511. The largest collection of diamonds in London are here, so security is tight and two days' notice of a proposed visit is essential. Visitors can see the evolution of a diamond from rough stone to glittering gem, as well as the collection itself. *Open by appointment only.* Charge.
⊖ Oxford Circus
🚌 1, 3, 6, 7, 8, 12, 13, 15, 15A, 16A, 25, 53, 73, 88, 113, 137, 159, 500, C2

Dickens House Museum   *3L5*

48 Doughty St WC1. 01-405 2127. Charles Dickens lived and worked here from April 1837 to December 1839. In that relatively short time he finished the last five chapters of 'Pickwick Papers', most of 'Oliver Twist', 20 monthly instalments of 'Nicholas Nickleby' and the first few pages of 'Barnaby Rudge', and so established his reputation as a writer. The house is cared for by The Dickens Fellowship, who publish 'The Dickensian' three times a year, which is packed with fascinating memorabilia. Also houses the best Dickens library in the world (an appointment is necessary to see the library). *Open 10.00–17.00 Mon–Sat. Closed Sun & Nat Hols.* Charge.

⊖ Russell Square, Chancery Lane (not Sun)

🚌 5, 17, 19, 38, 45, 55, 171, 171A, 243, 259

Dickens Inn   *4U6*

St Katharine's Way E1. 01-488 1226. Fine views of the yacht marina and Tower Bridge from this artfully converted warehouse. Exposed beams, antique furniture, a brass-topped bar and sawdust on the floor. Pub grub in The Tavern Room on the ground floor; traditional English and classical French dishes in the first-floor Pickwick Room; fish in various forms and sauces in the top-floor Dickens Room. *Tavern open normal licensing hours Mon–Sun. Restaurants open LD Mon–Sun.*

⊖ Tower Hill
Docklands Railway: Tower Gateway

🚌 15, 42, 56, 78, 278

Dickins and Jones   *3M3*

Regent St W1. 01-734 7070. Large fashion store with a good stock of British and continental men's and women's clothes, cosmetics and perfumes, knitting wools, costume jewellery, and with an excellent underwear and lingerie department. There is also a Shopping Adviser, a hairdressing salon, the Rose Restaurant, and three coffee shops. *Open 09.30–18.00 Mon–Wed, Fri & Sat; to 19.00 Thur. Closed Sun.*

⊖ Oxford Circus

🚌 3, 6, 12, 13, 15, 15A, 53, 88, 159, C2

Dillons The Bookstore   *1D5*

82 Gower St WC1. 01-636 1577. Lushly refurbished and still expanding, London's leading academic booksellers have now devoted half the store to general books. Enlarged sections on travel, arts, biography, literature. Also sells classical music, antiquarian and bargain books. Some 5½ miles of books and 150,000 titles of books. *Open 09.00–17.30 Mon & Wed–Fri; 09.30–17.30 Tue & Sat.*

⊖ Euston Square

🚌 14, 14A, 18, 24, 29, 30, 73, 134, 176, 253

Dingwall's Club   *1A3*

Camden Lock, Chalk Farm Rd NW1. 01-267 4967. Barge-horse stables, near a busy weekend market, converted into a lively music club with burger-style restaurant. Varied contemporary music from Mon–Sun eve and at lunchtime on Sat. *Open LD Mon–Sat, D Sun. Closed L Sun.*

⊖ Camden Town

🚌 24, 31, 168, Sun only 68

Dino's Restaurant   *2J5*

1 Pelham St SW7. 01-589 3511. Long-established eatery, with a bustling Italian atmosphere, in which to enjoy breakfasts, grills, pasta, veal and chicken dishes all day and all evening. *Open 08.30 –23.45 Mon–Sun.*

⊖ South Kensington

🚌 14, 30, 45, 49, 74

Dominion Theatre   *1E5*

Tottenham Court Rd W1. 01-580 9562. Huge cinema which stages seasons of live opera and rock concerts between the musicals and movies. Booking essential.

⊖ Tottenham Court Road

🚌 1, 7, 8, 14, 14A, 19, 22, 24, 25, 29, 38, 55, 73, 134, 153, 176

Donmar Warehouse   *3M4*

41 Earlham St WC2. 01-379 6565. Comfortable studio theatre which welcomes touring companies, mounts its own productions and is a mixture of fringe venue and small legitimate West End theatre. One of the Wyndham theatres (others are Albery, Criterion, Piccadilly and Wyndham's) and theatre tours are available.

⊖ Leicester Square

🚌 1, 14, 14A, 19, 22, 24, 29, 38, 55, 176

Dorchester Hotel *3N1*
Park La W1. 01-629 8888. Luxury
and efficiency in this large, 285-
room hotel. Eat English regional and
national dishes in the Grill Room or
dine and dance in the rococo Terrace Restaurant where chef Anton
Mossiman has made his name with
inventive, handsome nouvelle
cuisine. There is also a light, airy bar
and The Promenade which serves
teas to piano accompaniment.
● Hyde Park Corner
▨2B, 16, 30, 36, 73, 74, 82, 137,
500

Downing Street *3O4*
SW1. 17thC town houses built by
Sir George Downing. No 10, with
the policeman at the door, is the
official residence of the Prime
Minister, No 11 of the Chancellor of
the Exchequer.
● Westminster
▨3, 11, 12, 24, 29, 53, 70, 76, 77,
77A, 88, 109, 159, 170, C1

Draper's Company Hall *4S4*
Throgmorton Av EC2. Information
from City Information Centre, St
Paul's Churchyard EC4, 01-606
3030 extn 2456. The City Livery Hall
dates from 1667 but was largely
rebuilt in 1870. Tours to see the fine
staircase and collection of silver
plate may be booked in advance.
● Bank, Liverpool Street
▨6, 8, 9, 11, 22

Drury Lane, Theatre Royal *3M5*
Catherine St WC2. 01-836 8108.
Known as 'Drury Lane', although

the entrance is around the corner.
This is the richly decorated succes-
sor to three earlier theatres on the
site. Famous for lavish musicals –
'Oklahoma', 'My Fair Lady', '42nd
Street' – and for one of the best-
loved theatre ghosts, The Man in
Grey, who appears where building
work uncovered a male skeleton,
and whose presence is said to
herald a successful show.
● Covent Garden
▨1, 4, 5, 6, 9, 11, 13, 15, 15A, 68,
77, 77A, 168, 170, 171, 176, 188,
199, 501, 502, 513

Duke of York's Theatre *3N4*
St Martin's La WC2. 01-836 5122.
Attractive small theatre, with a
domed auditorium – the first
theatre to stage 'Peter Pan' and
many other J. M. Barrie offerings.
● Leicester Square
▨1, 3, 6, 9, 11, 12, 13, 15, 15A,
24, 29, 53, 77, 77A, 88, 109, 159,
170, 176, 199

Dulwich College Picture Gallery
College Rd SE21. 01-693 5254. England's first purpose-built art gallery, designed by Sir John Soane,
with natural light washing down
from above. Incorporates a
mausoleum for the benefactors
which is bathed in amber light and
has a slightly eerie sense of expec-
tancy. The collection includes important works by Rembrandt,
Rubens, Gainsborough, Cuyp, Watteau, Murillo, Poussin, Hogarth and
Van Dyck. *Open 10.00–13.00;*
14.00–17.00 Tue–Sat; 14.00–
17.00 Sun. Closed Mon & Nat Hols.
Charge.
● Brixton (then bus 3 or P4)
▨3, P4
⇌ West Dulwich, North Dulwich

Dulwich Park
SE21. 01-693 5737. A favourite garden of the late Queen Mary, wife of
George V, which is quite spectacular in early summer when the rhododendrons and azaleas are in
bloom. There is a pleasant boating
lake, tennis courts, and a marked
trail among the trees. *Open 07.30*
–dusk. Free.
● Brixton (then bus P4, 37 to North
Dulwich Station)
▨P4, 37 (to North Dulwich Stn),
12, 78, 176, 185 (to The Plough)
⇌ West Dulwich, North Dulwich

E

Earl's Court Exhibition Hall   2K2

Warwick Rd SW5. 01-385 1200. The 19-acre Exhibition Hall, designed by Howard Crane in 1937, regularly fills its mighty space with shows which attract visitors from all over the world. In January – the largest Boat Show in Europe; in February – Crufts judges pick Top Dog; in March – the Ideal Home Exhibition; in July – the Royal Tournament; in August – the Motor Cycle Show; in October, in odd-numbered years, the Motor Show; in December the farm machinery and puzzled livestock of the Smithfield Show. Bars and Buffet. Charge.
⊖ Earl's Court
🚌 30, 31, 74

East End

Extending from the borders of the City eastwards, north of the river, this old part of London has been traditionally associated with slums, poverty, docks, warehouses, warm-hearted Cockneys, vibrant street markets and night-time violence. It was in the Whitechapel district for three grisly months in 1888 Jack the Ripper committed his hideous crimes and achieved international notoriety.

Proximity to the docks has meant that for centuries the East End has been an immigrant area and each ethnic group has left its imprint – from the 17thC Huguenot weavers who settled in Spitalfields, to the 19th and early 20thC huge influx of Jewish refugees from Eastern Europe, to today's industrious, Asian community.

Extensive bomb damage during the last war paved the way for new building developments which have changed the landscape of the area. And further developments are currently taking place as the East End experiences the spin-off effects from the commercial revival of the whole docklands area.

The famous Petticoat Lane market is still lively (and worth a visit on Sunday morning) and many of the East End pubs still go in for regular and spontaneous sing-songs. There are also some interesting cultural centres including the Bethnal Green Museum of Childhood, the Geffrye Museum and the Whitechapel Art Gallery. Blooms Jewish restaurant is on-hand for sustenance of a salt-beef kind!
⊖ Aldgate, Aldgate East, Bethnal Green, Mile End, Shadwell, Shoreditch, Stepney Green, Wapping, Whitechapel
Docklands Railway: all stations from Tower Gateway
🚌 6, 8, 10, 15, 15A, 25, 55 (from Central London)

Economist Building   3N3

25 St James's St SW1. Alison & Peter Smithson, 1964–6. A very beautiful and harmonious group of buildings with its own raised piazza. The design was intended to demonstrate a general principle for the redevelopment of dense commercial areas and is a rare example of new buildings in an area with a traditional street pattern.
⊖ Green Park, Piccadilly Circus
🚌 9, 14, 14A, 19, 22, 25, 38, 55

Elfin Oak   2G3

Near Black Lion Gate, Kensington Gdns W2. An aged stump from Richmond Park, carved by Ivor Innes in the 1930s into a magic world of clambering gnomes, winged fairies, tiny animals and birds. Iron railings protect it from loving hands.
⊖ Queensway, Bayswater
🚌 12, 88

El Vino's Wine Bar   4S2

47 Fleet St EC4. 01-353 6786. Something of an institution. Musty and masculine haunt of lawyers and journalists, who are required to wear jacket, collar and tie at all times. Ladies were not permitted to buy drinks at the bar until 1982. Excellent French and German wine

list, snacks and a restaurant for cold lunches in the cellar. *Open Mon–Fri & L Sat, closed Sat eve & all Sun.*
e Temple (not Sun), Chancery Lane (not Sun), Blackfriars
🚌 4, 6, 9, 11, 15, 15A, 171A

Eltham Palace
Off Court Yd, Eltham SE9. 01-859 2112. A royal palace beloved of kings from Henry III to Henry VIII. Henry IV was married here – though Joan of Navarre was not present at the time since it was a proxy affair. Rebuilding in the 1930s, and the fact that it is now HQ of the Institute of Army Education, has done for the atmosphere, rather, but the restored Banqueting Hall with its hammerbeam roof and oriel windows is splendid. *Open 10.30–12.15 & 14.15–10.00 Thur & Sun. Closed Mon–Wed, Fri & Sat & 16.00 in winter.* Free.
🚌 21, 61, 61B, 124, 126, 160, 161, 228, 286, B1
🚆 Eltham

Empire Cinema (1, 2, 3) **3N4**
Leicester Sq WC2. 01-437 1234. Cavernous 'movie palace' with adjustable seats, perfect vision, Dolby stereo. Shows new releases – booking advisable.
e Leicester Square
🚌 1, 24, 29, 176

Epping Forest
Essex. Six thousand acres of natural woodland, six miles long and two miles wide, stretching from Chingford to Epping. This is mixed woodland with hornbeam, oak, ash, maple, beech and birch trees, sheltering a flourishing range of natural wildlife – a shade too flourishing in the case of the grey squirrels. Large enough to get thoroughly lost, though a detailed map of the area will enable you to find two ancient British camps – Loughton Camp and Ambersbury Banks – each at least 2,000 years old. *Open 24 hours.* Free.
e Loughton (then bus 201, 250)
🚌 201, 250
🚆 Chingford

Eros **3N3**
Piccadilly Circus W1. The famous arrow-firing cherub, by Sir Alfred

Gilbert in 1892, cleaned up by the GLC in 1985, is not Eros at all but the Angel of Christian Charity, a memorial to the philanthropic Lord Shaftesbury.
e Piccadilly Circus
🚌 3, 6, 9, 12, 13, 14, 14A, 15, 15A, 19, 22, 38, 53, 55, 88, 159

Euston Station **1C5**
Euston Rd NW1. Information on 01-387 7070. Modern structure, set back from the road behind lawns and a large forecourt, which dispatches trains north to Birmingham and Manchester, Liverpool, Glasgow and Inverness.
e Euston, Euston Square
🚌 14, 14A, 18, 30, 68, 73, 77, 77A, 168, 188
🚆 Euston

D. H. Evans **3M2**
318 Oxford St W1. 01-629 8800. A House of Fraser department store with fashions for men, women and children including top designer labels and upmarket high street fashions. Also has an accessories department, Astral sports and household goods. Cafe, restaurant, export scheme, shopping advisor. *Open 09.30–18.00 Mon–Wed & Fri; 09.30–20.00 Thur; 09.00–18.00 Sat.*
e Bond Street
🚌 1, 6, 7, 8, 12, 13, 15, 15A, 16A, 25, 73, 88, 113, 137, 159, 500

F

Fenchurch Street Station **4T5**
Railway Pl, Fenchurch St EC3. Information on 01-283 7171. Victorian rail terminal, built in 1841, from which trains leave for Tilbury and Southend.
⊖ Tower Hill
🚌 10, 15, 40
≢ Fenchurch Street

Fenton House Grove
Hampstead Grove NW3. 01-435 3471. Built c1693, its early history is unknown. It was bought by a merchant called Philip Fenton in 1793 and, though it passed through other hands, kept his name. It was bequeathed to the National Trust in 1952 by its last owner, Lady Binning, together with her pictures, furniture and European and Chinese porcelain. It also houses the Benton Fletcher collection of early musical instruments, most in such good working order that you

may well tour the house to the background strains of harpsichord or virginal. *Open 11.00–17.00 Mon –Wed, Sat & Nat Hols; 14.00– 17.00 Sun. Closed Dec & Jan; & Mon–Fri Nov, Feb & Mar. Charge.*
⊖ Hampstead
🚌 46, 210, 268

Flamsteed House
Old Royal Observatory, Greenwich Park SE10. 01-858 1167. Built by Wren and topped by the octagon room observatory, it has been furnished more or less as it may have been when the first Astronomer Royal lived in it. A series of modern galleries built on at the back show the history of time-keeping, navigation and surveying by means of displays of elegant instruments, with a ticking, whirring section of clocks and watches below. *Open 10.00 –18.00 Mon–Sat; 14.00–17.30 Sun. Closes 17.00 in winter.*
⊖ New Cross, New Cross Gate (then bus 53)
🚌 53, 54, 75
≢ Maze Hill

Flanagan's Fish Parlour **1D3**
100 Baker St W1. 01-935 0287. Blithely phoney Victorian dining rooms – with stalls and sawdust, Cockney songs, breezy service, spirited pianist, and tripe and onions, fish and chips, spotted dick and custard to eat. *Open LD Mon –Sun.*
⊖ Baker Street
🚌 1, 2B, 13, 18, 27, 30, 74, 82, 113, 159, 176

Fleet Street **4S2**
EC4. London's 'street of ink' (or 'shame') has been associated with printing since the days of Caxton. Despite the mounting exodus of the major newspaper groups, a few national and many provincial newspapers still have their offices in or near it.
 When Fleet Street leaves the City, past the two dragon guardians, it enters the world of the law because all around are the four Inns of Court (Middle and Inner Temple,

Lincoln's Inn and Gray's Inn), and the Royal Courts of Justice.

This is an intriguing, historic area, with numerous pubs and wine bars all heavily patronised by journalists and lawyers.
⊖ Blackfriars, Chancery Lane (not Sun), Temple (not Sun), Aldwych (Mon–Fri rush hours only)
🚍 4, 6, 9, 11, 15, 15A, 171A

Floris   3N3
89 Jermyn St SW1. 01-930 2885. Perfumiers to the Court of St James since the reign of George IV. Their very English flower perfumes have matching toiletries and there are gruffer preparations for men. *Open 09.30–17.30 Mon–Fri; 09.30–16.00 Sat. Closed Sun.*
⊖ Piccadilly Circus
🚍 3, 6, 9, 12, 13, 14, 14A, 15, 15A, 19, 22, 38, 53, 55, 88, 159

Fortnum and Mason   3N3
181 Piccadilly W1. 01-734 8040. World-famous, decorous department store with floor-walkers in morning dress, a food hall full of bottled exotica and delicatessen delicacies, superb hampers, and designer collection clothes. Watch the outside clock on the hour when four-foot-high figures of Messrs F and M emerge from doors and bow to each other to 18thC airs. *Open 09.00–17.30 Mon–Fri; 09.00–17.00 Sat. Closed Sun.*
⊖ Piccadilly Circus
🚍 14, 14A, 19, 22, 25, 38, 55

Foundling Hospital   4Q1
(Thomas Coram Foundation for Children)
40 Brunswick Sq WC1. 01-278 2424. The charitable foundation, set up by a sea captain in the 18thC to give shelter to homeless children, now functions as an adoption and fostering agency for children with special needs. Good collection of paintings, many by, or of, past governors. There are three Hogarths, a Gainsborough, original Handel scores and sad cases of trinkets left with children by destitute mothers. *Open 10.00–16.00 Mon–Fri. Closed Sat & Sun & during conferences – telephone first.* Charge.
⊖ Russell Square
🚍 68, 77, 77A, 168, 188

Foyles   3M4
119 Charing Cross Rd WC2. 01-437 5660. The largest of London's bookshops with an immense and wide-ranging stock, arranged rather perversely by publisher rather than author or subject. *Open 09.00–18.00 Mon–Wed, Fri & Sat; until 19.00 Thur. Closed Sun.*
⊖ Tottenham Court Road
🚍 1, 14, 14A, 19, 22, 24, 29, 38, 55, 176

Freud's House Museum
20 Maresfield Gdns NW3. 01-435 2002. This is where Sigmund Freud lived after his escape from the Nazis in Vienna in 1938 until his death just over a year later. His daughter Anna continued to reside and work in the house preserving her father's study and library as he had left them until her own death in 1982. The house has been maintained in its original style, adorned with distinctive Viennese painted furniture. Freud's study holds the famous analytical couch and chair, as well as his impressive collection of books and antiquities. Upstairs Anna Freud's room has a display of awards for her own work in the field of psychology. Freud's former bedroom, with letters and newspaper cuttings, now serves as a display room for temporary exhibitions on various aspects of psychology. The reception area sells copies of the Freud Penguin Library along with a number of postcards and souvenirs. *Open 10.00–17.00 Mon–Sat, 13.00–17.00 Sun. Closed Xmas.* Charge.
⊖ Finchley Road
🚍 13, 46, 82, 113

Fulham Palace
Fulham Palace Rd SW6. The oldest visible parts of the calm two-storey house and intimate collegiate courtyard are Tudor. Used as ecclesiastical offices and not visitable, though the extensive riverside grounds are open to the public, and contain a magical herb garden discovered through a narrow Tudor arch. Fourteen past bishops lie in the nearby yew-shadowed churchyard of All Saints. *Open 09.00–½ hour before dusk.* Free.
⊖ Putney Bridge
🚍 14, 22, 30, 74, 220

G

Garrick Theatre   3N4
Charing Cross Rd WC2. 01-379 6107. Built in 1897, named for the actor David Garrick, and said to be haunted by Arthur Bourchier, one of its earliest actor-managers. Puts on varied programmes.
⊖ Leicester Square, Charing Cross
🚌 1, 3, 6, 9, 11, 13, 15, 15A, 24, 29, 53, 77, 77A, 88, 109, 159, 170, 176, 199

Gate Cinema Notting Hill   2G2
Notting Hill Gate W11. 01-727 5750. The first Gate to open and to set the tone for showing outstanding films. Recently refurbished. *Late show Sat.* Membership at door.
⊖ Notting Hill Gate
🚌 12, 27, 28, 31, 52, 52A, 88

Gatwick Airport
Horley, Surrey. 0293 28822. Busy international airport with an 800-foot-high viewing gallery from which to watch most types of aircraft, including light planes. *Gallery open 09.00–19.50 Mon–Sun. Close dusk in winter.* Charge.
Green Line 727, 747, 777
≠ Gatwick Airport

Le Gavroche   3N1
43 Upper Brook St W1. 01-408 0881. One of the best restaurants in London, renowned for its luxurious atmosphere, imaginative haute cuisine, magnificent wine list, faultless service. It is essential to book – and to be prepared for very high prices. *Open LD Mon–Fri. Closed Sat & Sun*
⊖ Marble Arch
🚌 2B, 16, 30, 36, 73, 74, 82, 137, 500

Gay Hussar   3M3
2 Greek St W1. 01-437 0973. Intimate and sophisticated Hungarian restaurant in Soho, with some well-known politicians and publishers among its loyal devotees. Chilled wild cherry soup, roast saddle of carp and orange curd pancakes might be the order of the day. Book-

ing essential. *Open LD Mon–Sat. Closed Sun.*
⊖ Tottenham Court Road
🚌 1, 14, 14A, 19, 22, 24, 29, 38, 55, 176

Geffrye Museum   4Q6
Kingsland Rd E2. 01-739 8368. Named for a past Lord Mayor of London whose bequest founded the almshouses, built in 1715. These attractive buildings were converted into a museum of English furniture and woodwork early this century. It is arranged as a series of fully furnished period rooms so that you can assess the development of design from Georgian England to the 1930s. School visits are encouraged and projects and activities arranged in the holidays. *Open 10.00–17.00 Tue–Sat; 14.00–17.00 Sun. Closed Mon & Xmas.* Free.
⊖ Liverpool Street (then bus)
🚌 22, 22A, 48, 67, 149, 243, Sun only 243A, 263A, 279A

Geological Museum   2J5
Exhibition Rd SW7. 01-589 3444. The National Museum of Earth Science is a part of the Institute of Geological Sciences. Its collections are drawn from all over the world, though with one floor devoted entirely to British geology. Riveting displays of fossils, the world-famous gem and ornamental stone collection, a piece of moon rock, a stirring earthquake simulator, and Story of the Earth which describes the origin of the whole universe. *Open 10.00–18.00 Mon–Sat; 14.30–18.00 Sun.* Free.
⊖ South Kensington
🚌 14, 30, 45, 49, 74, C1

George Inn   4U4
77 Borough High St SE1. 01-407 2056. London's only remaining galleried coaching inn, first mentioned in John Stow's 'History of London' in 1590 and rebuilt, after fire damage, in 1676. Patronised by Dickens and featured in 'Little Dorrit'. The summer season of Shakespeare plays will resume as soon as the

immense building-work next door is completed. There are two bars, a wine bar, an à la carte grill room and a table d'hôte lunchtime restaurant. *Open LD Mon–Sun.*

⊖ London Bridge

🚌 10, 17, 21, 35, 40, 43, 44, 47, 48, 70, 133, P3

Globe Theatre *3M3*
Shaftesbury Av W1. 01-437 1592. Built in 1906, designed by W. G. R. Sprague with a French flavour and reproduction Regency staircase. Known for a wide variety of plays but especially 'quality' comedies.

⊖ Piccadilly Circus

🚌 14, 14A, 19, 22, 38, 55

Goldsmiths Hall *4S4*
Foster La EC2. Information from City Information Centre, St Paul's Churchyard EC4. 01-606 3030. Classical-style palazzo rebuilt in 1835 by Philip Hardwick for the company whose duty it is to assay gold and silver plate and stamp it with its own leopard-head hallmark. Occasional exhibitions and regular tours. Enquire at telephone number above.

⊖ St Paul's

🚌 4, 8, 22, 25, 141, 501, 502

Goodwins Court *3N4*
Just off St Martin's La WC2. Neat and complete row of bow-fronted 18thC shops.

⊖ Leicester Square

🚌 1, 24, 29, 176

Gordon's Wine Cellar *3N5*
47 Villiers St WC2. 01-930 1408. A 300-year-old cellar with a main bar and a tunnel-shaped inner sanctum. Only Quasimodo could be truly comfortable hunched against the damp curvature of the ancient stone walls, yet the candlelit atmosphere is so pleasant that customers return again and again. Good selection of wines, sherries, ports and madeiras; tempting hot and cold buffet. *Open Mon–Fri to 21.00. Closed Sat & Sun.*

⊖ Charing Cross, Embankment

🚌 1, 3, 6, 9, 11, 12, 13, 15, 15A, 24, 29, 53, 77, 77A, 88, 109, 159, 170, 176, 199

Gray's Inn *4R1*
Holborn WC1. 01-405 8164. Entrance from passage next to 22

High Holborn. An Inn of Court since the 14thC, although the oldest surviving buildings are 17thC. Francis Bacon had chambers here from 1577 until his death. It is said that he laid out the gardens and planted the Catalpas, now exceedingly venerable and supported on crutches. *Gardens open on summer weekday afternoons; Hall open by written application to the Under Treasurer.* Free.

⊖ Chancery Lane (not Sun), Holborn

🚌 5, 8, 17, 19, 22, 25, 38, 45, 55, 171, 171A, 243, 259, 501

Great Eastern Hotel *4S5*
Liverpool St EC2. 01-283 4363. The City Gates Bar and Restaurant – in this the City's only hotel – is *open every day all day* for full breakfasts, light lunches, coffees or teas. There is also the Entrecote Restaurant which is *open Mon–Fri only*, at lunchtime, for steak and apple pie, or the Abercrombie Bar for real ale and ploughman's lunches from *Mon–Fri.*

⊖ Liverpool Street

🚌 5, 6, 8, 9, 11, 22, 22A, 35, 47, 48, 78, 133, 149, 502, Sun only 243A, 263A, 279A

≉ Liverpool Street

Green Park *3O2*
SW1. A simple green space with trees for shade and deckchairs for

comfort. Henry VIII enclosed it as a deer park and later, in the 18thC, the fashionable gentry strolled within its bounds. The delicate gates opposite Buckingham Palace were made by Jean Tijou around 1690. *Open 05.00–24.00. Free.*
⊖ Green Park
🚌 9, 14, 14A, 19, 22, 25, 38, 55

Greenwich
SE10, SE3. Royal Greenwich once had a palace – in fact Henry VIII was born here. It was rebuilt, principally by Wren, as a Royal Naval Hospital and is now the Royal Naval College. Greenwich remains rich in history, much of it within the beautiful royal park which sweeps down to the river. Here are the National Maritime Museum, and the Old Royal Observatory where you can see the Zero Meridian from which Greenwich Meantime is calculated. In dry dock by the waterside are 'Cutty Sark' and Sir Francis Chichester's 'Gipsy Moth'.
Greenwich Theatre offers new and classic plays and has an art gallery, too. There are concerts in the Wren Chapel of the Royal Naval College from October to April and again during the Greenwich Festival in June. The Festival itself attracts numerous visitors to its concerts, events and exhibitions which involve most possible venues in the

area, including the open air. See separate entries for all the above.
⊖ Surrey Docks (then bus 1, 188), New Cross (then bus 177) Docklands Railway: Island Gardens then via foot tunnel
🚌 1, 177, 180, 188, 286
≹ Greenwich
Boats from Westminster and Charing Cross Piers

Greenwich Theatre
Crooms Hill SE10. 01-858 7755. Purpose-built with a large ground floor restaurant which has a bar in one corner and a wine bar in the other. Upstairs an airy space houses changing exhibitions of paintings. The theatre itself mounts a season of seven plays a year – new plays, revivals and classics, often with famous names in the cast.
⊖ Surrey Docks (then bus 1, 188), New Cross (then bus 177) Docklands Railway: Island Gardens (then via foot tunnel)
🚌 1, 177, 180, 188, 286
≹ Greenwich

Grosvenor House Hotel   3N1
Park La W1. 01-499 6363. Unobtrusive luxury in this large hotel with extensive conference facilities, its own garage, shopping arcade, swimming pools, restaurants and coffee house. The exclusive restaurant 90 Park Lane has nouvelle cuisine, The Pavilion is a coffee house-cum-brasserie with afternoon teas, and the informal Pasta House has fresh pasta daily.
⊖ Marble Arch
🚌 2B, 16, 30, 36, 73, 74, 82, 137

Guildhall   4S4
Off Gresham St EC2. 01-606 3030. The City is governed from this primarily 15thC building with a façade by George Dance, 1789, and later restoration by Sir Giles Gilbert Scott. You may view the medieval Great Hall unless a council meeting is in progress. The library is wonderfully rich in works on London and the art gallery has occasional exhibitions from visiting art societies. *Open 09.30–17.30 Mon–Sat. Closed Sun. Free.*
⊖ Bank
🚌 6, 8, 9, 11, 15A, 21, 25, 43, 76, 133, 141, 149, 501, 502

Guildhall Art Gallery   *4S4*
Aldermanbury EC2. 01-606 3030.
Has its own entrance by the side of
the Guildhall and uses its two floors
of exhibition space to display the
works of professional artists in a
programme of 10 or 12 different
shows a year. Pictures are usually
for sale. *Opening times vary.
Closed between exhibitions.* Free.
⊖ Bank
🚌 6, 8, 9, 11, 15A, 21, 25, 43, 76,
133, 141, 149, 501, 502

Guinness Book of World   *3N3*
Records Exhibition
Trocadero, Piccadilly W1. 01-439
1791. For those who like to go to
extremes – compare yourself with
the tallest man and smallest
woman, use VDUs to check your
knowledge of sporting records,
watch videos of people eating more
than anyone else, diving from
higher into less water than anyone
else, and collecting more bees on
the chin than ever before recorded.
Plentiful cafes and other facilities in
the encompassing Trocadero complex. *Open 10.00–21.30 Mon–
Sun.* Charge.
⊖ Piccadilly Circus
🚌 3, 6, 9, 12, 13, 14, 14A, 15, 15A,
19, 22, 38, 53, 55, 88, 159

Gunnersbury Park Museum
Gunnersbury Park, Pope's La W5.
01-992 1612. The fine rooms of this
one-time home of a branch of the

Rothschild family are used for a
series of regularly changing exhibitions on local history, archaeology
and topography. There is also a
transport collection of aged bikes
and chariots and a fully equipped
Victorian kitchen. The grounds are
now a public park with a lakeful of
waterfowl, a pleasant cafe, and a
'Temple' used for craft exhibitions
by day and popular concerts by
night (summer only). *Open 13.00
–17.00 Mon–Fri; 14.00–18.00 Sat,
Sun & Nat Hols. Closed mornings &
16.00 in winter.* Free.
⊖ Acton Town (then bus E3)
🚌 E3

H

Habitat   1D5
196 Tottenham Ct Rd W1. 01-631
3880. Not so much a shop, more a
way of life! Modern furniture,
household goods and kitchen
equipment in brightly coloured,
simple but striking designs. Also
has other branches. *Open 10.00
–18.00 Mon; 09.30–18.00 Tue,
Wed & Fri; 09.30–19.30 Thur;
09.00–18.00 Sat. Closed Sun.*
⊖ Warren Street
🚌14, 14A, 18, 24, 27, 29, 30, 73,
134, 137, 176, 253

Hainault Forest
Essex. 01-500 3106. Once a part of
the great forest of Essex, known as
Waltham Forest, this area is now a
country park of 1,100 acres of extensive woodland with a lake, two
18-hole golf courses, a playing field
and facilities for angling, riding, pic-
nicking, cross-country running and
orienteering. *Open 24 hours.* Free.
⊖ Hainault (then bus 247)
🚌247 (also 62 at certain times)

Ham House
Richmond, Surrey. 01-940 1950. A
richly baroque Stuart house on the
banks of the Thames outside Richmond, now administered by the
Victoria and Albert Museum and
offering the best glimpse of 17thC
life at that social level to be found
anywhere in England. Portraits by
Lely and Kneller, tapestries,
cabinets of miniatures, Chinese
porcelain, fine pieces of furniture
and attractive formal gardens, in
which the Orangery has become a
pleasant tea room. *Open 14.00–
18.00 Tue–Sun. Closed mornings,
Mon, Nat Hols & 16.00 in winter.*
Charge.
⊖ Richmond (then bus 71)
🚌71
⇌ Richmond

Hamleys   3M3
188–196 Regent St W1. 01-734
3161. London's largest toy shop
with four floors richly stocked with
delights for all ages – from dolls to
electronic games, tiny pocket-

money novelties to vast model railway set-ups. *Open 09.00–17.30
Mon–Wed, Fri & Sat; 09.00–20.00
Thur. Also open some Nat Hols.*
⊖ Oxford Circus
🚌3, 6, 12, 13, 15, 15A, 53, 88,
159, C2

Hampstead Heath
NW3. The 790 acres of the heath
sprawl over sandy hills and dip into
wooded valleys. Dick Turpin ranged
over it and drank, or hid, in most of
the inns on its borders. There are
wonderful views over London from
here, as well as ponds, 10 tennis
courts, an Olympic track and grass
ski-ing. The Bank Holiday fair is
famous and so are Kenwood
House, the 16thC Spaniard's Inn
and Jack Straw's Castle. Open-air
concerts are held here in summer.
Open 24 hours. Free.
⊖ Hampstead
🚌46, 210, 268

Hampstead Theatre Club
Swiss Cottage Centre, Avenue Rd
NW3. 01-722 9301. One of the leading club theatres which has acquired a respectability at variance
with its controversial and experimental productions. Has passed several excellent productions

on to the West End and to television. Bar and coffee bar.
⊖ Swiss Cottage
🚌 13, 31, 46, 82, 113, 268, C11

Hampstead Village
NW3. High society came to the country village of Hampstead in the 18thC when a mineral spring was discovered and thought to have healing properties, and most of the attractive houses and alleyways date from this period. Constable lived and worked here and so did Keats and Galsworthy. Still very much a village, and still popular with writers and artists of all persuasions.
⊖ Hampstead
🚌 46, 210, 268

Hampton Court Palace
Hampton Court, Middx. 01-977 8441. Begun by Cardinal Wolsey in 1514, enlarged by Henry VIII, repaired by Charles II, extended by Sir Christopher Wren under William and Mary, with further interior decoration carried out on the orders of Queen Anne, George I and George II. The State Apartments were first opened to the public by Queen Victoria.

Vast and grand, on a prime riverside site, its sweeping grounds contain the famous Maze. Interior treasures include paintings by Giorgione, Titian, Tintoretto and early primitives, wall and ceiling paintings by Thornhill, Vanbrugh and Verrio, 16th and 17thC tapestries, the Chapel Royal, the magnificent Tudor Great Watching Chamber, and the Great Hall with its superb hammerbeam roof.

The Cartoon Gallery was badly damaged by fire in 1986 and will be closed to the public for some years until rebuilding and restoration work is completed.

There is also a licensed restaurant and cafeteria. *Open 09.30 –18.00 Mon–Sun. Closed Nat Hols in winter.* Charge.
⊖ Hammersmith (then bus 267)
🚌 111, 131, 216, 267
Green Line 715, 718
🚆 Hampton Court

Hard Rock Cafe   *302*
150 Old Park La W1. 01-629 0382. One of London's most popular, long-established hamburger joints.

Vast room on two levels with huge wooden tables and non-stop blaring rock music. The hamburgers and steaks are excellent – all prime meat. Expect a very long queue outside or have a drink at the bar while you wait. *Open LD Mon–Sun.*
⊖ Hyde Park Corner
🚌 2B, 9, 14, 14A, 16, 19, 22, 25, 30, 36, 38, 52, 52A, 55, 73, 74, 82, 137, 500

Harrods   *2H6*
Knightsbridge SW1. 01-730 1234. World-famous department store which prides itself on selling virtually everything – furniture, musical instruments, superb men's, ladies' and children's fashions, up-to-the-minute styles in the Way In boutique, expensive fabrics from Switzerland, Italy and France, gem stones, silver, books and exotic pets. There are also the magnificent marbled Edwardian food halls where displays of fish have become an art form, banking halls, a restaurant and various cafes and juice bars. *Open 09.00–17.00 Mon & Tue, Thur & Fri; 09.30–19.00 Wed; 09.00–18.00 Sat. Closed Sun.*
⊖ Knightsbridge
🚌 9, 14, 19, 22, 30, 52, 52A, 73, 74, 137, C1

Harvey Nichols   *3O1*
Knightsbridge SW1. 01-235 5000. Major department store with stylish clothes from top British, American and continental designers, housewares, home furnishings, haberdashery, perfumery and pleasant

cafeteria for coffees, light lunches, teas. *Open 09.30–18.00 Mon & Tue, Thur–Sat; to 19.00 Wed. Closed Sun.*
⊖ Knightsbridge
🚌 9, 14, 19, 22, 30, 52, 52A, 73, 74, 137, C1

Hatchards *3N3*
187 Piccadilly W1. 01-439 9921. Reliable and knowledgeable bookshop established in 1797, with a calm and dignified atmosphere. Good stock of books on most subjects, apart from academic or technical. Large paperback section downstairs, excellent children's section upstairs, also rare and art books. *Open 09.00–17.30 Mon–Fri; 09.00 –13.00 Sat. Closed Sat afternoon & Sun.*
⊖ Piccadilly Circus
🚌 9, 14, 14A, 19, 22, 38, 55

Hatfield House
Hatfield, Herts. 070 72 62823. A mellow and completely preserved Jacobean mansion with a magnificent interior built in 1607–11 by Robert Cecil, 1st Earl of Salisbury. It is still the home of the Cecil family. The Tudor Old Royal Palace nearby was the home of Queen Elizabeth I. Superb collection of 16th, 17th and 18thC portraits, manuscripts and relics. Lavish Elizabethan banquets are held all year round, enquire on 070 72 62055. *Open Mar–Oct 12.00–17.00 Tue–Sat; 14.00– 17.30 Sun; 11.00–17.00 Nat Hols. Closed Oct–Mar.* Charge.
Green Line 797
🚉 Hatfield

Haymarket (Theatre Royal) *4N4*
Haymarket SW1. 01-930 9832. Founded in the 18thC as 'the little theatre in the Hay', it moved in the 1820s to the present building with its grand Palladian Nash exterior and pretty gilded interior. Sometimes enlivened by the ghost of Mr Buckstone, Queen Victoria's favourite actor-manager, who no doubt approves of the policy to present plays of quality.
⊖ Piccadilly Circus
🚌 3, 6, 9, 12, 13, 14, 14A, 15, 15A, 19, 22, 38, 53, 55, 88, 159

Hayward Gallery *3N5*
South Bank SE1. 01-928 3144. Can be picked out from the rest of the

South Bank complex by the kinetic sculpture it wears on its head. Administered by the Arts Council who mount major changing exhibitions of British, American and European art. *Open 10.00–20.00 Mon –Thur; 10.00–18.00 Fri & Sat; 12.00–18.00 Sun.* Charge.
⊖ Waterloo
🚌 1, 4, 5, 68, 70, 76, 149, 168, 171, 171A, 176, 177, 188, 199, 501, 502, 507

Heals *1D5*
196 Tottenham Court Rd W1. 01-636 1666. Five famous floors of furniture, furnishings, pictures and kitchenware – the best of British and continental designs. *Open 10.00–18.00 Mon; 09.30–18.00 Tue, Wed & Fri; 09.30–19.00 Thur; 09.00–18.00 Sat.* Closed Sun.
⊖ Goodge Street, Warren Street
🚌 14, 14A, 18, 24, 27, 29, 30, 73, 134, 137, 176, 253

Heathrow Airport (London Heathrow)
01-759 4321. Major international airport, extremely busy, with a viewing terrace above Queen's Building (between Terminals 1 & 2) from which to watch the planes. There is also a roof garden, a small children's play area and several levels of refreshments. *Viewing terrace opens 10.00–18.00 Mon–*

Sun; closes 16.00 in winter.
Charge.
⊖ Heathrow Terminals 1, 2, 3 and
Heathrow Terminal 4
🚌105, 111, 140, 202, 223, 285,
Airbus A1, A2

Heinz Gallery **1E3**
RIBA Drawings Collection, 21 Port-
man Sq W1. 01-580 5533. The
Royal Institute of British Architects'
extensive collection of drawings
may be viewed by appointment
from *10.00–13.00 Mon–Thur.*
From time to time, there are public
exhibitions arranged around specific themes. *Exhibitions open 10.00
–20.00 Mon–Thur; 10.00–18.00
Fri & Sat; 12.00–18.00 Sun. Closed
between exhibitions, except by
appointment.* Charge.
⊖ Marble Arch
🚌1, 2B, 13, 30, 74, 82, 113, 159

Henry VIII's Wine Cellar **3O4**
Whitehall SW1. This Tudor wine
cellar, built for Cardinal Wolsey, is,
in company with the Banqueting
House, a remnant of the Tudor
Palace of Whitehall. *Guided tours
on Sat afternoon from Mar–Sep.*
Apply in writing to the Department
of the Environment, Room 10/14,
St Christopher House, Southwark
St SE1. 01-928 3666, extn 4673.
⊖ Charing Cross
🚌3, 11, 12, 24, 29, 53, 77, 77A,
88, 109, 159, 170

Her Majesty's Theatre **3N4**
Haymarket SW1. 01-930 6606. A
fine Victorian baroque theatre
founded by Sir Herbert Beerbohm
Tree. Successful productions include 'West Side Story', 'Fiddler on
the Roof' and 'Amadeus'.
⊖ Piccadilly Circus
🚌3, 6, 9, 12, 13, 15, 15A, 53, 88,
159

Highgate
NW3. Attractive largely 18thC hill-
top village whose residents are on a
level with the cross on top of St
Paul's. It shares with Hampstead an
arty-literary reputation; Coleridge
and A. E. Housman lived here.
⊖ Archway (then bus)
🚌143, 210, 271

Highgate Cemetery
Swains La N6. Everyone thinks of
Karl Marx, and his tomb is here, in

the newer eastern section. But in
the older western section is the
great Egyptian gateway (which has
loomed menacingly in Hammer
House of Horror movies), won-
drous funerary sculpture and native
woodland rich in wild flowers and
birds. *Open 09.00–17.00 Mon–
Sat; 14.00–17.00 Sun. Closes
16.00 in winter. Tours on the hour
from 10.00–15.00.*
⊖ Archway
🚌143, 210, 271

Hilton Hotel **3O2**
22 Park La W1. 01-493 8000. Modern luxurious hotel overlooking
Hyde Park. The Roof Restaurant
has splendid views, buffet lunches
and dinner dances. There is also the
mock-Tudor London Tavern, the
Scandinavian sandwich shop and
Trader Vic's with its Polynesian
food, cocktails in bowls with float-
ing flowers and South Seas decor.
⊖ Hyde Park Corner
🚌2B, 16, 30, 36, 73, 74, 82, 137,
500

Hippodrome **3N4**
Hippodrome Corner WC2. 01-437
4311. Peter Stringfellow's most lavish night club with rainbow-laser
ceiling, smoke machines, a huge
video machine, flying speakers, a
magic stage, six bars, a restaurant,
live dancing acts nightly, three live
bands a week, and a young clientele
of wonderful weirds, juvenile aris-
tos and pop stars. Selective and
idiosyncratic admission vetting.
Open 21.00–03.00 nightly.
⊖ Leicester Square
🚌1, 24, 29, 176

HMSO Bookshop **4S1**
49 High Holborn WC1. 01-211
5656. The retail outlet for the publications of Her Majesty's Stationery Office. This is where to buy
venerable 'Hansard' – the verbatim
record of the daily proceedings in
both chambers of the Houses of
Parliament. Also carries parliamen-
tary publications from overseas
(EEC, UN and others), the full range
of Ordnance Survey maps, National
Heritage publications and regional
guides. *Open 08.30–17.00 Mon–
Fri.*
⊖ Chancery Lane (not Sun)
🚌8, 17, 22, 25, 45, 46, 171, 171A,
243, 259, 501

HMV Record Store   3M3
150 Oxford St W1. 01-631 3423.
The biggest record store in Europe
with a comprehensive stock of
music of every kind. Four floors of
records, compact discs, videos,
cassettes, books, T-shirts and
stereo accessories. *Open 09.30–
18.00 Mon–Wed, Fri & Sat; 09.00
–20.00 Thur. Closed Sun.*
⊖ Oxford Circus
🚌 1, 7, 8, 25, 73

Hogarth's House
Hogarth La, Great West Rd W4.
01-994 6757. This was William
Hogarth's country house from 1749
until the night before he died 15
years later and it contains an unrival-
led collection of prints, 'visual writ-
ings' satirising the life of his day.
'The Harlot's Progress' and 'Mar-
riage à la Mode' are here, together
with jolly 'Beer Street' and dismal
'Gin Lane'. *Open 11.00–18.00 Mon
& Wed–Sat; 14.00–18.00 Sun.
Closed Tue, Good Fri & 16.00 Oct
–Apr. Free.*
⊖ Hammersmith (then bus 290),
Turnham Green (then walk)
🚌 290

Holland Park   2G1
W8. Once the private park of Holland House, a Jacobean mansion
which was the seat of the Whig
Foxes – Lords Holland from the
18thC. Largely destroyed in World
War II, the remaining wing is a
youth hostel. The Orangery and Ice
House hold changing exhibitions of
paintings and ceramics from March
to November, and the Court
Theatre in the courtyard presents
opera and ballet during July. This
area, with its attendant Dutch and
rose gardens, is floodlit every night.
The northern part is 28 acres of
verdant woodland where tree-
creepers, owls and green wood-
peckers live among 3,000 species
of trees and plants. *Area around
house closes 24.00. Rest of park
closed dusk.*
⊖ Holland Park, High Street
Kensington
🚌 9, 12, 27, 28, 31, 33, 49, 73, 88,
C1

Holy Trinity Church   2H6
Brompton Rd SW7. 01-581 8255.
Behind Brompton Oratory stands
this Victorian Gothic parish church,
consecrated in 1892. The choir, of
mainly professional singers, give
concerts in and around London and
there are sometimes exhibitions in
the crypt. Donation welcome.
⊖ South Kensington
🚌 14, 30, 74, C1

Holy Trinity Church   5W3
Sloane Square SW1. 01-730 7270.
A living and lovely church and also a
memorial to the Arts and Crafts
Movement of the 1890s. The grace-
ful design is by J. D. Sedding and
the east window was planned by
Burne-Jones with glass by William
Morris. Occasional concerts. Dona-
tion welcome.
⊖ Sloane Square
🚌 11, 19, 22, 137, C1

Horniman Museum
100 London Rd SE23. 01-699 2339.
Given to the LCC in 1901 by
Frederick Horniman of the famous
tea firm, together with his personal
collection of ethnography and natural history. Though enlarged since,
it has retained the special charm
peculiar to such places with its
masks and stuffed tigers, mummies and musical instruments. In
the aquarium there are tree frogs,
piranhas and a working beehive.
There is an animal enclosure and
nature trail in the park at the back.
*Open   10.30–18.00   Mon–Sat;
14.00–18.00 Sun. Closed Xmas.
Free.*
🚌 12, 12A, 63, 176, 185, 194, P4,
Sun only 12B, 194A
⇌ Forest Hill

Horse Guards **304**
Whitehall SW1. The building is by
William Kent, 1750–60, and Horse
Guards Parade is the scene of the
ceremony of Trooping the Colour
every June. A daily spectacle is the
changing of the Queen's Life
Guard, on their splendid black
horses, *at 11.00 Mon–Sat & 10.00
Sun.*
⊖ Westminster, Charing Cross
🚌 3, 11, 12, 24, 29, 53, 77, 77A,
88, 109, 159, 170

House of Fraser **2H3**
63 Kensington High St W8. 01-937
5432. Barkers no more, but this
landmark store has been lavishly
refurbished to show off both its
beautiful art deco features and its
quality merchandise. Cosmetics
and fragrance hall, up-market
fashions, household and electrical
goods, hairdressing salon, bureau
de change, restaurant. *Open 09.30–
20.00 Mon–Fri; 09.00–18.00 Sat.*
⊖ High Street Kensington
🚌 9, 27, 28, 31, 33, 49, 52, 52A,
73, C1

House of St Barnabas **3M3**
1 Greek St W1. Early Georgian town
house at one corner of Soho Square
with fine wood carving and rococo
plasterwork inside. Now owned by
a charity caring for London's desti-
tutes. *Open Mon morning & Thur
afternoon.* Donation appreciated.
⊖ Tottenham Court Road
🚌 1, 7, 8, 14, 14A, 19, 22, 24, 25,
29, 38, 55, 73, 134, 176

Houses of Parliament **3P4**
St Margaret St SW1. 01-219 3000.
More properly the New Palace of
Westminster, by Barry and Pugin
1840–68. The grand and glorious
Gothic structure was built around
the 11thC Westminster Hall,
whose 14thC timber roof rivals any
in Europe. Still has royal status.
Tour the building when the house is
not sitting, or listen from the Stran-
gers Gallery when it is. Write to
your MP for an invitation, or join the
queue outside. *Open 09.00–17.50
Mon–Sat. Closed Sun.* Free.
⊖ Westminster
🚌 3, 11, 12, 24, 29, 53, 70, 77,
77A, 88, 109, 159, 170, C1

Hyatt Carlton Tower **3P1**
Cadogan Pl SW1. 01-235 5411.
Sophisticated hotel, with a high
standard of cuisine and service.
Ambitious, largely French menu in
the Chelsea Room, notable roast
beef in the Rib Room.
⊖ Sloane Square
🚌 11, 19, 22, 137, C1

Hyde Park **3N1**
W2. The most informal of the royal
parks, appropriated by Henry VIII
from the Abbot of Westminster and
used as a royal hunting ground until
it was opened to the public during
the reign of James I. The Great
Exhibition of 1851 was staged here,
in Paxton's Crystal Palace which originally stood between Knightsbridge and Rotten Row.
A wild bird sanctuary, various
sporting facilities, the fine artificial
lake called the Serpentine with its
Lido, hire-boats and restaurants at
either end, and the famous Speaker's Corner are among the Park's
many attractions.
The Household Cavalry Review is
held here in spring, the London to
Brighton Veteran Car Rally begins
here in autumn, and military bands
play rousing music on summer Sun-
days.
⊖ Marble Arch, Lancaster Gate,
Hyde Park Corner
🚌 2B, 6, 7, 8, 9, 12, 14, 14A, 15,
15A, 16, 16A, 19, 22, 25, 30, 36, 38,
52, 52A, 55, 73, 74, 82, 137, 500

ICA   3N4
(Institute of Contemporary Arts)
12 Carlton House Ter SW1. 01-930
0493. Recorded information 01-930
6393. The three galleries hold three
simultaneous exhibitions of paintings, drawings or photographs. The
cinema screens foreign, avant-
garde and unusual films and there is
a children's cinema club at
weekends. The cinematheque
shows low-budget films and videos
and there is also a video library. The
studio theatre changes shape to
suit productions and there are
lunchtime and evening talks and
seminars. Fully licensed healthfood
restaurant.   *Open   12.00–23.00
Mon–Sun*. Charge (for day or
annual membership).
⊖ Charing Cross, Piccadilly Circus
▦3, 6, 9, 12, 13, 15, 15A, 53, 88,
159

Imperial War Museum   3P6
Lambeth Rd SE1. 01-735 8922. An
extremely   popular   national
museum on all aspects of warfare –
military and domestic – concerning
Britain and the Commonwealth
from 1914. Housed in the central
portion of the old Bethlehem Royal
Hospital for the Insane – or Bedlam.
There is also an art gallery, film
shows at weekends, and reference
departments of documents, film,
photographs, printed books and
sound records, open for study by
appointment. The museum's two
out-stations are 'HMS Belfast' in
the Port of London and Duxford
Airfield in Cambridge. *Open 10.00
–18.00 Tue–Sat;   14.00–17.30
Sun. Closed Mon, Nat Hols & 17.00
in winter*. Free.
⊖ Lambeth North
▦3, 10, 44, 109, 159

Inn on the Park Hotel   3O2
Park La W1. 01-499 0888. Luxurious modern hotel of international
standing, with views over Hyde
Park and two haute cuisine restaurants. Despite its relative new-
ness, it has much of the charm and
comfortable appeal of an older
establishment.
⊖ Hyde Park Corner
▦2B, 9, 14, 14A, 16, 19, 22, 25,
30, 36, 38, 52, 52A, 55, 73, 74, 82,
137, 500

Ismaili Centre   2J5
1–7 Cromwell Gdns SW7. Founded
by His Highness, the Aga Khan, the
architecturally acclaimed Ismaili
Centre is the principal Islamic Cultural and Religious Centre in London.
Within it is the Zamana Gallery, an
independent exhibition area with its
own entrance in Cromwell Rd. *Centre not open to public*. (For Zamana
Gallery see separate entry.)
⊖ South Kensington
▦14, 30, 74, C1

J

Jack Straw's Castle
North End Way NW3. 01-435 8885. Rebuilt in the 1960s on the site of the original pub, which was named for Wat Tyler's comrade who was hanged outside. Unusual weatherboard frontage, marvellous views over Hampstead Heath, a sunny courtyard, snack bar, cocktail bar and upstairs Carvery. *Open LD Mon –Sat & L Sun. Closed D Sun.*
⊖ Hampstead
▦ 210, 268

Jaeger   3M3
204 Regent St W1. 01-734 8211. Famous for well-cut, smart English clothes. A reliable source of cashmere, camel-hair coats and pure wool knitteds. Also cocktail and evening wear. Men's clothes, too. *Open 09.30–18.00 Mon & Tue, Thur–Sat; to 19.00 Wed. Closed Sun.*
⊖ Oxford Circus
▦ 3, 6, 12, 13, 15, 15A, 53, 88, 159, C2

Jewel Tower   3P4
Old Palace Yd SW1. 01-937 9561. Discreet amidst the Gothic finery of Westminster Abbey and the Houses of Parliament stands this 14thC fragment of the old Palace of Westminster. Once Edward III's treasure house, it now displays medieval carvings. *Open 10.00– 17.30 Mon–Sat. Closed Sun.* Free.
⊖ Westminster
▦ 3, 11, 12, 24, 29, 53, 70, 77, 77A, 88, 109, 159, 170, C1

Jewish Museum   15C
Woburn House, Upper Woburn Pl WC1. 01-387 3081. A small museum in an upstairs room of the Jewish Communal Centre, whose aim is to illustrate Jewish life, history and religion. Two audio-visual programmes on religion and ritual are shown at varying times, often to suit visiting groups. *Open 12.30– 15.00 Mon–Thur; 10.30–12.45 Sun. Closed Fri, Sat, Nat & Jewish Hols.* Free.
⊖ Euston, Euston Square
▦ 14, 14A, 18, 30, 68, 73, 77A, 168, 188

Joe Allen's   3M5
13 Exeter St WC2. 01-836 0651. Fashionably crowded, especially after the theatre, this large converted warehouse restaurant follows the pattern of its New York and Paris counterparts. Dim lights, slick and friendly service, killer cocktails, blackboard menu of steak, chilli, spinach salad, pecan pie. Reservations wise. *Open LD Mon–Sun.*
⊖ Charing Cross (then any bus along the Strand)
▦ 1, 4, 5, 6, 9, 11, 13, 15, 15A, 68, 77, 77A, 168, 170, 171, 176, 188, 199, 501, 502

John Lewis   3M2
Oxford St W1. 01-629 7711. Department store with the largest dress fabric department in Europe, a large furnishing fabric department, furniture, china, glass, bureau de change, export bureau and interpreters. Many branches – 'never knowingly undersold'. *Open 09.00–17.30 Mon–Wed, Fri & Sat; 09.30–20.00 Thur.*
⊖ Bond Street, Oxford Circus
▦ 1, 6, 7, 8, 12, 13, 15, 15A, 16A, 25, 73, 88, 113, 137, 159, 500

Dr Johnson's House   4S2
17 Gough Sq, off Fleet St EC4. 01-353 3745. The industrious Dr J. lived here from 1748–1759 and it was in the attic that much of the famous 'Dictionary' was compiled, with the help of six copyists. The furnishings and effects include a first edition of the great work, contemporary portraits, and the last will and testament. *Open 11.00–17.30 Mon–Sat. Closed Sun, Nat Hols & 17.00 in winter.* Charge.
⊖ Chancery Lane (not Sun), Blackfriars
▦ 4, 6, 9, 11, 15, 15A, 17, 45, 63, 76, 141, 171A, 502

Keats House

Wentworth Pl, Keats Grove NW3. 01-435 2062. A pair of semi-detached houses in which Keats spent much of his most prolific period, 1818–21. This is where he wrote 'Ode To A Nightingale', 'Lamia', 'La Belle Dame Sans Mercie', 'On A Grecian Urn', and became engaged to Fanny Brawne next door. There is a wealth of memorabilia – letters, pictures and annotated books. The Keats Memorial Library is open by appointment only. *Open 10.00–13.00 & 14.00 –18.00 Mon–Sat; 14.00–17.00 Sun.* Free.
⊖ Hampstead
🚌 24, 46, 168, C11
⇌ Hampstead Heath

Kensal Green Cemetery

Harrow Rd W10. Its 56 acres of splendid stone and marble tombs trace the decline of the 'classic' and the introduction of the Gothic style. Wilkie Collins, the two Brunels, Princess Sophia, the Duke of Sussex, G. K. Chesterton, Thackeray and Trollope lie here.
🚌 18, 52
⇌ Kensal Green

Kensington Gardens   2G4

W8. 01-937 4848. Originally laid out as the private gardens of Kensington Palace, this lovely spread of 275 acres of tree-lined walks, luxuriant flower beds and the man-made Long Water and Round Pond adjoins Hyde Park. It is the most endearingly fey of London's royal parks, and probably the one that appeals most to children, with its Elfin Oak, ornamental ducks and swans, pets' cemetery and statue of Peter Pan. *Open 07.30–dusk.*
⊖ Queensway, High Street Kensington
🚌 9, 12, 33, 49, 52, 52A, 73, 88, C1

Kensington Market   2H3

Kensington High St W8. Large shop front behind which are grouped a complex of stalls selling off-beat clothes, jewellery, antiques and records. Stallholders prepared to buy, sell and barter. *Open 10.00–18.00 Mon–Sat.*
⊖ High Street Kensington
🚌 9, 27, 28, 31, 33, 49, 52, 52A, 73, C1

Kensington Palace   2G3

Kensington Gdns W8. 01-937 9561. Queen Victoria and Queen Mary were born here, and this is where Victoria received the news of her accession. The Prince and Princess of Wales, Princess Margaret, Prince Michael of Kent and the Duke and Duchess of Gloucester still have apartments in the private wings. Bought in 1689 by William III, house and gardens are rich in the work of the famous who refurbished them – William Kent, Sir Christopher Wren, Grinling Gibbons, Nicholas Hawksmoor. There are also paintings from the royal collection, busts, furniture and ornaments and the Court Dress Collection. *Open 10.00–17.00 Mon–Sat; 14.00–17.00 Sun. Closed some Nat Hols.* Charge.
⊖ Queensway, High Street Kensington, Notting Hill Gate
🚌 9, 12, 33, 49, 52, 52A, 73, 88, C1

Kentish Town City Farm

1 Cressfield Clo, off Grafton Rd NW5. 01-482 2861. Horses, pigs, chickens, sheep, goats, rabbits, a nature area and an exhibition. Children have reasonably close encounters with the animals and may see work in progress if they arrive at the appropriate times. *Open most of the time – enquire.* Free.
⊖ Kentish Town
🚌 27, 134, 137, 214, C2

Kenwood House

Hampstead La NW3. 01-348 1286/7. A fine Adam house at the edge of Hampstead Heath with lawns that slope down to a lake. Bequeathed to the nation by the first Earl of Iveagh, together with his collection of paintings which includes works by Gainsborough, Reynolds, Vermeer, Rembrandt, Frans Hals, Van

Dyck, Turner and Joseph Wright of Derby. Music and poetry recitals are held in the Orangery on spring and autumn evenings, and in summer symphony concerts compete with the birdsong at the lakeside (details on 01-633 1707). *Open 10.00–19.00 Mon–Sun. Closes 16.00 or 17.00 in winter.* Free.
⊖ Archway (then bus 210), Golders Green (then bus 210)
🚌210

Kew Gardens
Kew Rd, Richmond, Surrey. 01-940 1171. More properly – the Royal Botanical Gardens, Kew. An important research institute and a wonderful sight with more than 25,000 species and varieties of plants grown over its 300 acres. An arboretum, alpine, water and rhododendron gardens, magnificent cast-iron and glass palm house and temperate house by Decimus Burton, a herbarium, tropical orchid house and a library of rare books on botany and exploration. Two attractive cafeterias. *Open 10.00–dusk (or 20.00 in summer).* Small charge.
⊖ Kew Gardens
🚌27, 65, 90B, Sun only 7

Kew Palace
Kew Gardens, Richmond, Surrey. 01-940 7333. The Dutch House, as it is sometimes called, was built in 1631 for the merchant Samuel Fortrey. In 1802 George III and Queen Charlotte used it while they awaited the building of a new summer palace, which was never completed. The Queen loved the chunky brick house and died here in 1818. There are portraits, furniture and royal knick-knacks and, outside, formal gardens laid out in the 1960s in 17thC style. *Open 11.00–17.30 Mon–Sun. Closed Oct–Mar, Good Fri & May Day.* Charge.
⊖ Kew Gardens
🚌27, 65, 90B, Sun only 7

King's Cross Station   *1B6*
Euston Rd NW1. Information on 01-278 2477. Mainline station built by Cubitt in 1851 and topped by the clock tower from the original Crystal Palace. The trains go to Leeds, York, Newcastle and Edinburgh.

⊖ King's Cross, St Pancras
🚌14A, 17, 18, 30, 45, 46, 63, 73, 77A, 214, 221, 259, C11
🚅 King's Cross

King's Head Theatre
115 Upper St N1. 01-225 1916. Arguably the best-known of the pub theatres, presenting musicals, reviews, new plays, revivals. Buy a ticket for performance only, or for a meal as well, in which case you watch the show from your table. The pub itself has live music seven nights a week. *Open LD Mon–Sun. Theatre Mon–Sat lunchtime & eve.*
⊖ Angel
🚌4, 19, 30, 38, 43, 73, 171A, 277, 279, Sun only 263A, 279A

King's Road   *5X1*
Chelsea SW3. Once a private royal track from St James's towards Hampton Court Palace, much later one of the places where the Swinging Sixties swung. Still exciting, especially on a Saturday when the young and colourful fill the boutiques and antique shops and drink coffee and wine at pubs and pavement cafes. An essential stop on the shopping circuit for the latest fashions, which are often the last word! Indigenous wildlife includes flame-coated Chelsea pensioners and flame-haired punks.
⊖ Sloane Square
🚌11, 19, 22, 45, 49

L

Lamb and Flag 3M4
33 Rose St WC2. 01-836 4108. 300-year old pub, once known as 'The Bucket of Blood' because of the bare fist fights upstairs – and perhaps too because Dryden got the once-over downstairs for writing satirical ballads about Charles II's mistress. Now a popular mellow bar. *Open normal licensing hours Mon–Sun.*
⊖ Leicester Square
🚌 1, 24, 29, 176

Lambeth Palace 3P5
SE1. Begun in the early 13thC, although most of the present structure with its castellated gatehouse and high protective wall is medieval. The London residence of the Archbishop of Canterbury for 700 years and *not open to the public* – although groups are occasionally admitted on application to the Secretary.
⊖ Victoria (then bus 10, 507)
🚌 3, 10, 44, 77, 159, 170, 507

Lancaster House 3O3
Stable Yard, St James's SW1. Early 19thC town house, decorous without but lushly, ripely baroque within. Lavishly painted ceilings and breathtaking staircase. Used as a government hospitality centre. *Open Sat & Sun afternoons in summer. Closed Mon–Fri & winter.* Free.
⊖ St James's Park, Green Park
🚌 9, 14, 14A, 19, 22, 25, 38, 55

Laura Ashley 3I0
9 Harriet St SW1. 01-235 9796. Romantically styled dresses, skirts and nightgowns in distinctively patterned cottons and subtle-coloured corduroys for girls who want to look like an 18thC poet's vision of a milkmaid. Several branches. *Open 09.30–18.00 Mon & Tue; 09.30–19.00 Wed; 09.30–18.00 Thur & Fri; 09.00–18.00 Sat. Closed Sun.*
⊖ Knightsbridge
🚌 19, 22, 137, C1

Law Courts 4S2
Strand WC2. 01-936 6000. An elaborate fairy-tale castle, with spire, turrets and statues, built by Street in 1874–80 to house the Royal Courts of Justice. Admission only to visitors aged 16 and over. *Open 10.00–16.00 Mon–Fri. Closed Sat & Sun.* Courts not in session *Aug* & *Sep* but open to public. Free.
⊖ Temple (not Sun), Charing Cross (then bus 6, 9, 11, 15, 15A)
🚌 4, 6, 9, 11, 15, 15A, 171A

Leadenhall Market 4T5
Gracechurch St EC3. Horace Jones built the superb glass and iron hall in 1881, on the site of the old Roman basilica and forum, which still shelters a lively general market. *Open 09.00–17.00 Mon–Fri.*
⊖ Bank, Monument
🚌 8, 10, 15, 15A, 21, 25, 35, 40, 43, 47, 48, 133, 501

Leather Lane Market 4R2
Leather Lane EC1. Once specialised in the sale of cured skins – now a busy general market, with lively patter from the stallholders and few leather stalls left. *Open 11.00–15.00 Mon–Sat.*

⊖ Farringdon, Chancery Lane (not Sun)
🚌5, 8, 17, 18, 22, 25, 45, 46, 55, 63, 171, 221, 243, 259, 501

Leicester Square   *3N4*
WC2. Pedestrianised and commercial, flanked by four major cinemas, the Swiss Centre and several eating places with their sights set on tourists. The first statue of Charlie Chaplin stands to the west, under trees raucous with starlings at dusk. London's Chinatown lies just behind, on the north side.
⊖ Leicester Square
🚌1, 24, 29, 176

Leighton House   *2H1*
12 Holland Park Rd W14. 01-602 3316. Designed by Aitchison in 1865, in collaboration with Lord Leighton, as the latter's home and studio. Now an intimate museum of high Victorian art, with an exquisite Arab Hall on the ground floor and the finest collection of Leighton paintings in any one place. Music recitals, poetry readings and lectures are held in the barrel-vaulted studio above. *Open 11.00–17.00 Mon–Sat. Free.*
⊖ High Street Kensington (then bus)
🚌9, 27, 28, 31, 33, 49, 73, C1

Liberty's   *3M3*
Regent St W1. 01-734 1234. This architecturally remarkable department store, with its half-timbered façade and Tudor-style interior, is world-famous for its own distinctive printed fabrics. There are also china and glass departments, furniture, fashions, oriental carpets and fashion jewellery, especially in Cameo Corner. *Open 09.30–18.00 Mon–Wed, Fri & Sat; to 19.00 Thur. Closed Sun.*
⊖ Oxford Circus
🚌3, 6, 12, 13, 15, 15A, 53, 88, 159, C2

Lillywhites   *3N3*
Lower Regent St SW1. 01-930 3181. Excellent general stock of top English and continental equipment and clothes for most sports, especially skiing, tennis, golf and cricket. For each sport, a pro is available to advise on purchases. *Open 09.30 –18.00 Mon–Wed, Fri & Sat; to 19.00 Thur. Closed Sun.*

⊖ Piccadilly Circus
🚌3, 6, 9, 12, 13, 14, 14A, 15, 15A, 19, 22, 38, 53, 55, 88, 159

Lincoln's Inn   *4S1*
WC2. One of the four great Inns of Court, a compact Dickensian world of squares, gardens and barristers' chambers, whose records go back to 1422. The 15thC Old Hall and the 17thC Chapel by Inigo Jones may be viewed on application to the Gatehouse in Chancery Lane.
⊖ Holborn, Chancery Lane (not Sun)
🚌5, 8, 17, 18, 19, 22, 25, 38, 45, 46, 55, 68, 77, 77A, 153, 171, 171A, 188, 243, 259, 501

Linley Sambourne House   *2H2*
18 Stafford Ter W8. Administered by The Victorian Society which was formed here (1 Priory Gdns W4, 01-994 1019). An unspoiled Victorian house. Linley Sambourne, who lived here from 1879–1910, was chief political cartoonist for 'Punch' and the decor and furnishings remain unchanged since he sat at the drawing board in his study. *Open by appointment Mar –Oct. Charge.*
⊖ High Street Kensington
🚌9, 27, 28, 31, 33, 49, 73, C1

Little Angel Marionette Theatre
14 Dagmar Passage, Cross St N1. 01-226 1787. Marionettes are the

puppets worked by strings – and this is their only permanent London venue. The excellent shows – at weekends and in the school holidays – are put on by the resident company or visiting puppeteers. Booking essential.

⊖ Angel

🚌 4, 19, 30, 38, 43, 73, 171, 171A, 277, 279, Sun only 263A, 279A

Little Venice

W2. A section of Regent's Canal, lined with brightly painted houseboats and flanked by large Victorian houses and plane trees which reflect in the green water. It was christened Little Venice by the poet Robert Browning. There are pleasant pubs along here and a somewhat arty fraternity.

⊖ Warwick Avenue

🚌 6, 18, 46

Liverpool Street Station   4G5

Liverpool St EC2. Information on 01-283 7171. 19thC station built to serve the east and north-east London suburbs. Trains go to Cambridge, Colchester, Norwich and Harwich Harbour.

⊖ Liverpool Street

🚌 5, 6, 8, 9, 11, 22, 22A, 35, 47, 48, 78, 133, 149, 502, Sun only 243A, 263A, 279A

≠ Liverpool Street

Lloyds of London   4T5

Lime St EC3. 01-623 7100. World-famous international insurance market, particularly concerned with shipping. It has recently removed to this brand new Richard Rogers designed building which looks a little like an oil refinery. The Lutine Bell still rings once for bad news of a ship, twice for good, and there is now a visitors viewing area. *Tours between 10.00–16.00 Mon–Fri.* Minimum age 14. Free.

⊖ Bank, Monument

🚌 15A, 25

London Apprentice

62 Church St, Old Isleworth, Middx. 01-560 6136. Famous 16thC Thames-side pub named for the apprentices from London's Docks who spent their one-day-off-a-year rowing down to it for a pint or so. Lovely interiors, flowery patio, good restaurant (01-560 3538). *Open LD*

Tue–Fri, D Sat, L Mon. Closed L Sat, LD Sun, D Mon.

⊖ Gunnersbury (then bus 267)

🚌 37, 267

≠ Isleworth (then bus 37)

London Bridge   4T4

SE1. Concrete construction completed in 1973. Its 1830s predecessor now spans an artificial lake in Arizona. The 13thC stone bridge which preceded that one carried houses and shops and is famous from old woodcuts.

⊖ Monument, London Bridge

🚌 10, 15, 17, 21, 35, 40, 43, 44, 47, 48, 70, 133, 501, 513, P3

London Bridge Station   4U5

Borough High St SE1. Information on 01-928 5100. 19thC station dispatching trains to the south and south-east London suburbs – Kent, Sussex, and East Surrey.

⊖ London Bridge

🚌 10, 17, 21, 35, 40, 43, 44, 47, 48, 70, 133, 501, 513, P3

≠ London Bridge

London Dungeon   4U5

34 Tooley St EC1. 01-403 0606. Gruesomely realistic exhibition of the dark side of British history in a dank vaulted cellar. Sacrifices, tortures, plagues, murders, executions – everything you need for a really vivid nightmare or several. Unsuitable for those of a sensitive disposition. *Open 10.00–17.30 Mon–Sun.* Charge.

⊖ London Bridge

🚌 10, 17, 21, 35, 40, 43, 44, 47, 48, 70, 133, 501, 513, P3

London Experience   3N3

Trocadero, Piccadilly W1. 01-734 0555. A 35-minute multi-media show on the history of London – film (including old news reel films), slides, video and special effects. High points are the Plague, the Great Fire, the Blitz and Jack the Ripper, but there is plenty of pageantry and glamour as well. *Shows every 40 mins from 10.20 –22.20, Mon–Sun.* Charge.

⊖ Piccadilly Circus

🚌 3, 6, 9, 12, 13, 14, 14A, 15, 15A, 19, 22, 38, 53, 55, 88, 159

London Mosque   1C2

Hanover Gate NW1. The religious centre for London's Muslims is a

graceful building on the edge of Regent's Park, completed in 1978.
⊖ Marylebone, Baker Street
🚌 13, 74, 82, 113

London Telecom Tower   *3L3*
Maple St W1. 198 metres of telecommunications gadgetry and mast. Transmits radio, television and telephone signals around the country and, via a Goonhilly Down satellite link-up, around the world.
⊖ Goodge Street, Warren Street, Great Portland Street
🚌 14, 18, 24, 29, 30, 73, 134, 137, 176

London Toy & Model Museum   *2F4*
23 Craven Hill W2. 01-262 7905. Restored Victorian house with an international collection of model trains, a collection of Victorian and Edwardian tin toys, a mock-up of a Victorian nursery and, in the garden, a carousel, two miniature working railways – electric and steam – and a 56-seater bus. Cafe too. *Open 10.00–17.30 Tue–Sat; 11.00–17.30 Sun. Closed Mon.* Charge.
⊖ Lancaster Gate
🚌 12, 88

London Transport Museum *3M5*
The Piazza, Covent Garden WC2. 01-379 6344. Buses, trams, trolleybuses, tube trains, tickets, posters, photographs – in fact, everything you could want to see and know about London's public transport. The fascinating history of London's transport is told by way of audio-visual displays, working exhibits and gleamingly preserved historic vehicles of road and rail. Visitors are encouraged to try out some of the controls themselves. *Open 10.00–18.00 Mon–Sun* (last admission 17.15). Charge.
⊖ Covent Garden
🚌 1, 6, 9, 11, 13, 15, 15A, 68, 77, 77A, 168, 170, 176, 199

London Visitor & Convention Bureau   *3P2*
Victoria Station Forecourt SW1. 01-730 3488. Comprehensive travel and tourist information for London and England. Most languages spoken. Also instant hotel reservations, theatre and tour bookings, sales of tourist tickets, guidebooks and maps. *Open 09.00–20.30 Mon–Sun.*
⊖ Victoria
🚌 2, 2B, 10, 11, 14A, 16, 24, 25, 29, 36, 36B, 38, 39, 52, 52A, 55, 70, 185, 500, 507, C1
🚆 Victoria

Lord's Cricket Ground   *1C1*
St John's Wood Rd NW8. 01-289 1615. Thomas Lord's Marylebone Cricket Club – the MCC – was founded in 1787 in Dorset Square and moved here in 1814. This, the most famous cricket ground in the world has a museum housed in the racquets court. *Open on match days only.* Charge.
⊖ St John's Wood
🚌 13, 74, 82, 113, 159

Lumiere Cinema   *3N4*
St Martin's La WC2. 01-836 0691. Premiere release cinema for quality films.
⊖ Leicester Square
🚌 1, 24, 29, 176

Lyric Theatre   *3N3*
Shaftesbury Av W1. 01-437 3686. The oldest theatre in Shaftesbury Avenue, built in 1888, presenting straight plays and comedies, usually by established writers.
⊖ Piccadilly Circus
🚌 14, 14A, 19, 22, 38, 55

Lyric, Hammersmith
King St W6. 01-741 2311. Rebuilt in its original Victorian-style inside a modern block. There is also an adaptable studio theatre, a bar and a wine-bar-style restaurant, and regular exhibitions of pictures and prints. Productions range from classic through to modern and fringe.
⊖ Hammersmith
🚌 9, 11, 27, 33, 72, 73, 91, 220, 266, 267, 283, 290, 295

M

Madame Tussaud's   3L1
Marylebone Rd NW1. 01-935 6861.
Tableaux of wax images of the
famous and notorious – royalty,
sporting stars, politicians, pop
stars, murderers, actors. The
Chamber of Horrors has the original
moulds made by Madame Tussaud
herself of heads severed during the
French Revolution. Also a mock-up
of the gun deck of Nelson's 'Victory' at the height of the Battle of
Trafalgar, complete with sound and
smoke effects. *Open 10.00–18.00
Mon–Sun; closes 17.40 in winter.*
Charge (a special ticket includes
admission to The Planetarium next
door; the queue at Madame Tussaud's can be avoided if you buy
one of the joint LT sightseeing tour
and Madame Tussaud's tickets at a
LT Travel Information Centre – see
page 5 for details).
⊖ Baker Street
▦ 1, 2B, 13, 18, 27, 30, 74, 82,
113, 159, 176

Magpie and Stump   4S3
18 Old Bailey EC4. 01-248 3819.
Pleasant old pub with two downstairs bars and one upstairs bar, set
opposite the Old Bailey and often
full of crime reporters, barristers
and the friends of the committed or
acquitted. When old Newgate Prison – parts of whose walls are incorporated in the Old Bailey – still
stood, the gentry used to hire window space here to watch the public
hangings. Bar snacks at lunchtime
and in the evening. *Open Mon–Fri.
Closed Sat & Sun.*
⊖ St Paul's
▦ 4, 8, 22, 25, 141, 501, 502

Mansion House   4T4
Walbrook EC4. 01-626 2500. Fine
Palladian building, completed in
1752, which is the official residence
of the Lord Mayor of London and
scene of his annual banquets. The
Egyptian Hall – sumptuous, though
devoid of Egyptian architectural features – is worth seeing. Apply in
writing for appointment to view.
Free.

⊖ Bank, Mansion House
▦ 6, 8, 9, 11, 15A, 21, 22, 25, 43,
76, 133, 149, 501

Maples   3L3
145 Tottenham Court Rd W1. 01-
387 7000. 50,000 square feet of
furniture store, stocking all types
and styles – including reproduction
and modern. Oriental and English
carpets and rugs, soft furnishing
fabrics and customer services
which include curtain-making, con-
tract and design. *Open 09.00–
17.30 Mon–Sat. Closed Sun.*
⊖ Warren Street
▦ 14, 14A, 18, 24, 27, 29, 30, 73,
134, 137, 176, 253

Mappin and Webb   3M3
170 Regent St W1. 01-734 3801.
Senior shop of a prestigious chain
selling high-quality jewellery and silver. *Open 09.00–17.30 Mon–Fri;
09.30–17.00 Sat. Closed Sun.*
⊖ Oxford Circus, Piccadilly Circus
▦ 3, 6, 12, 13, 15, 15A, 53, 88,
159

Marble Arch   6M1
W2. This impressive arch, though
small by Arc de Triomphe standards, with its finely-wrought
gates, is now no more than a landmark. It was originally designed by
Nash as a gateway to Buckingham
Palace, but declared too narrow and
moved here as an entrance to Hyde
Park. It was then stranded by road
widening in the early 1900s.
⊖ Marble Arch
▦ 2B, 6, 7, 8, 12, 15, 15A, 16,
16A, 30, 36, 73, 74, 82, 88, 137,
500

Marble Hill House
Richmond   Rd,   Twickenham,
Middx. 01-892 5115. Standing in
pleasant grounds near the Thames,
this attractive English Palladian
house was built for Henrietta
Howard, mistress of George II and
later Countess of Suffolk. The furnishings date from the Countess's
time and there are portraits from
the school of Van Dyck. Tea rooms

in the coach house. *Open 10.00
–17.00 Mon–Thur, Sat & Sun.
Closed Fri & Xmas.* Free.
⊖ Richmond (then bus)
🚌33, 37, 90B, 202, 270, 290
⭐ St Margarets

Marks and Spencer **3M1**
Oxford St W1. 01-935 7954. The
Marble Arch branch is one of the
largest shops of many in this internationally-famous and popular high
street chain which sells separates,
knitteds, dresses, suits, underwear, home furnishings, gifts,
books and fine foods. No fitting
rooms but clothes may be returned
for exchange or refund (keep the
receipt). *Open 09.00–18.00 Mon
–Wed, Fri & Sat; to 19.30 Thur.
Closed Sun.*
⊖ Marble Arch
🚌2B, 6, 7, 8, 12, 15, 15A, 16A,
30, 73, 74, 82, 88, 137, 500

Marlborough House **3N4**
Marlborough Gate, Pall Mall SW1.
01-930 8071. Charming 18thC red
brick Wren building, added to by
Pennington in the 19thC, which
was built for the first Duke of Marlborough and is now the Commonwealth Centre. *Tours at 11.00 &
15.00 Mon–Fri by telephone application to Administration Officer.*
Charge.
⊖ Charing Cross
🚌1, 3, 6, 9, 11, 12, 13, 15, 15A,
24, 29, 53, 77, 77A, 88, 109, 159,
170, 176, 199

Martinware Pottery Collection
Southall Library, Osterley Park Rd,
Middx. 01-574 3412. A room in the
reference library displays some of
the heavily distinctive bowls, heads
and quizzically grotesque birds
made by the Martin brothers in
Southall from 1873–1923. *Open
09.00–19.30 Tue, Thur & Fri; 09.00
–16.45 Wed & Sat. Closed Mon &
Nat Hols.* Free.
⊖ Hounslow West (then bus 232)
Hounslow Central (then bus 120)
🚌105, 120, 195, 232

May Fair Hotel
Stratton St W1. 01-629 7777.
Smart, well-appointed hotel, a
stone's throw from Berkeley
Square. Restrained decor, an à la
carte restaurant, a good coffee

shop, and incorporating the intimate May Fair Theatre.
⊖ Green Park
🚌9, 14, 14A, 19, 22, 25, 38, 55

May Fair Theatre **3N2**
Stratton St W1. 01-629 3036. Luxurious and intimate theatre in the
May Fair Hotel, not open per-
manently but taken by companies
for short seasons.
⊖ Green Park
🚌9, 14, 14A, 19, 22, 25, 38, 55

Mayflower
117 Rotherhithe St SE16. 01-237
4088. Tudor inn which was christened The Shippe but changed its
name when the 'Mayflower', which
set off from this part of the river,
reached America. You can stand on
the jetty and ponder on the Pilgrim
Fathers. Unusually, the pub is
licensed to sell English and American postage stamps alongside the
more usual beers and spirits. Has a
seafood restaurant and bar snacks
are always available. *Pub open normal licensing hours Mon–Sun. Restaurant open LD Mon–Sat & L Sun;
closed D Sun.*
⊖ Rotherhithe
🚌47, 70, 188, Sun only 47A

MCC Memorial Gallery **1C1**
Lord's Cricket Ground, St John's
Wood Rd NW8. 01-289 1611. Exhibition on the history of cricket
from its beginnings to the present
day housed in the old racquets
court. *Open 10.30–17.00 Mon–Sat
on match days. Other times by
appointment only.* Donation.
⊖ St John's Wood
🚌13, 74, 82, 113, 159

McDonald's **3N4**
57 Haymarket SW1. 01-930 9302.
Famous hamburger chain with
branches all over London. Spotless-
ly clean, fast service, mostly take-
away but with seating areas for
those with nowhere to take it away
to. Also fruit pies, and milk shakes
almost too thick to climb up the
straw. *Open LD Mon–Sun.*
⊖ Piccadilly Circus
🚌3, 6, 9, 12, 13, 14, 14A, 15, 15A,
19, 22, 30, 53, 55, 88, 159

Mermaid Theatre **4T3**
Puddle Dock, Blackfriars EC4. 01-
236 5568. Lord Bernard Miles' crea-
tion, established in the late 50s as

an Elizabethan-style theatre across the river from the site of Shakespeare's Globe. New plays, revivals, musicals, riotous Christmas shows, children's shows, a restaurant and two bars.
⊖ Blackfriars
▤45, 59, 63, 76, 141

Minema Cinema   *2H6*
45 Knightsbridge SW7. 01-235 4225. Minimal in size but with maximum comfort – regular programmes of modern classics.
⊖ Knightsbridge
▤9, 14, 19, 22, 30, 52, 52A, 73, 74, 137

Mitre Hotel
Hampton Court Bridge, Middx. 01-979 2264. A large and popular pub, with an enormous riverside garden, which is open all day in summer even when the pub cannot serve alcohol. Bar snacks every day and full meals in the Steak House Restaurant. *Open LD Mon–Sun.*
⊖ Hammersmith (then bus 267)
▤111, 131, 216, 267, 511
Green Line 715, 716, 718, 726
⇌ Hampton Court

Mitre Tavern, Ye Olde   *4S2*
1 Ely Pl EC1. 01-405 4751. Built in the 16thC by the Bishops of Ely to house their servants and rebuilt in the 18thC. Panelled walls, small bars and gentle lighting. Elizabeth I is said to have danced around the old cherry tree, preserved in the corner (it was out of doors at the time). *Open Mon–Fri. Closed Sat & Sun.*
⊖ Chancery Lane (not Sun), Farringdon
▤8, 17, 22, 25, 45, 46, 171, 171A, 221, 243, 259

The Monument   *4T5*
Monument St EC3. Wren's monument to the Great Fire of London. It is 202 ft high – the distance from its base to the fire's origin in Pudding Lane. 311 steps lead to a literally breathtaking view on top. *Open 09.00–17.00 Mon–Sat. Closed Sun.* Charge.
⊖ Monument
▤10, 15, 21, 35, 40, 43, 47, 48, 501

Moss Bros   *3N5*
Bedford St WC2. 01-240 4567. Make uniforms for officers in all the services and hire out men's ceremonial and formal wear. Wise to make hiring arrangements a week in advance. Also retails men's and women's clothes. *Open 09.00–17.30 Mon–Wed, Fri & Sat; to 19.00 Thur. Closed Sun.*
⊖ Leicester Square
▤1, 24, 29, 176

Mothercare   *3M1*
461 Oxford St W1. 01-629 6621. From maternity clothes to clothes and equipment for babies and toddlers, at competitive prices. Several branches. *Open Mon–Wed 09.30 –17.30; Thur 09.30–19.00; Fri 09.00–17.30; Sat 09.00–18.00. Closed Sun.*
⊖ Marble Arch, Bond Street
▤1, 2B, 6, 7, 8, 12, 13, 15, 15A, 16A, 30, 73, 74, 82, 88, 113, 137, 159, 500

Museum of London   *4T6*
London Wall EC2. 01-600 3699. Relics and reconstructions of the City of London from its Roman beginnings, through its Elizabethan and Dickensian stages to the present. Shops, docks and death masks, coronations, jewellery and the Great Fire, china, glass, weapons and the Lord Mayor of London's ceremonial coach. Licensed restaurant for hot dishes, snacks and other refreshments. *Open 10.00–18.00 Tue–Sat; 14.00–18.00 Sun. Closed Mon.* Free.
⊖ Barbican (not Sun), St Paul's
▤4, 141, 502, Sun only 279A

Museum of Mankind   *3N3*
6 Burlington Gdns W1. 01-437 2224. The British Museum's Department of Ethnography, with huge collections of carvings, masks, clothing, weapons and artefacts from Africa, Australia, the Pacific Islands, the Americas and parts of Asia and Europe. Also film shows linked to current exhibitions, and a bookshop. *Open 10.00–17.00 Mon–Sat; 14.30–18.00 Sun. Closed Nat Hols.* Free.
⊖ Piccadilly Circus
▤9, 14, 14A, 19, 22, 38, 55

N

Nag's Head 3M5
10 James St WC2. 01-836 4678.
Famous and lively Edwardian pub
with a strong theatrical flavour. Real
ale and good home-cooking, especially at Sunday lunchtime. *Open
Mon–Sun (no food D Sun & Mon).*
⊖ Covent Garden
🚌1, 24, 29, 176

National Army Museum 5X2
Royal Hospital Rd SW3. 01-730
0717. The story of the British Army
from 1480 to the present, of the
Indian Army up to partition in 1947
and of other Commonwealth
armies until the time of their inde-
pendence, can be traced in the four
galleries. There are uniforms, medals and decorations, weapons,
models, dioramas, an art gallery and
a shop for books and model soldiers. The books, manuscripts,
maps, drawings and photographs
stored in the reading room may be
consulted on application to the
Director. *Open 10.00–17.30 Mon
–Sat; 14.00–17.30 Sun.* Free.
⊖ Sloane Square
🚌39

National Film Theatre 3N5
South Bank SE1. 01-928 3232. The
two cinemas show rare foreign
films, classic revivals, and run seasons specialising in the work of one
director or one star. The bookshop
is a must for serious students of
movie history. The licensed buffet
does a nice line in snacks. Also a
club; children have their own membership and own weekend programmes.
⊖ Waterloo
🚌1, 4, 5, 68, 70, 76, 149, 168,
171, 171A, 176, 177, 188, 199,
501, 502, 507

National Gallery 3N4
Trafalgar Sq WC2. 01-839 3321.
The imposing mid-19thC building
by William Wilkins houses a rich
collection of important paintings in-
cluding many masterpieces. Here
are pictures by Ucello and Botticelli,
Titian, Veronese, Tintoretto, Bellini,
Montegna, Rembrandt, Frans Hals,
Cuyp, Rubens, Van Dyck, Caravag-
gio, Poussin, Turner, Constable,
Gainsborough, Watteau, Frago-
nard, Canaletto, Tiepolo, El Greco,
Velasquez, Murillo, Goya, Monet,
Manet, Degas and Renoir. There is
the cartoon and 'The Virgin of the
Rocks' by Leonardo da Vinci,
Goya's 'Duke of Wellington',
Monet's 'Waterlilies', Philipe de
Champaigne's sumptuous 'Cardinal Richelieu'. Constable's 'Hay
Wain', Turner's 'Fighting Temer-
aire'. If dazed by all the possibilities
join a guided tour *(11.30 Mon–Fri).*
There are also lectures, audio-visual
shows, special exhibitions, an interesting shop and a pleasant restaurant. *Open 10.00–18.00 Mon–
Sat; 14.00–18.00 Sun. Closed
some Nat Hols.* Free.
⊖ Charing Cross
🚌1, 3, 6, 9, 11, 13, 15, 15A, 24,
29, 53, 77, 77A, 88, 109, 159, 170,
176, 190

Natural History Museum 2J5
Cromwell Rd SW7. 01-589 6323. A
cathedral-like, twin-towered building by Alfred Waterhouse, 1873–

80, with a superb Romanesque interior housing the national collections of zoology, entomology, palaeontology, mineralogy and botany. Here are the famous dinosaur replicas backed up by pushbutton VDUs explaining their evolution, not to mention reptiles, scorpions, birds, mammals and minerals. The human biology display includes a walk-in womb, and other important presentations are Origin of Species, Man's Place in Evolution and British Natural History. Regular films, lectures, special exhibitions, and good gift and book shops. Small cafeteria. *Open 10.00 –18.00 Mon–Sat; 14.30–18.00 Sun. Closed Nat Hols in winter & spring.* Charge.
⊖ South Kensington
🚍 14, 30, 45, 49, 74, C1

National Maritime Museum
Romney Rd SE10. 01-858 4422. The world's largest museum on its subject. The beautiful buildings – the Queen's house by Inigo Jones at their centre – are set in a sloping riverside park with the Old Royal Observatory on the hill behind. Life-size displays and packed showcases cover all imaginable aspects of Britain's maritime history. Shipbuilding, battles, trade and exploration – scale models, actual vessels, navigational instruments and weapons.

Up by the Old Royal Observatory is the house of the first Astronomer Royal, Flamsteed.

In the Meridian Building is a unique display of instruments used for measuring time and the beginnings of the understanding of space, as well as the famous Meridian line from which Greenwich Mean Time is measured. The bookshop is good and the Dolphin Coffee Shop restorative. *Open 10.00–18.00 Mon –Sat; 14.00–17.00 Sun. Closed 17.00 Oct–Easter.* Charge.
⊖ Surrey Docks (then bus 1, 188) Docklands Railway: Island Gardens (then via foot tunnel)
🚍 1, 177, 180, 188, 286
⇌ Maze Hill

National Portrait Gallery   **3N4**
2 St Martin's Pl WC2. 01-930 1552. Fascinating collection of contemporary portraits of major figures in British history – in which the sub-

jects are more important than the quality of the painting. Spans from Richard II to Bob Geldof, with many important literary, political and scientific figures in between. The ground floor is devoted to the 20thC and includes some very recent and exciting revolving displays arranged by theme. Special exhibitions from time to time. *Open 10.00–17.00 Mon–Fri; 10.00–18.00 Sat; 14.00 –18.00 Sun. Closed Nat Hols.* Free (occasional charge for special exhibitions).
⊖ Charing Cross
🚍 1, 3, 6, 9, 11, 13, 15, 15A, 24, 29, 53, 77, 77A, 88, 109, 159, 170, 176, 199

National Postal Museum   **4S3**
King Edward St EC1. 01-432 3851. One of the largest and most significant stamp collections in the world, on the upper floors of a major Post Office where current first day covers are on sale. Here are The Phillips Collection of 19thC British stamps; The Post Office Collection of all stamps issued under its aegis since 1840, plus proof sheets, designs, recent issues and the stamp archives of the Royal Mint. There is also The Berne Collection of almost

every stamp or piece of postal stationery issued anywhere in the world since 1878. *Open 10.00–16.30 Mon–Thur; 10.00–16.00 Fri. Closed Sat, Sun & Nat Hols.* Free.
⊖ St Paul's
⛟4, 8, 22, 25, 141, 501, 502

National Theatre 4U2
South Bank SE1. 01-928 2252. Within the massive concrete structure are three theatres: the large Olivier with its open-thrust stage; the smaller Lyttelton with its proscenium arch; and the adaptable little Cottesloe, which is now rarely open, awaiting an improvement of the Arts Council grant. There are bars and coffee bars on every floor, the Lyttelton Buffet, and Ovations Restaurant and Wine Bar (01-928 2033 extn 531), a bookstall, art gallery and live music often to be seen and heard in the foyer. *Open 09.30–23.00 Mon–Sun.*
⊖ Waterloo
⛟1, 4, 5, 68, 70, 76, 149, 168, 171, 171A, 176, 177, 188, 199, 501, 502, 507

Nat West Tower 4S5
25 Old Broad St EC2. London's tallest building, designed by a master of architectural overkill, Richard Seifert. The Nat West logo is on the roof, visible only from the air.
⊖ Liverpool Street
⛟6, 8, 9, 11, 22, 149, 502

Nelson's Column 3N4
Trafalgar Sq WC2. The whole square commemorates Lord Nelson and his last, greatest naval victory at Trafalgar in 1805. The focal point is the 185-ft column topped by a statue of the Admiral and guarded by Landseer's amiable lions. At the base of the column are four bronze reliefs cast from French cannon captured in Nelson's famous battles.
⊖ Charing Cross
⛟1, 3, 6, 9, 11, 13, 15, 15A, 24, 29, 53, 77, 77A, 88, 109, 159, 170, 176, 199

New West End Synagogue 2F3
St Petersburgh Pl W2. The twin cupolas of the imposing building give a somewhat Moorish air to this late 1870s version of early Gothic by Audesley and Joseph.
⊖ Queensway, Bayswater
⛟12, 88

Next 3M3
160 Regent St W1. 01-434 2515. One of an ever-growing chain of shops selling bright, smart and competitively priced clothes for men and women. This major branch also has home furnishings and a pleasant café. *Open 09.30–18.00 Mon–Sat; to 20.00 Thur. Closed Sun.*
⊖ Oxford Circus, Piccadilly Circus
⛟3, 6, 12, 13, 15, 15A, 53, 88, 159

London Transport 24-hour information service
For any information on travel in Greater London – routes, fares, times – telephone 01-222 1234 at any time of the day or night.

O

Odeon Cinema *3N4*
Haymarket SW1. 01-930 2738/
2771. Mainly new releases but also
revivals in separate performances.
⊖ Piccadilly Circus
🚌3, 6, 9, 12, 13, 14, 14A, 15, 15A,
19, 22, 38, 53, 55, 88, 159

Odeon Cinema *2H2*
Kensington High St W8. 01-602
6644. Mainly new releases, some
recent revivals.
⊖ High Street Kensington (then
bus or walk)
🚌9, 27, 28, 33, 49, 73

Odeon Cinema *3N4*
Leicester Sq WC2. 01-930 6111.
New releases. Booking wise.
⊖ Leicester Square
🚌1, 24, 29, 176

Odeon Cinema *3M1*
Marble Arch W2. 01-723 2011.
Claimed to be the most advanced
cinema in Britain, with closed-
circuit TV. Premieres and blockbus-
ters.
⊖ Marble Arch
🚌2B, 6, 7, 8, 12, 15, 15A, 16,
16A, 30, 36, 73, 74, 82, 88, 137,
500

Old Bailey *4S3*
EC4. 01-248 3277. More properly,
The Central Criminal Court. The impressive buildings are on the site of
old Newgate Prison and some of its
stones are incorporated in the lower walls. The public (only those age
14 and over) may watch the trials.
*Open 10.30–13.00 & 14.00–16.00
Mon–Fri. Closed Sat & Sun.* Free.
⊖ St Paul's
🚌4, 8, 22, 25, 141, 501, 502

Old Curiosity Shop *4S1*
13–14 Portsmouth St WC2. 01-405
9891. Tudor-style building which is
believed to have inspired Dickens'
'Old Curiosity Shop'. Sells antiques
and souvenirs. *Open 09.30–17.30
Mon–Sat. Closed Sun.*
⊖ Holborn
🚌5, 68, 77, 77A, 168, 171, 188,
501

Old Royal Observatory
Greenwich Hill SE10. 01-854 4422.
On a green hill above and behind
the riverside National Maritime
Museum. Among a group of buildings made up of the Great Equa-
torial Building with the world's
seventh largest refracting tele-
scope; the Altazimuth Pavilion; the
South Building with its planetarium;
and Flamsteed House and the Meridian Building, the only two which
are open to the public. *Open 10.00
–18.00 Mon–Sat; 14.00–17.00
Sun. Closes 17.00 Oct–Easter.*
Charge (includes entry to Maritime
Museum).
⊖ New Cross, New Cross Gate
(then bus 53)
🚌53, 54, 75
≥ Maze Hill

Old St Thomas's Hospital *4U4*
Operating Theatre
The Chapter House, St Thomas' St
SE1. 01-407 7600. The only surviving early 19thC operating theatre in
Britain. Also houses contemporary
surgical instruments, pictures of
people being separated from their
limbs, and a garret atop a spiral stair
full of herbs dried by the hospital

apothecary. *Open 12.30–16.00 Mon, Tue & Fri, or by appointment.* Charge.
⊖ London Bridge
🚌 10, 17, 21, 35, 40, 43, 44, 47, 48, 70, 133, 501, P3
⇌ London Bridge

Old Vic Theatre 4U2
Waterloo Rd SE1. 01-928 7616. Built in 1818 and run for many years by Lilian Baylis who presented opera, concerts and drama, especially Shakespeare. The home of the National Theatre Company from 1962–1976, then of the Prospect Theatre Company. Refurbished in late Victorian style in the early 1980s by its Canadian purchaser who puts on popular well-attended shows.
⊖ Waterloo
🚌 1, 4, 5, 68, 70, 76, 149, 168, 171, 171A, 176, 177, 188, 199, 501, 502, 507
⇌ Waterloo

Olympia 2J1
Hammersmith Rd W14. 01-603 3344. Gargantuan hall staging regular, popular shows and exhibitions. Among them are: the Fine Arts and Antiques Fair in early June; the Festival for Mind, Body and Spirit in late June; the Cat Club Show in early December and International Show Jumping in late December. Bars and snack bars inside. Charge.
⊖ Kensington Olympia, West Kensington (then walk)
🚌 9, 27, 28, 33, 49, 73, 91

Orange Tree Theatre
45 Kew Rd, Richmond, Surrey. 01-940 3633. Early Victorian pub with leaded windows and marble columns, above which is an 80-seat theatre in which the Richmond Fringe gives evening performances from September to April and rehearsed play readings during May. Pleasant restaurant in which it is wise to reserve dinner. *Open Mon –Sun. Restaurant closed Sun.*
⊖ Richmond
🚌 27, 65, Sun only 7

Osterley Park House
Isleworth, Middx. 01-560 3918. An out-station of the Victoria and Albert Museum and one of the most perfect examples of 18thC decor and furniture in the country. Built by Sir Thomas Gresham in the 1570s, refurbished by Robert Adam in the 1760s, presented to the nation in 1949. Adam interior design, Gobelins tapestries, Reynolds portraits, lovely grounds and a cafeteria in the stable block. *Open 14.00–18.00 Tue–Sun. Closed Mon, winter Nat Hols & 16.00 in winter.* Charge.
⊖ Osterley
🚌 91

Oxford Street 3M1
W1. Here is the largest choice of modern mass-produced clothes and shoes in London, sold through clothes chains such as C & A, Benetton, Next and Marks and Spencer and shoe chains such as Saxone, Dolcis, Derber and Ravel, all of which reappear periodically down its length. The street is also punctuated by large department stores – Selfridges, John Lewis and D. H. Evans among them.
⊖ Oxford Circus (centre), Bond Street (centre), Marble Arch (western end), Tottenham Court Road (eastern end)
🚌 2, 2B, 3, 6, 7, 8, 12, 13, 15, 15A, 16A, 30, 53, 73, 74, 82, 88, 113, 137, 159, 500, C2

P

Paddington and Friends   **1E2**
22 Crawford Pl W1. 01-262 1866.
Small shop which is a magnet for
the fans of Michael Bond's world-
famous Paddington Bear. Bears
and books and benefactions are
here, both large and small. *Open
10.00–17.00 Mon–Sat. Closed
Sun.*
⊖ Edgware Road
🚌 6, 7, 8, 15, 15A, 16, 16A, 18, 27,
36, 176

Paddington Station   **1E1**
Praed St W2. Information on 01-262
6767. Railway cathedral engineer-
ing at its best, by Brunel, the Gothic
ornament by Wyatt and Owen
Jones and the adjoining Renaiss-
ance-Baroque hotel by the younger
Hardwick. Trains go west – to Bath,
Bristol, Cardiff, Hereford, Swansea,
Devon and Cornwall.
⊖ Paddington
🚌 7, 15, 15A, 18, 27, 36
≷ Paddington

Palace Theatre   **3M4**
Shaftesbury Av W1. 01-437 6834.
Large and grand. Its first manager,
Richard D'Oyly Carte, intended it to
become the home of English opera,
but it staged music-hall and, more
recently, such smash hit musicals
as 'Jesus Christ Superstar', 'Oklahoma', 'Song and Dance', 'On Your
Toes' and 'Les Misérables'.
⊖ Leicester Square
🚌 1, 14, 14A, 19, 22, 24, 29, 38,
55, 176

Palladium Theatre   **3M3**
8 Argyll St W1. 01-437 7373. Variety
shows par excellence, international
names, a panto every Christmas
and all the glitter of the Royal Command Performance.
⊖ Oxford Circus
🚌 1, 3, 6, 7, 8, 12, 13, 15, 15A,
16A, 25, 53, 73, 88, 113, 137, 159,
500, C2

Pall Mall   **3N4**
SW1. Early 19thC opulence,
reflected in the cushioned world of
gentlemen's clubs. Here are The

Traveller's Club and the Reform
Club, both fine buildings by Sir
Charles Barry.
⊖ Piccadilly Circus
🚌 3, 6, 9, 12, 13, 14, 14A, 15, 15A,
19, 22, 38, 53, 55, 88, 159

Pan Bookshop   **2K4**
158–162 Fulham Rd SW10. 01-373
4997. Revamped and refurbished,
London's original late night bookshop stocks all Pan paperbacks, so
if Pan have it in print you'll get it
here. Also other publishers' paperbacks, new hardbacks and coffee
table books. *Open 10.00–22.00
Mon–Sat; 14.00–21.00 Sun.*
⊖ South Kensington
🚌 14, 45, 49

Park Lane   **3N1**
W1. In the 18thC a select lane bor-
dered by small palaces and large
mansions, now a busy dual car-
riageway with some of the mansions taken over by luxury hotels –
The Dorchester, Grosvenor House
and the flashier (and newer) London
Hilton are all here.
⊖ Marble Arch (northern end),
Hyde Park corner (southern end)
🚌 2B, 16, 30, 36, 73, 74, 82, 137

Passmore Edwards Museum
Romford Rd E15. 01-519 4296. Collections of Essex archaeology, local
history, geology and biology. Good
collection of Bow porcelain. *Open
10.00–18.00 Mon–Fri; 10.00–
13.00 & 14.00–17.00 Sat; 14.00
–17.00 Sun & Nat Hols. Free.*
⊖ Stratford
🚌 25, 86, 225

Penguin Bookshop   **3N4**
Unit 10, The Market, Covent Garden WC2. 01-379 7650. If by any
chance a Penguin in print is not
present, it can be summoned within 24 hours. Paperbacks from most
other publishers and some hardbacks, too. *Open 10.00–20.00
Mon–Sat. Closed Sun.*
⊖ Covent Garden
🚌 1, 6, 9, 11, 13, 15, 15A, 77, 77A,
170, 176, 199

Penhaligon's 3M5

41 Wellington St WC2. 01-836 2150. Traditional and pricey perfumes, hand-made fragrances and toilet waters based on English flowers either alone – Bluebell – or in groups – Victorian Posy. *Open 10.00–18.00 Mon–Fri; 10.00–17.00 Sat. Closed Sun.*
⊖ Covent Garden
🚌 1, 4, 6, 9, 11, 13, 15, 15A, 77, 77A, 170, 171, 171A, 176, 199

Percival David Foundation 1D5
of Chinese Art
53 Gordon Sq WC1. 01-387 0670. In 1950 Sir Percival David gave a fine library and a priceless collection of Sung, Yuan, Ming and Ch'ing dynasty Chinese ceramics to the University of London. They are housed here not solely for serious students but for anyone wanting to enjoy the cool serenity of their presence. *Open 14.00–17.00 Mon; 10.30–17.00 Tue–Fri; 10.30–13.00 Sat. Closed Sun. Free.*
⊖ Euston, Euston Square
🚌 14, 14A, 18, 30, 68, 73, 77A, 168, 188

Peter Jones 5W3
Sloane Sq SW1. 01-730 3434. One of the most architecturally successful of London's department stores with its clear curved glass frontage. Furniture and furnishing fabrics, glass, china, linen, clothes, interpreters and an airy, friendly cafeteria at tree-top height. *Open 09.00–17.30 Mon & Tue, Thur & Fri; to 19.00 Wed; 09.30–13.00 Sat. Closed Sun.*
⊖ Sloane Square
🚌 11, 19, 22, 137, C1

Peter Pan's Statue 2G5
Near Long Water, Kensington Gdns W8. J. M. Barrie's famous celebration of arrested development here reproduced in bronze by Sir George Frampton. The nymphs and rabbits clambering up the pedestal are burnished as high as young fingers can reach to stroke.
⊖ High Street Kensington
🚌 9, 33, 49, 52, 52A, 73, C1

Petticoat Lane Market 4S6
Radiates from Middlesex St E1. Huge bustling complex, too famous now for amazing bargains, but lively and stocked with pretty well every-thing. Some of the side streets specialise – Brick Lane has furniture and electrical goods and Club Row (which needs constant vigilance by the RSPCA) has pets. *Open 09.00–14.00 Sun. Closed rest of week.*
⊖ Liverpool Street, Aldgate, Aldgate East
🚌 5, 6, 8, 9, 10, 11, 15, 22, 25, 35, 40, 42, 44, 47, 47A, 48, 67, 78, 149, 225, 243A, 253, 263A, 279A

Phoenix Theatre 3M4
Charing Cross Rd WC2. 01-836 2294. Large theatre offering comedies, straight plays and musicals. It opened with 'Private Lives', and Noel Coward and Gertrude Lawrence played here during the 30s.
⊖ Tottenham Court Road
🚌 1, 14, 14A, 19, 22, 24, 29, 38, 55, 176

Photographer's Gallery 3M4
8 Gt Newport St WC2. 01-836 7860. Lively exhibitions and good stocks of photographic books and postcards. Two doors down at No 5 is another gallery, prints for sale and a small coffee bar. *Open 11.00–19.00 Tue–Sat. Closed Sun & Mon. Free.*
⊖ Leicester Square
🚌 1, 24, 29, 176

Piccadilly Circus 0N0
W1. Celebrated confluence of roads, originally by Nash, with the famous winged cherub at its centre. He isn't really Eros, he's the Angel of Christian Charity, a memo-

rial to the philanthropic Lord Shaftesbury. The whole area is being gradually lifted out of a distinctly tawdry phase by redevelopment; the new Trocadero complex of shops, cafes and exhibitions is here now, and even Eros has been polished. Still *the* meeting place for the international brigade.
⊖ Piccadilly Circus
🚌3, 6, 9, 12, 13, 14, 14A, 15, 15A, 19, 22, 38, 53, 55, 88, 159

Piccadilly Theatre   3N3
Denman St W1. 01-437 4506. A pre-war theatre which showed the first season of 'talkies' in Britain. Transformed into a cabaret theatre in 1983.
⊖ Piccadilly Circus
🚌3, 6, 9, 12, 13, 14, 14A, 15, 15A, 19, 22, 38, 53, 55, 88, 159

Picketts Lock Centre
Picketts Lock La N9. 01-803 4756. Large sports centre with facilities for soccer, hockey, tennis and golf and, indoors, gymnastics, badminton, basketball, hockey, netball, volley ball, martial arts, roller-skating, shooting, bowls and swimming. Tuition available in most sports. *Open 09.30–22.00 Mon–Sun.*
🚌W8
⇌ Lower Edmonton (then bus W8)

Pied Piper Video Cafe   3M3
8 Argyll St W1. 01-734 5776. Adolescents' dream eatery – a large basement restaurant plastered with screens of various dimensions showing continuous pop videos. American-style food; hamburgers, spare ribs and huge salads are served to accompany the bombardment of sights and sounds. *Open 12.00–24.00 Mon–Sun all year.*
⊖ Oxford Circus
🚌1, 3, 6, 7, 8, 12, 13, 15, 15A, 16A, 25, 53, 73, 88, 113, 137, 159, 500, C2

The Place   3M1
17 Duke's Rd WC1. 01-387 0161. Home base of the London Contemporary Dance Theatre which presents an annual season of new and often experimental choreography. Visiting fringe theatre, too, and classes for amateurs in the evenings and at weekends.

⊖ Euston
🚌14, 14A, 18, 30, 68, 73, 77A, 168, 188

Planetarium   1D3
Marylebone Rd NW1. 01-486 1121. The beginner's guide to the universe – stars, planets, galaxies are represented hourly on the domed ceiling with full commentary. There are evening shows in the adjoining Laserium (01-935 3726). *Open 11.00–16.30 Mon–Sun.* Charge. (Special ticket includes admission to Madame Tussaud's.)
⊖ Baker Street
🚌1, 2B, 13, 18, 27, 30, 74, 82, 113, 159, 176, T1

Players Theatre Club   3N5
Villiers St WC2. 01-839 1134. Victorian music hall is alive and well and presenting for your delectation, rollicking frolicsome festivities of a hilarious and multifarious nature. Two bars, a supper room, and drinks and sandwiches served during the performance. Full membership must be taken out in person, *48 hours* before the show; temporary membership available at the door. *Open Tue–Sat. Closed Mon.*
⊖ Charing Cross, Embankment
🚌1, 3, 6, 9, 11, 12, 13, 15, 15A, 24, 29, 53, 77, 77A, 88, 109, 159, 170, 176, 199

Plaza Cinema (1, 2, 3, 4)   3N3
Lower Regent St W1. 01-437 1234. Varied programmes – usually with new releases.
⊖ Piccadilly Circus
🚌3, 6, 9, 12, 13, 14, 14A, 15, 15A, 19, 22, 38, 53, 55, 88, 159, T1

Polka Children's Theatre
240 The Broadway, Wimbledon SW19. 01-543 4888. The shows often involve mime, puppets, masks, clowns and noisy audience participation. There is also an exhibition of toys, a small playground, workshops and classes for adults and children and the Polka Pantry for suitably gooey treats. *Open 10.00–16.30 Tue–Fri; 11.00–18.00 Sat. Closed Sun.*
⊖ Wimbledon
🚌57, 80, 93, 131, 155, 156, 200

Pollock's Toy Museum   3L3
1 Scala St W1. 01-636 3452. Three rickety floors of small creaking

rooms packed with a magical mix of bygone toys, including Victorian cut-out theatres, ancient dolls and decrepit Teddy bears. Scale models and Pollock's own famous toy theatres are on sale on ground level. *Open 10.00– 17.00 Mon–Sat. Closed Sun.*
⊖ Goodge Street
▥ 14, 14A, 24, 29, 73, 134, 176

Portobello Road Market   2F2
W11. The famous welter of glorious junk lies heaped enticingly on stall after stall every Saturday. During the week the permanent antique shops come into their own. Abundant fruit and veg, too. *Full market 09.00– 17.00 Sat only.*
⊖ Ladbroke Grove, Notting Hill Gate
▥ 7, 12, 15, 15A, 52, 52A, 88

Postman's Park   4S3
Churchyard of St Botolph, Aldersgate St EC1. On the enclosing walls, Victorian tile tablets commemorate the courage of ordinary individuals. The glowering bronze minotaur in the centre is by Michael Ayrton.
⊖ Barbican (not Sun), St Paul's
▥ 4, 8, 22, 25, 141, 501, 502, Sun only 279A

Primrose Hill
NW8. 01-486 7905. This 200-foot-high grassy hill, with its fine views over London, is a minor royal park. The up-currents attract all manner of kite and glider enthusiasts.
⊖ Camden Town
▥ 31, 74, C11
⇌ Primrose Hill

Prince Charles Cinema   3N4
Leicester Pl, Leicester Sq WC2. 01-437 8181. Small cinema showing new releases. *Late shows Fri & Sat.*
⊖ Leicester Square
▥ 1, 24, 29, 176

Prince Edward Theatre   3M4
Old Compton St W1. 01-734 8951. One-time cabaret spot, cinema and casino – now a large theatre showing hit musicals. 'Evita' was here.
⊖ Tottenham Court Road
▥ 1, 14, 14A, 19, 22, 24, 29, 38, 55

Prince Henry's Rooms   3M6
17 Fleet St EC4. 01-353 7323. Above the archway to Inner Temple Lane is the oldest domestic building in London, dating from 1610. The room which is open to visitors has a fine Jacobean ceiling and a small exhibition of Pepysiana, on loan from Pepys' house in Huntingdon. *Open 13.45– 17.00 Mon–Fri; 13.45 –16.30 Sat. Closed mornings & Sun. Charge.*
⊖ Temple (not Sun), Blackfriars
▥ 4, 6, 9, 11, 15, 15A, 171A

Prospect of Whitby
57 Wapping Wall E1. 01-481 1095. Historic and famous dockland tavern dating back to the reign of Henry VIII. Its famous customers have included the notorious Judge Jeffries, Samuel Pepys and Rex Whistler. It has beams and wood panelling, a restaurant terrace overlooking the Thames, inventive à la carte menu upstairs, good bar snacks and live music nightly downstairs. *Open Mon–Sun. Restaurant closed L Sat, D Sun.*
⊖ Wapping
▥ 22A, 56, 278

**Public Records Office   3M6
Library**
Chancery La WC2. 01-405 0741. The search rooms contain legal documents and government archives from 'Domesday Book' to 1800. The ever-popular census returns are held at the Land Registry Building in Portugal St, nearby. *Open 09.30– 17.00 Mon–Fri. Closed Sat & Sun. Free.*
⊖ Chancery Lane (not Sun), Temple (not Sun)
▥ 4, 6, 9, 11, 15, 15A, 171A

Purcell Room   4U1
South Bank SE1. 01-928 3191. The smallest of the three South Bank concert halls, whose intimate atmosphere is ideal for chamber music and solo recitals. Bar and coffee bar – more facilities at the Royal Festival Hall nearby.
⊖ Waterloo
▥ 1, 4, 5, 68, 70, 76, 140, 168, 171, 171A, 176, 177, 188, 199, 501, 502, 507

Q

Queen Elizabeth Hall **4U1**
South Bank SE1. 01-928 3191. Shares its foyer with the Purcell Room and uses its larger space for symphony, orchestral and big band concerts. More facilities at the Royal Festival Hall nearby.
⊖ Waterloo
🚍1, 4, 5, 68, 70, 76, 149, 168, 171, 171A, 176, 177, 188, 199, 501, 502, 507

Queen's Chapel **3O3**
St James's Palace, Marlborough Rd SW1. Designed by Inigo Jones in 1623 for Charles I's Queen, Henrietta Maria. The coffered timber ceiling has been beautifully restored. Open on application to the Administrative Officer, Marlborough House SW1, or for occasional public services.
⊖ Green Park
🚍9, 14, 14A, 19, 22, 25, 38, 55

Queen's Elm **2K5**
241 Fulham Rd SW3. 01-352 9157. The pub is so-called because Queen Elizabeth I took shelter under a nearby elm in 1567. Has numbered many writers among its clientele, including Laurie Lee whose signed books may be bought over the bar. *Open Mon –Sun.*
⊖ Fulham Broadway (then bus 14 or walk), South Kensington (then bus 14 or walk)
🚍14, 45, 49

Queen's Gallery **5W4**
Buckingham Palace, Buckingham Palace Rd SW1. 01-930 4832 extn 351. The one-room gallery, formerly a private chapel, is reached by a side entrance and gives no access to the rest of the palace. The priceless paintings and drawings of the royal collection make public appearances here in small, regularly changed exhibitions. *Open 11.00 –17.00 Tue–Sat; 14.00–17.00 Sun. Closed Mon.* Charge.
⊖ Victoria
🚍2, 2B, 10, 11, 14A, 16, 24, 25, 29, 36, 36B, 38, 39, 52, 52A, 55, 70, 82, 185, 500, 507, C2

Queen's House
National Maritime Museum, Romney Rd SE10. 01-858 4422. A Palladian masterpiece by Inigo Jones which is now the central building of the Maritime Museum. The carved beams in the Great Hall are original, but the ceiling painting of the school of Thornhill replaces earlier panels – now at Marlborough House. Currently being refurbished as a stately home. *Open 10.00–18.00 Mon–Sat; 14.00–17.00 Sun. Closed 17.00 Easter–Oct.* Charge.
⊖ Surrey Docks (then bus 1, 188) Docklands Railway: Island Gardens (then by foot tunnel)
🚍1, 177, 180, 188, 286
⇌ Maze Hill

Queen's Ice Skating Club **2F3**
17 Queensway W2. 01-229 0172. Glamorous rather disco-like atmosphere in which to show off the fancy footwork. Tuition available. *Open 10.00–12.00, 14.00–17.00, 19.00 –22.00 Mon–Sun.* Charge (for membership and skate hire).
⊖ Queensway, Bayswater
🚍12, 88

Queens Theatre **3M4**
Shaftesbury Av W1. 01-734 1166. Twin to the Globe. Particularly successful between the wars, but still presents good drama and varied productions.
⊖ Piccadilly Circus
🚍3, 6, 9, 12, 13, 14, 14A, 15, 15A, 19, 22, 38, 53, 55, 88, 159

R

RAF Museum
Aerodrome Rd, Hendon NW9. 01-205 2266. This first national museum to cover all aspects of the RAF and its predecessor the RFC was opened in 1972 on a former wartime airfield. As well as several genuine old aircraft there are displays of equipment, documents and paintings. The Battle of Britain Museum and Bomber Command Museum share the site. *Open 10.00–18.00 Mon–Sat; 14.00–18.00 Sun. Closed Nat Hols.* Free.
⊖ Colindale
🚌 226

Rangers House
Chesterfield Walk, Blackheath SE10. An attractive late 17thC villa, once home to the 4th Earl of Chesterfield and later to General Lord Wolsey. The Suffolk collection of portraits from Stuart and Jacobean England are painted in such detail that they serve as valuable reference material on contemporary court dress. Furniture and antique musical instruments of the same periods are gradually being acquired. *Open 10.00–17.00 Mon–Sun.* Free.
⊖ New Cross, New Cross Gate (then bus 53)
🚌 53, 54, 75
🚊 Maze Hill

Regent's Park   *1B2*
NW1. Originally part of Henry VIII's royal hunting grounds, the park took its present handsome form when the Prince Regent appointed John Nash to connect it by way of Regent Street to the now demolished Carlton House. The design of 1812–26 was never completed, but the 470 acres of lawns and lakes were encircled by elegant Regency terraces and imposing gateways.
   Here you will find the Grand Union Canal – called Regent's Canal at this point – the Zoo, a boating lake with 30 species of wildfowl, the London Mosque and, in the Inner Circle, Queen Mary's lovely rose gardens with their bandstand and the Open Air Theatre (01-486 2431). In good weather, you can watch performances primarily of Shakespearean plays, *from May–Aug. Open 05.00–dusk.* Free.
⊖ Regent's Park, Baker Street, Great Portland Street
🚌 2B, 13, 18, 27, 30, 74, 82, 113, 159, 176, C2, Sat only 3

Regent Street   *3H3*
W1. One great curve of elegance when built by Nash in 1813, now almost entirely rebuilt into a sedate shopping street for good clothes, china, glass, toys, jewellery and tourism.
⊖ Piccadilly Circus, Oxford Circus
🚌 3, 12, 13, 15, 15A, 53, 88, 159, C2

Reject Shop   *3L3*
209 Tottenham Court Rd W1. 01-580 2895. And after Habitat, there's life! Kitchen equipment, china, glass, gifts and household bits and pieces at very good prices, rejected because of minuscule flaws. Branches in Beauchamp Place, Brompton Road and King's Road as well.

Open 09.30–18.00 Mon–Wed, Fri & Sat; to 19.00 Thur. Closed Sun.
○ Goodge Street
▨ 14, 14A, 18, 24, 27, 29, 30, 73, 134, 137, 176, 253

Richmond Park
Surrey. 01-940 0654. A royal park of 2,500 acres, first enclosed as a hunting ground by Charles I in 1637, in which herds of dappled deer live wild, squirrels drop half-chewed acorns on early morning joggers, grown-ups ride horses and children sail boats on the Pen Ponds, which are well stocked with fish. The Isabella Plantation, in the heart of the park, is a magic garden of high trees, tiny waterfalls and miniature rustic bridges. Lovely views of the Thames Valley; also golf, polo and football. *Open 07.00–½ hour before dusk.* Free.
○ Richmond (then bus 65, 71)
▨ 65, 71
⇌ Richmond

Riverside Studios
Crisp Rd W6. 01-748 3354. The ex-BBC studios have been converted to provide two studio theatres – one for drama and dance, one for bands and special stage shows. There are also dance classes and workshops, a bookshop and an art gallery. Drinks, snacks and light meals are available from a self-service counter in the huge foyer with its plentiful chairs and tables.
○ Hammersmith
▨ 9, 11, 33, 72, 73, 220, 283, 295

Ritz Hotel   3N3
Piccadilly W1. 01-493 8181. Edwardian baroque grandeur and elegance in a period hotel which has always been a rendezvous for visiting celebrities. Stylish international restaurant, exuberant cocktail bar, essential to dress correctly. Casino, too.
○ Green Park
▨ 9, 14, 14A, 19, 22, 25, 38, 55

Ronnie Scott's   3M4
47 Frith St W1. 01-439 0747. This is the most famous and respected jazz club in London where you can be sure to see all the top jazz bands, mainly from the USA. The lighting is subtle, the atmosphere is crowded and mellow, but it is advisable to book. On the menu – chicken,

steaks, pasta and salads. *Open 20.30–03.00 Mon–Sat. Closed Sun.* Charge.
○ Leicester Square, Piccadilly Circus, Tottenham Court Road
▨ 1, 14, 14A, 19, 22, 24, 29, 38, 55, 176

Rotten Row   2G6
Hyde Park W2. Originally 'Route en Roi', the King's route to Kensington Palace; now a wide sandy ride where those who have access to horses exercise them daily.
○ Knightsbridge
▨ 9, 14, 19, 22, 30, 52, 52A, 73, 74, 137

Royal Academy of Arts   3N3
Burlington House, Piccadilly W1. 01-734 9052. Much dignified research and study is conducted in private rooms here by the Academy itself and by the Society of Antiquaries, the Royal Society of Chemistry, the Geological Society, the Royal Astronomical Society and the Linnean Society. The public galleries present a series of important loan exhibitions throughout the year, containing work by major artists. The Summer Exhibition in *May–Aug* displays the work of new and aspiring, living artists. *Open 10.00–18.00 Mon–Sun.* Charge.
○ Piccadilly Circus
▨ 9, 14, 14A, 19, 22, 38, 55

Royal Albert Hall   2H4
Kensington Gore SW7. 01-589 8212. Oval, Victorian domed hall, perhaps best known for the summer 'Prom' concerts. Throughout the year, stages orchestral, choral and pop concerts, sporting events and even large meetings. One of London's premier all-purpose auditoria. There's also a newly introduced guided tour which includes views of the amphitheatre from a private box and the Queen's box regally dressed for a gala concert. Gift shop, refreshments and annual theme exhibitions.
○ Knightsbridge (then bus 52, 52A, 73), South Kensington (then bus C1 or walk)
▨ 9, 33, 49, 52, 52A, 73, C1

Royal College of Arms   4T4
Queen Victoria St EC4. Discreet brick building of 1671, behind splendid gates, wherein the three Kings

of Arms, six Heralds and four Pursuivants arrange matters ceremonial and heraldic and store the official records of English and Welsh genealogy. *Not open to the general public.*
⊖ Blackfriars, Mansion House
🚌 6, 9, 11, 15, 15A, 76

Royal College of Music   **2H5**
Prince Consort Rd SW7. 01-589 3643. Holds a wide range of recitals – solo, symphonic, full operas – all by students. The Donaldson Museum, with its old musical instruments, including Handel's spinet, is *open on Mon and Wed in term time. Open by appointment.* Free.
⊖ Knightsbridge (then bus 52, 52A, 73), South Kensington (then walk)
🚌 9, 33, 49, 52, 52A, 73, C1

Royal College of Surgeons   **3M5**
Lincoln's Inn Fields WC2. 01-405 3474. The collection on anatomy, physiology and pathology assembled by the 18thC surgeon John Hunter is on display here – though not to children under 14. *Open by appointment only.* Free.
⊖ Chancery Lane (not Sun)
🚌 4, 6, 8, 9, 11, 15, 15A, 22, 25, 68, 77, 77A, 168, 171, 171A, 188

Royal Court Theatre   **5W3**
Sloane Sq SW1. 01-730 1745. This is where John Osborne's 'Look Back in Anger' launched a new wave of drama in the 50s, and experimental work is still staged here. The studio Theatre Upstairs, 01-730 2554, also puts on new plays and rehearsed play readings. Two bars, snack bar and bookstall.
⊖ Sloane Square
🚌 11, 19, 22, 137, C1

Royal Exchange   **4S5**
Threadneedle St and Cornhill EC3. 01-606 2433. The premises of the Financial Futures Exchange. Originally planned in 1564, as a meeting place for merchants, by Sir Thomas Gresham whose family emblem of a golden grasshopper crouches on top of this third building on the site.
⊖ Bank
🚌 6, 8, 9, 11, 15A, 21, 22, 25, 40, 76, 133, 149, 501

Royal Festival Hall   **4U1**
South Bank SE1. 01-928 3191. Built for the Festival of Britain in 1951 and now a part of the South Bank Arts complex. Orchestral and choral concerts are staged in the 3,000-seat concert hall, and the large foyers offer exhibitions, bars, a wine and salad bar, a licensed restaurant, a book and score shop and music on occasional lunchtimes. *Open all day*
⊖ Waterloo
🚌 1, 4, 5, 68, 70, 76, 149, 171, 176, 177, 188, 199, 501, 502, 507

Royal Garden Hotel   **2H3**
Kensington High St W8. 01-937 8000. Modern, imposing and smart hotel with good food in all three restaurants – one of which, The Roof Restaurant, has lovely views over Kensington Gardens and a dance floor. Morning coffee and full afternoon tea, as well as snacks, are served in The Garden Room. *Open LD Mon–Sun.*
⊖ High Street Kensington
🚌 9, 27, 28, 31, 33, 49, 52, 52A, 73, C1

Royal Horticultural Society Halls   **5W5**
Vincent Sq SW1. 01-834 4333. Sixty exhibitions of flowers and plants are held here annually, clustered in spring, summer and au-

tumn. The Society was founded in 1805 to promote the knowledge of horticulture and botany and has an extensive library *(by appointment only). Open daily when shows are on.*
θ St James's Park
▨ 10, 507

Royal Mews   *5W4*
Buckingham Palace Rd SW1. 01-930 4832. The home of the royal horses and of the state coaches, including the elaborate golden coronation coach and the fairytale glass coach. *Open 14.00–16.00 Wed & Thur. Closed during Ascot week.* Charge.
θ Victoria
▨ 2, 2B, 10, 11, 14A, 16, 24, 29, 36, 36B, 38, 39, 52, 52A, 55, 70, 82, 185, 500, 507, C1

Royal Naval College
Greenwich SE10. Box office: 01-317 8687. There is a season of classical concerts in the beautiful Wren Chapel from October to April and again during the Greenwich Festival in June. Although it is traditional to view the Painted Hall – structure by Wren, painted by Thornhill – in the interval the rest of the college is out of bounds.
θ Surrey Docks (then bus 1, 88)
Docklands Railway: Island Gardens (then by foot tunnel)
▨ 1, 177, 180, 188, 286
≋ Maze Hill

Royal Opera Arcade   *3N4*
Between Pall Mall and Charles II St SW1. London's first arcade, designed in 1816 by John Nash. Pure Regency, with its bow-fronted shops, glass-domed vaults and elegant lamps.
θ Piccadilly Circus
▨ 3, 6, 9, 12, 13, 14, 14A, 15, 15A, 19, 22, 38, 53, 55, 88, 159

Royal Opera House   *3M5*
Floral St WC2. 01-240 1066. 24-hour recorded information on: 01-240 1911. England's foremost opera house, a splendid construc-

tion by Barry, is often referred to simply as 'Covent Garden'. It is home to the Royal Opera Company and the Royal Ballet Company and provides a suitably lavish setting for the great names who perform here. Cold buffet and drinks are served in all the bars. Champagne in the Crush Bar is *de rigueur.*
θ Covent Garden
▨ 1, 6, 9, 11, 13, 15, 15A, 77, 77A, 170, 176, 199 (to Strand)

Rules   *3N5*
35 Maiden La WC2. 01-836 5314. Famous Edwardian restaurant. Edward VII dined Lily Langtry in an upstairs room and Thackeray and Dickens ate here in their day. Electric chandeliers now, but authentic panelling, pictures and playbills. Roast beef or jugged hare are recommended. *Open LD Mon–Fri. Closed Sat & Sun.*
θ Charing Cross
▨ 1, 6, 9, 11, 13, 15, 15A, 77, 77A, 170, 176, 199

Rumours Cocktail Bar   *3M5*
33 Wellington St WC2. 01-836 0038. Once a flower market, now a large pillared and mirrored room in which to try an imaginative range of new and classic cocktails in the lively and rather fashionable setting of Covent Garden. Very much a venue for the now-people with sturdy eardrums! *Open Mon–Sat & Sun eve only.*
θ Covent Garden
▨ 1, 4, 5, 6, 9, 11, 13, 15, 15A, 68, 77, 77A, 168, 170, 171, 171A, 176, 188, 199, 501, 502

Russian Orthodox Church   *2H5*
Ennismore Gdns SW7. The Patriarchal Church of the Dormition and All Saints was designed in the 1840s by Vulliamy in Early Christian style. The rich interior has sgraffito work by Heywood Sumner, one of the leaders of the Arts and Crafts movement.
θ Gloucester Road
▨ 49, 74

Sadler's Wells Theatre **4Q2**
Rosebery Av EC1. 01-837 1672.
This venerable theatre, the birth-
place of the Royal Ballet Company
who are now based at the Royal
Opera House, engages visiting
companies to present seasons of
opera and dance. The name comes
from a well discovered in 1683 by a
Mr Thomas Sadler – it still exists,
under a trap-door at the back of the
stalls.
⊖ Angel
19, 38, 171, 171A, 279

St Andrew's Church **4S2**
Holborn Circus EC1. Wren's largest
parish church, built in 1686 but res
tored after bombing in World War II
with a cool, simple, modern interior.
The pulpit, font, organ, and tomb of
Thomas Coram come from the
chapel of his 18thC Foundling Hospital.
⊖ Chancery Lane (not Sun),
Farringdon
8, 17, 22, 25, 45, 171A, 221,
243, 259, 501

St Andrew Undershaft **4S5**
Church
Leadenhall St EC3. Early 16thC East
Anglian Gothic – once oversha-
dowed by a maypole. The monument to John Stow, London's first
historian, is annually furnished with
a fresh quill pen by the Lord Mayor.
⊖ Aldgate, Bank
15A, 25

St Bartholomew the Great **4S3**
Church
West Smithfield EC1. 01-606 5171.
Great indeed, and the oldest church
in London (apart from the chapel in
the Tower). It is the Norman choir of
the Augustinian Priory founded in
1123, together with St Bartholomew's Hospital, by Rahere, a
courtier of Henry I.
⊖ St Paul's
4, 8, 22, 25, 141, 501, 502

St Bride's Church **4T2**
Fleet St EC4. 01-353 1301. Known
as the printers' church, its crypt

museum (itself part Roman part
Saxon) is warmed by the heat of
Reuters press agency next door.
This is the Wren church whose
tiered spire has been the model for
countless wedding cakes. Restored after war damage; Christ
almost dances in the stained glass
window in the Wren-style altar-
piece. *Museum open 09.00–17.00
Mon–Sun.* Donation appreciated.
⊖ Blackfriars
4, 6, 9, 11, 15, 15A, 17, 45, 59,
63, 76, 141, 502

St Bride's Printing **4T2**
Library
St Bride's Institute, Bride La EC4.
01-353 4660. A public reference library of books on graphic design,
papermaking, printing, binding and
everything to do with the construction of books. Occasional special
exhibitions. *Open 09.30–17.30
Mon–Fri.*
⊖ Blackfriars
4, 6, 9, 11, 15, 15A, 17, 45, 59,
63, 76, 141, 502

St Clement Danes Church **4T2**
Strand WC2. 01-242 8282. The
church of the nursery rhyme whose
carillon includes 'Oranges and
Lemons' in its repertoire. Built for
the Danes in the 9thC, rebuilt by
Wren, destroyed in 1941, rebuilt
again in the 50s and now the central
church of the RAF.
⊖ Temple (not Sun), Charing Cross
(then any bus along the Strand),
Holborn (then bus 68, 77, 77A, 501
to Aldwych)
4, 6, 9, 11, 15, 15A, 171

St Dunstan in the West **4S2**
Church
Fleet St EC4. 01-242 6027. Rebuilt
in 1832 as a copy of All Saints
Church in York. The clock with its
two striking jacks is 17thC and the
statue of Queen Elizabeth I is the
only known, contemporary three-
dimensional likeness of her.
⊖ Temple (not Sun), Charing Cross
(then bus 6, 9, 11)
4, 6, 9, 11, 15, 15A, 171A

St George's Cathedral   **3P6**
Lambeth Rd SE1. 01-928 5256. This Roman Catholic cathedral, barrack-like from without but gracious within, was designed by Pugin in the 1840s and never completed. It was destroyed by bombing in 1941 and rebuilt by Romily Croze, who adapted the original plans.
⊖ Lambeth North
🚌3, 10, 12, 44, 45, 63, 68, 109, 141, 171, 176, 177, 188, 199

St Giles Cripplegate   **4S4**
Church
Fore St EC2. 01-606 3630. The massive Barbican surrounds this church where Cromwell was married and Milton is buried. Its interior was almost wholly rebuilt after bombing. Behind it stands a corner bastion of the Roman city wall. 'Cripple-gate' comes from 'crepel', Anglo-Saxon for a kind of pedestrian underpass used for entry after curfew.
⊖ Barbican (not Sun), St Paul's
🚌4, 141, 502, Sun only 279A

St James's Church   **3N3**
Piccadilly W1. 01-734 5244. A Wren church restored in 1954 after bomb

damage. The reredos and font garlanding are by Grinling Gibbons. A place of tremendous activity with craft markets in the courtyard, music, lectures, exhibitions, events – and they do fit in church services, too. Very pleasant little cafe.
⊖ Piccadilly Circus
🚌9, 14, 14A, 19, 22, 38, 55

St James's Palace   **3N4**
Pall Mall SW1. In warm red brick with blue diapering, its Tudor gatehouse gives on to courtyards and buildings planned for Henry VIII, but with important additions by Wren and others. Still officially a royal residence – foreign ambassadors and commissioners are 'accredited to the Court of St James'.
⊖ Green Park, St James's Park
🚌9, 14, 14A, 19, 22, 38, 55

St James's Park   **3O3**
SW1. 01-930 1793. The oldest of the royal parks and one of the most attractive and most romantic with its long lake, delicate bridge and weeping willows. Especially rich in bird life, including 20 species of ducks and geese and, on Duck Island, some magnificent pelicans who have occasionally to be disciplined for eating pigeons and upsetting the tourists. The present design is mainly by Nash, and Buckingham Palace, Carlton House Terrace, the domes and spires of Whitehall, and Westminster Abbey overlook it with apparent approval. *Open 05.00–24.00. Free.*
⊖ St James's Park
🚌10, 11, 24, 29, 70, 507, C1 (to Victoria Street)

St John's Church   **4R3**
Clerkenwell
St John's Sq EC1. 01-253 6644. Mostly 18thC but the crypt is part of the original 12thC priory church of the Order of St John of Jerusalem. Used by the St John's Ambulance Brigade for ceremonies and services. Apply to curator for admission.
⊖ Farringdon
🚌5, 55, 243, 277, 279

St John's Church   **3P4**
Smith Square
SW1. 01-222 1061. 18thC church whose curious appearance has been likened to an upside-down

footstool. Has regular lunchtime and evening concerts – solo recitals, chamber, orchestral and choral works. The crypt has exhibitions of works by contemporary artists and a good licensed buffet and restaurant.
⊖ Westminster
🚌 3, 10, 77A, 88, 159, 507

St John's Gate Museum   4R3
St John's Sq EC1. 01-253 6644 extn 35. The old gatehouse of the Priory of St John of Jerusalem is now a small museum on all aspects of the Knights Hospitallers. The St John Ambulance Brigade was launched from the gatehouse in 1837 – and the museum is in the hands of the Order of St John. *Open 10.00– 18.00 Tue, Fri & Sat. Closed Mon, Wed, Thur, Sun & Nat Hols.* Free.
⊖ Farringdon
🚌 5, 55, 243, 277, 279

St Katharine's Dock   4U6
St Katharine's Way, Tower Bridge E1. No longer a commercial dock, but three inter-linked basins which form a yacht haven and an appropriate setting for the Thames Maritime Museum with its tug, lightship, sailing barges and Captain Scott's 'Discovery'. Some warehouses survive – converted into souvenir shops, the Dickens Tavern and the Warehouse Restaurant. Charge to enter ships.
⊖ Tower Hill
Docklands Railway: Tower Gateway
🚌 15, 42, 56, 78, 278

St Margaret Church   3O4
Westminster
Parliament Sq SW1. 01-222 6382. Somewhat dwarfed by the massive bulk of Westminster Abbey is this parish church of the House of Commons, rebuilt in the 16thC with a splendid east window and some wondrous modern stained glass by John Piper.
⊖ Westminster
🚌 3, 11, 12, 24, 29, 53, 77, 77A, 88, 109, 159, 170, C1

St Margaret Pattens   4T5
Church
Rood La, Eastcheap EC3. 01-623 6630. The locally-made pattens, or shoes, are displayed in a cabinet in this Wren church of 1684–9, with

its unusual canopied pews and punishment bench for naughty children.
⊖ Monument
🚌 10, 15, 40, Sun only 44

St Martin-in-the-Fields   3N4
Church
Trafalgar Sq WC2. 01-930 1862. This is the parish church of Buckingham Palace (though not used as such) and above the congregation is a Royal Box complete with fireplace. Puts on regular lunchtime music recitals and Christmas choral concerts.
⊖ Charing Cross
🚌 1, 3, 6, 9, 11, 12, 13, 15, 15A, 24, 29, 53, 77, 77A, 88, 109, 159, 170, 176, 199

St Martin's Theatre   3M4
West St, Cambridge Circus WC2. 01-836 1443. Intimate playhouse with unusual polished teak doors. 'The Mousetrap' continues its record run here.
⊖ Leicester Square
🚌 1, 14, 14A, 19, 22, 24, 29, 38, 55, 176

St Mary-le-Bow Church   4S4
Cheapside EC2. 01-248 5139. Bow Bells still ring out from this Wren

church, gutted in 1941 and rebuilt by Laurence King. The modern rood is a present from Germany. The 11thC crypt, with its quiet chapel, houses the Ecclesiastical Court of Arches, the Archbishop of Canterbury's appeal court.
⊖ Bank, Mansion House
🚌 8, 22, 25

St Mary le Strand Church   3M5
Strand WC2. A perfect small baroque church, built 1714–17 by James Gibb, perched nervously on an island in the middle of the busy road.
⊖ Temple (not Sun), Holborn (then bus 68, 77, 77A, 188, 501 to the Aldwych), Charing Cross (then any bus along the Strand)
🚌 1, 4, 5, 6, 9, 11, 13, 15, 15A, 68, 77, 77A, 168, 170, 171, 171A, 176, 188, 199, 501, 502

St Michael Paternoster   4T4
Church
College Hill EC4. Dick Whittington lies buried in this recently restored Wren church. The tower is used as an office by the Mission to Seamen.
⊖ Cannon Street (not evenings or weekends), Mansion House
🚌 6, 9, 11, 15, 15A, 17, 76, 149

St Michael-upon-Cornhill   4T5
Church
Cornhill EC3. 01-626 8841. First-rate choir, also lunchtime organ recitals and choral evenings. Send s.a.e. for list of events. Magnificent peal of bells, too. A Wren church restored by Scott.
⊖ Bank
🚌 15A, 25

St Olave Church   4T5
8 Hart St EC3. 01-488 4318. A 15thC survivor of the Great Fire. The arch of skulls in the churchyard indicates that the dead from the Plague were buried here as were Samuel Pepys and, so says the parish register, Mother Goose.
⊖ Aldgate
🚌 10, 40, Sun only 44

St Pancras Old Church   1B6
Pancras Rd NW1. 01-387 8818. On the third oldest Christian site in Europe stands this small country-style church with 4thC foundations and Saxon altar stone. Atmospheric

churchyard. *Open for services Wed & Sun.*
⊖ King's Cross St Pancras
🚌 46, 214

St Pancras Station   1C6
Euston Rd NW1. Information on 01-387 7070. Gothic extravaganza by Sir George Gilbert Scott. The vast pinnacled frontage was once a grand hotel but now houses offices. The 19thC train shed is an impressive feat of engineering, its glass and iron tunnel vault spanning 243 feet without supporting pillars. The trains from here go to the Midlands.
⊖ Kings' Cross St Pancras
🚌 14A, 17, 18, 30, 45, 46, 63, 73, 77A, 214, 221, 259, C11
≋ St Pancras

St Paul's Church   3M4
Covent Garden
Covent Garden WC2. 01-836 5221. The actors' church. Built by Inigo Jones in the 1630s it contains memorials to Marie Lloyd, Boris Karloff, Sybil Thorndike, Lewis Casson and many more.
⊖ Covent Garden
🚌 1, 6, 9, 11, 13, 15, 15A, 77, 77A, 170, 176, 199

St Paul's Cathedral   4S3
EC4. 01-248 4619/2705. Sir Christopher Wren's greatest work, built from 1675–1710. The superb dome and porches are dwarfed by modern building, but the interior has lost nothing with its magnificent stalls by Grinling Gibbons, ironwork by Tijou, paintings by Thornhill, mosaics by Salviati and Stephens. Rich in memorials to the great and famous – soldiers, artists, statesmen. The crypt, the largest in Europe, has a worthwhile museum. It is worth the heart-pounding climb to the Whispering Gallery not only for the weird phenomenon but to get a different view of the whole. Holds occasional lunchtime organ recitals and the choir is exceptional.
⊖ St Paul's, Mansion House
🚌 4, 6, 8, 9, 11, 15, 15A, 17, 22, 25, 76, 141, 501, 502

St Peter-upon-Cornhill   4S5
Church
Bishopsgate Corner EC3. 01-626 9483. Built by Wren on the City's oldest church site. Holds regular

performances of Elizabethan music and of medieval plays at Christmas.
⊖ Bank
🚌 15A, 25

St Sophia's Cathedral 2F3
Moscow Rd W2. Oldrid Scott, son of Sir George Gilbert Scott, designed this red brick Byzantine Cathedral of the Greek Orthodox Church in 1877. The lovely mosaic work inside is by Boris Anrep.
⊖ Bayswater, Queensway
🚌 12, 88

St Stephen's Church 4T4
Walbrook EC4. 01-626 2277. The parish church of the Lord Mayor of London and a centre for the Samaritans, 01-283 3400, formed to help the suicidally desperate. One of Wren's masterpieces, its beautifully restored dome was possibly a prototype for St Paul's.
⊖ Bank, Cannon Street (not evenings or weekends)
🚌 6, 8, 9, 11, 15, 15A, 21, 22, 25, 43, 76, 133, 149, 501

St Stephen's Tavern 3O4
10 Bridge St SW1. 01-930 3230. Parliament's pub or the MPs' local, with a division bell to summon drinking Members back across the road to vote. Three bars, with food available at lunchtime during the week. Good place to spot famous faces and listen to the gossip of political journalists. *Open Mon–Sat & Sun morning. Closed Sun evening.*
⊖ Westminster
🚌 3, 11, 12, 24, 29, 53, 70, 77, 77A, 88, 109, 159, 170, C1

Samuel Pepys 4T3
Brooks Wharf, 48 Upper Thames St EC4. 01-248 3048. A warehouse converted into a rambling pub with a two-tiered, river-view terrace bar and a spacious cellar bar with a well-stocked food counter. The light airy restaurant has good river views, and transcriptions of Pepys' diaries and an original letter are on display among the old lamps and prints. *Pub open normal licensing hours Mon–Sun. Restaurant open LD Mon–Fri & D Sat; closed L Sat and all Sun.*
⊖ Mansion House
🚌 6, 9, 11, 15, 15A, 17, 76, 149

Savill Gardens
Windsor Great Park, Windsor, Berks. 0784 35544. The 35 acres of woodland garden were created by Sir Eric Savill in the 1930s. Beautiful throughout the spring and summer with azaleas, roses, herbaceous borders, alpine plants and a lake. *Open 10.00–18.00 Mon–Sun. Closed Oct–Mar.* Free.
Green Line 700, 701, 718, 726
➔ Windsor and Eton Riverside, Windsor and Eton Central (then walk)

Savoy Hotel 3N5
Strand and Embankment WC2. 01-836 4343. World-famous hotel with stylish decor, lovely river views and famous faces at the tables. Outstanding cuisine in Grill Room or River Room Restaurant, and classy cocktails in the American Bar.
⊖ Charing Cross (then any bus along the Strand), Temple (not Sun)
🚌 1, 6, 9, 11, 13, 15, 15A, 77, 77A, 170, 176, 199

Savoy Theatre 3N5
Strand WC2. 01-836 8888. Built by Richard D'Oyly Carte as a home for the comic operas of Gilbert and Sullivan – now presenting a wide variety of plays and musicals. Attached to the Savoy Hotel.
⊖ Charing Cross (then any bus along the Strand), Temple (not Sun)
🚌 1, 6, 9, 11, 13, 15, 15A, 77, 77A, 170, 176, 199

Science Museum   2H5

Exhibition Rd SW7. 01-589 3456.
Vast national collection on science
and its applications to industry.
Most of the items on display are
real, not models, and large numbers
still function and are demonstrated
daily. Transport and exploration,
meteorology and time measure-
ment, telecommunications and
computing, space exploration and
the Apollo 10 capsule, and The
Wellcome Museum of the History
of Medicine are all here. Lectures,
film shows, special school holiday
events, a museum shop and a
cafeteria round off the experience.
*Open   10.00–18.00   Mon–Sat;
14.30–18.00 Sun. Closed Nat Hols
in winter & spring.* Voluntary
charge.
⊖ South Kensington
🚌14, 30, 45, 49, 74, C1

Scotch House   2H6

2 Brompton Rd SW3. 01-581 2151.
Those who are entitled to wear the
tartan will find the appropriate one
here. Also Fair Isle, Shetland and
Pringle knitwear and top quality
Scottish tweeds for men, women
and children. *Open 09.00–17.30
Mon, Tue & Thur; 09.00–18.30
Wed; 09.00–18.00 Fri & Sat.
Closed Sun.*
⊖ Knightsbridge
🚌9, 14, 19, 22, 30, 52, 52A, 73,
74, 137, C1

Selfridges   3M1

400 Oxford St W1. 01-629 1234.
Established since 1909, this is one
of the most comprehensive of the
large department stores with lavish
food halls and glamorous displays
of clothes, toys, furniture, household goods, books and a large and
fragrant perfumery. Also a downstairs coffee shop and an upstairs
cafeteria. *Open 09.00–18.00 Mon
–Wed, Fri & Sat; 09.00–19.30
Thur. Closed Sun.*
⊖ Bond Street, Marble Arch
🚌1, 2B, 6, 7, 8, 12, 13, 15, 15A,
16A, 30, 73, 74, 82, 88, 113, 137,
159, 500

Serpentine   2G6

Hyde Park W2. A fine artificial lake,
created with the Long Water to the
west by damming the old Westbourne River. There are boats to
hire from the north bank, restaurants at either end, fishing,
ornamental ducks, and prom-
enades and deckchairs all around.
Park open 05.00–24.00 Mon–Sun.
Small charge for boat hire.
⊖ Knightsbridge, Lancaster Gate
🚌9, 12, 52, 52A, 73, 88, C1

Serpentine Gallery   2G5

Kensington Gdns W8. 01-402 6075.
The old Kensington Gardens tea
house is a lovely setting for a variety
of exhibitions of contemporary art
which change monthly. The Serpentine restaurant, buffet and bars
are only a duck's waddle away.
*Open   10.00–18.00   Mon–Sun.
Closed dusk in winter and between
exhibitions.* Free.
⊖ Knightsbridge (then walk)
🚌9, 52, 52A, 73, C1

Serpentine Restaurants   2G5

Hyde Park W2. 01-723 8784. An
elaborate modern structure, with
lovely views over the water and the
park. The Serpentine Restaurant
has a full à la carte menu and is *open
for lunch and dinner all year.* The
Pergola Restaurant serves light
meals, salads and steaks and is
open 12.00–18.00 summer only.
The Cocktail Bar is *open all year
during normal licensing hours.* The
Plant Bar is *open for summer drinking only.* The Serpentine Buffet is a
cafeteria, *open all day, all year, until
16.00 in winter or 18.00 in summer.*
⊖ Knightsbridge (then bus 52, 52A,
73), South Kensington (then walk)
🚌9, 52, 52A, 73, C1

Shaftesbury Theatre   **3M4**
Shaftesbury Av WC2. 01-836 6596.
Was acquired in the spring of 1983
by a company of some of the best of
British comedy actors, and is now a
Theatre of Comedy.
⊖ Tottenham Court Road, Holborn
▥7, 8, 14, 14A, 19, 22, 25, 29, 38,
55, 73, 134, 176

Shaw Theatre   **1C6**
100 Euston Rd NW1. 01-388 1394.
The permanent home of the New
Shaw Theatre Company, which presents a varied programme of plays,
musicals, concerts and children's
events, punctuated by a lavish
Christmas pantomime and a summer season by the National Youth
Theatre. Regular lunchtime concerts in the bar.
⊖ Euston
▥14, 14A, 18, 30, 68, 73, 77, 77A,
168, 188

Shepherd Market   **3N2**
W1. Mayfair's village centre – a picturesque little 18thC quarter of tiny
streets and alleys and a diminutive
piazza, with market stalls, antique
shops, pubs and eating houses.
⊖ Green Park
▥9, 14, 14A, 19, 22, 25, 38, 55

Sherlock Holmes   **3N4**
10 Northumberland St WC2. 01-
930 2644. Upstairs, next to the restaurant, is a perfect reconstruction
of Holmes' study, and down in the
bar are all manner of relevant cuttings and curios, including the head
of the legendary 'Hound of the Bas-
kervilles'. *Restaurant open LD Mon
–Fri & D Sat; closed L Sat & all Sun.
Pub open normal licensing hours
Mon–Sun.*
⊖ Charing Cross, Embankment
▥1, 3, 6, 9, 11, 12, 13, 15, 15A,
24, 29, 53, 77, 77A, 88, 109, 159,
170, 176, 199

Sheraton Park Tower   **2H6**
101 Knightsbridge SW1. 01-235
8050. Modern hotel with an interesting circular design, by Richard
Seifert. Behind the attractive shrub-
bery growing out of concrete con-
tainers on the forecourt is a stylish
coffee shop. The Restaurant offers
an all-day service of breakfast,
lunch, afternoon tea, pre-theatre
and main dinners. Wide range of
international cuisine.

⊖ Knightsbridge
▥9, 14, 19, 22, 30, 52, 52A, 73,
74, 137, C1

Shooter's Hill
SE18. 01-856 3610. Hundreds of
acres of woodland and open parkland which encompass Oxleas
Woods, Jackwood and Eltham
Parks. Castlewood has a folly
erected in 1784 to commemorate
the Indian exploits of Sir William
James. *Open 24 hrs. Free.*
▥89, 178
⇌ Lewisham (then bus 89, 178)

Simpsons of Piccadilly   **3N3**
203 Piccadilly W1. 01-734 2002. A
department store specialising in top
quality men's and women's clothes
especially knitwear and sports-
wear. *The place to get country*
casuals. Also good quality luggage
and handbags. *Open 09.00–17.30
Mon–Wed, Fri & Sat; 09.00–19.00
Thur. Closed Sun.*
⊖ Piccadilly Circus
▥9, 14, 14A, 19, 22, 38, 55

Simpson's in the Strand   **3N5**
100 Strand WC2. 01-836 9112. Very
English restaurant in the grand style
– booking and correct dress are
essential. The roast beef and mut-
ton are unfailingly splendid – remember to tip the carver – and may
be followed by treacle roll or a
savoury. The Stilton is always
creamy and there is vintage port by
the glass to accompany it. *Open LD
Mon–Sat. Closed Sun.*
⊖ Charing Cross (then any bus
along the Strand), Temple (not
Sun)
▥1, 6, 9, 11, 13, 15, 15A, 77, 77A,
170, 176, 199

Sir John Soane's Museum   **4S1**
13 Lincoln's Inn Fields WC2. 01-405
2107. The eccentric and inventive
Neo-Classical architect (1753–
1837) designed here his own house
to accommodate his uniquely
obsessive collection of antiquities
and architectural models; among
them the 1370BC sarcophagus of
Seti I and 12 Hogarth pictures.
*Open 10.00–17.00 Tue–Sat.
Closed Sun, Mon & Nat Hols. Free.*
⊖ Holborn
▥5, 7, 8, 22, 25, 38, 55, 68, 77A,
171, 171A, 188

W. H. Smith, Sloane Square   5W2

36 Sloane Sq SW1. 01-730 0351.
One of a nation-wide, high street
chain of booksellers, stocked best
for popular titles and paperbacks.
Also sells stationery, magazines,
toys, records and cassettes. *Open
09.00–18.30 Mon, Thur & Fri;
09.30–18.30 Tue; 09.00–19.00
Wed; 09.00–18.00 Sat. Closed
Sun.*
⊖ Sloane Square
🚌 11, 19, 22, 137, C1

Smithfield Market   4S3

EC1. The world's largest wholesale
meat market on a site originally
called Smooth Field. The 19thC Ital-
ianate-style buildings are interesting, but for most people this is 10-
acres of sheer horror. *Open 05.00
–12.00 Mon–Fri. Closed Sat & Sun.*
⊖ Barbican (not Sun), Farringdon
🚌 8, 22, 25, 63, 221, 243, 259

Society of Genealogists   2J4

37 Harrington Gdns SW7. 01-373
7054. The library contains a huge
collection of copies of parish regis-
ters, which those researching their
ancestry may consult for a fee. Or,
for a larger fee, the Society will
undertake the research itself. *Open
10.00–17.00 Mon–Fri.* Charge.
⊖ Gloucester Road
🚌 49

Soho   3M3

W1. London's oldest foreign quarter is changing character. For decades, a curious mixture of charm
and corruption, the area is gradually
acquiring a cleaner-cut image. As
the tide of erotica is turned back,
the increasing influence of the
young upwardly mobile media set
can be seen in the mushrooming of
hyped up wine bars, brasseries and
drinking clubs.
But the continental ambience is still
very much alive – from bustling Berwick Street Market which offers
the cheapest fruit and veg in the
West End to the paper lanterns and
wind-dried ducks of Chinatown.
Here also are countless, excellent
foreign and ethnic restaurants,
quality delicatessens and patiss-
eries.
Sex in its most indelicate and expensive forms lingers on – porno
movies, sex shops, live shows, top-
less bars and 'young models' of all
ages. Avoid the over-priced titilla-
tion and this is the perfect area to
eat in before or after a visit to one of
the many theatres or cinemas
which lie around its edges.
Soho was once a hunting ground
and 'So-ho' was the rallying cry of
the huntsmen.
⊖ Piccadilly Circus, Leicester
Square, Oxford Circus, Tottenham
Court Road
🚌 1, 7, 8, 14, 14A, 19, 22, 24, 29,
38, 55, 73, 176

Sotheby's   3M2

34–35 New Bond St W1. 01-493
8080. Famous auctioneers who
began as rare book specialists,
but now dispose of anything that
comes under the heading of antiques or works of art – with a turn-
over that runs into millions of
pounds. *Open 09.00–16.30 Mon
–Fri. Closed Sat & Sun.*
⊖ Bond Street
🚌 25

South Bank Arts Centre   4U1

South Bank SE1. The massive concrete group contains the National
Theatre, the Royal Festival Hall and
Queen Elizabeth Hall, the Purcell
Room, the National Film Theatre,
the Hayward Gallery (each with
their separate entries in this guide),
together with bookstalls, bars,
snack bars, restaurants, a riverside
terrace and live entertainment in
the theatre foyers. *Open 09.00–
23.30 Mon–Sun.*
⊖ Waterloo
🚌 1, 4, 5, 68, 70, 76, 149, 168,
171, 171A, 176, 177, 188, 199,
501, 502, 507

South London Art Gallery

Peckham Rd SE5. 01-703 6120.
Temporary exhibitions, sometimes
of new work, sometimes made up
from its own collection of the work
of British artists from 1700, which
includes many pictures of local relevance. *Open 10.00–18.00 Tue–
Sat; 15.00–18.00 Sun. Closed Mon
& between exhibitions.* Free.
⊖ Elephant and Castle (then bus
12, 171), Oval (then bus 36, 36B)
🚌 12, 36, 36B, 171

South Molton Street   3M2

W1. Traffic-free shopping street
with tables set temptingly outside

the restaurants in warm weather. Some very expensive dress shops are here and also slightly more moderately priced young fashions. Pleasant, civilised ambience.
⊖ Bond Street
🚌6, 7, 8, 12, 13, 15, 15A, 16A, 25, 73, 88, 137, 159, 500

Spaniards Inn
Hampstead La NW3. 01-455 3276. Renowned 16thC inn, once the residence of the Spanish Ambassador to the court of James I. Dick Turpin stayed here and other regular customers included Shelley, Keats, Byron and, of course, Charles Dickens. Lovely rose garden and good food both at lunchtime and in the evening. *Open Mon–Sun.*
⊖ Archway (then bus 210), Golders Green (then bus 210)
🚌210

Speaker's Corner   *2F6*
Hyde Park W2. At the Marble Arch corner of the park. Every Sunday, in celebration of the British right of free speech, unknown orators express strong and often strange views on life, death and politics. At least half the wit and insight comes from the hecklers. *Every Sun.*
⊖ Marble Arch
🚌2B, 6, 7, 8, 12, 15, 15A, 16, 16A, 30, 36, 73, 74, 82, 88, 137

Spitalfields   *4R6*
Commercial St E1. Five acres of wholesale fruit, vegetable and flower market, undercover and with extensive underground chambers. Large quantities of bananas are ripened here, having travelled green from their native countries. *Open from 04.30 Mon–Sat. Closed Sun.*
⊖ Liverpool Street
🚌5, 6, 8, 22, 22A, 35, 47, 48, 67, 78, 149, Sun only 243A, 263A, 279A

Steam Museum
Green Dragon La, Brentford, Middx. 01-568 4757. Five gigantic beam engines are under steam every weekend in this huge Victorian pumping house. There is a working forge here, too, and a collection of old traction engines, not to mention a tea room for those who prefer their steam rising from a cup. *Open 11.00–17.00 Sat & Sun*

& Nat Hols. Closed Mon–Fri. Charge.
⊖ Gunnersbury (then bus 237, 267)
🚌65, 237, 267
⇌ Kew Bridge

Stock Exchange   *4S5*
Old Broad St EC2. 01-588 2355. Capitalism in action and computerised! The dealers in negotiable securities began their transactions in a coffee house, but moved here into formal premises in 1901. There is a visitors' gallery and a daily film show which explains all. *Open 09.30–15.15 Mon–Fri. Closed Sat & Sun.* Free.
⊖ Bank
🚌6, 8, 9, 11, 149

Strand   *3N5*
WC2. Once truly a strand, a riverside walk, before the river was embanked and pushed south wards. With Fleet Street as its continuation, it links the City with Westminster. In Tudor times great mansions stood along it, their gardens reaching to the Thames. One of these was York House and when George Villiers, Duke of Buckingham, had to sell it to pay his debts, he asked to be remembered in the streets on the site. This accounts for George Court, Villiers Street, Duke Street, York Place (formerly Of Alley) and Buckingham Street.
⊖ Temple (not Sun), Charing Cross
🚌1, 4, 5, 6, 9, 11, 13, 15, 15A, 68, 77, 77A, 168, 170, 171, 171A, 188, 199, 501, 502

Strand Theatre   **3M5**
Aldwych WC2. 01-836 2661. Large
theatre staging a mixture of major
comedies, straight plays and
musicals.
⊖ Temple (not Sun), Charing Cross
🚌1, 4, 5, 6, 9, 11, 13, 15, 15A, 68,
77, 77A, 168, 170, 171, 171A, 176,
188, 199, 501, 502

Sun Inn
7 Church Rd, Barnes SW13. 01-876
5893. Famous, crowded and popular pub with the young. Rebuilt in
1750 on an old pub site, opposite
Barnes Pond with its lush rushes,
ducks and surrounding trees. Country inn atmosphere within easy
reach of London. Doesn't go in for
meals but has good sandwiches.
Open Mon–Sun.
⊖ Hammersmith (then bus 9)
🚌9
⇌ Barnes Bridge

The Swiss Centre   **3N4**
1 New Coventry St W1. 01-734
1291. Don't be perturbed by the
chiming of bells or the midday
crowing of a cock as you enter this
complex. Outside the Swiss Tourist
Centre is a glockenspiel and clock
with 25 bells surrounded by moving
wooden figures. As well as the
time, the clock shows the signs of
the zodiac and the phases of the
moon. Inside the centre is a selection of shops and restaurants specialising in Swiss delicacies: on the
ground level there is Gourmet Corner, selling Swiss meats, cheeses
and chocolates along with truffles,
bread and patisserie made on the
premises. *Open 09.30–21.00 Mon
–Sat, 11.00–18.00 Sun.*
Downstairs is a spacious basement
holding four restaurants. The Chesa
is the most up-market with a Swiss

and international menu; the Tavern,
very popular, serves raclette, meat
and fish dishes; the Rendez-vous
emphasises fondues, be it cheese
or chocolate; and finally the Locan-
da where you can be sure of fast
service, fresh salads and good business lunches. *Restaurants open
12.00–24.00 Mon–Sat, 12.00–
23.00 Sun.*
Around the corner on Wardour
Street the Swiss Imbiss serves
breakfast, pastries and savoury
snacks. *Open 08.30–23.30 Mon–
Sat, 12.00–21.00 Sun.*
Centre closed Xmas day.
⊖ Leicester Square, Piccadilly
Circus
🚌1, 3, 6, 9, 12, 13, 14, 14A, 15,
15A, 19, 22, 24, 29, 38, 53, 55, 88,
159, 176

Syon House and Park
London Rd, Brentford, Middx. 01-
560 0884. Tudor house, set in 55
acres of parkland which is owned
by the Percys, dukes of Northumberland. The present Duke still
lives here for part of the year. The
interior design is by Robert Adam,
with paintings by Huysmans, Lely
and Van Dyck, and the views
stretch across the river to Kew Gardens. Within the grounds is the
London Butterfly House, in which
exotic specimens fly free and land
on visitors. There is also an excellent garden centre and the Heritage
Collection of historic British cars.
*House open Easter–Sep 12.00–
17.00 Sun–Thur, Oct 12.00–17.00
Sun only; Butterfly House open
Mar–Oct 10.00–17.00 Mon–Sun;
Grounds open all year 10.00–18.00
or dusk Mon–Sun.* Charge.
⊖ Gunnersbury (then bus 237, 267)
🚌117, 203, 237, 267, Sun only E2
⇌ Syon Lane

T

Tate Gallery   **5X6**
Millbank SW1. 01-821 1313. This
classical 19thC building by Sidney
R. J. Smith has been enlarged three
times to provide adequate housing
for the national collection of British
art from the 16thC to the present
day, and its rich store of foreign
paintings from 1880. The Gallery
was born in 1889 when Sir Henry
Tate, of Tate and Lyle Sugar, bequeathed his collection of British
paintings to the nation. Here are
works by Blake, Turner, Hogarth,
the Pre-Raphaelites, Francis Bacon,
Picasso, Chagall, Mondrian and
Degas and sculpture by Moore and
Hepworth. You will also see examples of Op Art, Pop Art, Abstract
Art, Minimal Art and Conceptual
Art, including amongst them works
of controversial art. Wander at will
or enjoy film shows, lectures and
guided tours. In the basement there
is a licensed cafeteria and also the
Rex Whistler room where historical
English dishes are beautifully presented. The adjoining Clore Gallery
opens in late 1987 to exhibit the
Turner Bequest. *Open 10.00–
18.00 Mon–Sat; 14.00–18.00 Sun.
Closed Nat Hols.* Free.
⊖ Pimlico
🚌 77A, 88, or 2, 2B, 36, 36B, 185
(to Bessborough Gardens)

Telecom Technology   **4T3**
Showcase
Baynard House, 135 Queen Victoria
St EC4. 01-248 7444. Lively
museum of the history of telecommunications, with working examples of modern chip-operated technology, archaic set-ups of early telephone exchanges, and glimpses of
the bright future of fibre optics.
*Open 10.00–16.30 Mon–Thur.
Closed Fri, Sat, Sun & Nat Hols.*
Free.
⊖ Blackfriars
🚌 45, 59, 60, 70, 141

The Temple   **4T2**
Inner Temple, Crown Office Row
EC4. 01-353 8462; Middle Temple,

Middle Temple La EC4. 01-353
4355. You may wander around the
courtyards, alleys and manicured
gardens of these ancient inns of
court by privilege, not by right. Visit
on a winter afternoon to see London's last lamplighter igniting the
19thC gas lamps. *Open 10.30–
16.00 Mon–Fri. Closed weekends,
Nat Hols & legal vacations.* Free.
⊖ Temple (not Sun), Blackfriars
🚌 4, 6, 9, 11, 15, 15A, 171A

The Temple Church   **4T2**
Inner Temple La EC4. This 12th–
13thC early Gothic round church,
built by the Knights Templar, has a
chillingly romantic air with its stone
effigies of knights lying in stately
wait below grey marble pillars.
⊖ Temple (not Sun), Blackfriars
⊖ 4, 6, 9, 11, 15, 15A, 171A

Temple of Mithras   **4T4**
Queen Victoria St EC4. Mithraic
temples were always underground.
This one was raised to its present
site from 18 feet below Walbrook
and has lost something in the trans-
lation. The finds from the site are in
the Museum of London.
⊖ Mansion House, Bank
🚌 6, 9, 11, 15A, 76, 149

Thames Barrier
Unity Way, Eastmoor St SE10. This
impressive piece of modern engineering was set up as a bulwark
against dangerously high tides
which were causing floods as far up
river as Richmond. The Thames
Barrier Centre houses an exhibition
and an audio-visual presentation,
explaining the technology involved.
There is also a souvenir shop and
cafeteria. *Open 10.00–17.00 Mon
–Sun.* Free.
⊖ New Cross, New Cross Gate
(then bus 177)
🚌 177, 180
🚢 Woolwich Dockyard

Theatre Museum   **3M5**
Russell St WC2. 01-831 1227. This
eagerly-awaited outpost of the Victoria and Albert Museum is sche-

duled to open in April 1987. Within three large gallery spaces will be displayed the most extensive theatrical costume collection in the world, as well as scenery, props, photos, playbills and backstage equipment. Has its own theatre, a box office for all London theatres, a shop and licensed cafe. *Open 11.00 –19.00 Tue–Sun. Shop, cafe and ticketmaster booking until 20.00 Tue–Sat, to 19.00 Sun. Closed Mon.* Charge (free to Friends of the V & A).
⊖ Covent Garden
🚌 1, 6, 9, 11, 13, 15, 15A, 77, 77A, 170, 176, 199 (all go to the Strand)

Theatre Royal, Stratford East
Gerry Raffles Sq E15. 01-534 0310. Joan Littlewood's brainchild is fighting a winning battle against financial problems. It offers drama, variety, Christmas pantos, Sunday concerts and rehearsed play readings of productions too expensive to stage. Bar and snack bar open before the show. *Closed Sun & Mon.*
⊖ Stratford
🚌 10, 25, 69, 86, 108, 158, 173, 225, 238, 262A, 276, 278, S1, S2

Top Shop　　3M3
214–21 Oxford St W1. 01-636 7700. Huge and colourful shop, with a resident DJ, selling bright, inexpensive clothes and accessories for men and women. Popular styles for every whim or occasion. Other branches dotted round the West End. *Open 10.00–18.30 Mon –Wed & Fri; 10.00–20.00 Thur; 09.00–18.00 Sat. Closed Sun.*
⊖ Oxford Circus
🚌 1, 3, 6, 7, 8, 12, 13, 15, 15A, 16A, 25, 30, 53, 73, 88, 113, 137, 159, 500, C2

Tottenham Court Road　　3L3
W1. These days the road is best known for electronics. Hi-fis, videos and all their high-tech relations can be priced, compared and cross-checked within the confines of one road. There are also furniture and household shops here, including the 50,000 square feet of Maples, and camera shops.
⊖ Tottenham Court Road (south end), Goodge Street (centre), Warren Street (north end)
🚌 14, 14A, 24, 29, 73, 134, 176, 253

Tower Bridge　　4U6
EC3. Splendid Victorian Gothic structure with hydraulically operated drawbridge by Jones and Wolfe Barry, 1894. The lattice-work footbridges with their wonderful river views are open to the public. *Open Apr–Oct 10.00–18.30 Mon –Sun; Nov–Mar 10.00–16.45 Mon –Sun. Charge.*
⊖ Tower Hill
Docklands Railway: Tower Gateway
🚌 15, 42, 56, 78, 278 (north side), 42, 47, 70, 78, 188 (south side)

Tower Hotel　　4T6
St Katharine's Way E1. 01-481 2575. A large modern hotel, its lounge, bar and restaurant offering good views of the river and of St Katharine's Dock. *Open LD Mon –Sun.*
⊖ Tower Hill
Docklands Railway: Tower Gateway
🚌 15, 42, 56, 78, 278

Tower of London　　4T6
Tower Hill EC3. 01-709 0765. This grim and famous fortress looks deceptively pale and innocent from outside. Red-clad Yeomen warders, or Beefeaters, and black ravens guard the Bloody Tower, the Traitor's Gate, the armoury, the executioner's block and axe, the instruments of torture, the tragic graffiti and, of course, the Crown Jewels. The massively plain Norman chapel of St John is the oldest church in London. It is now possible to walk almost all the way around the curtain wall of the inner ward, visiting most of the outer towers.

To watch the ancient ritual of the Ceremony of the Keys, when the Tower is locked for the night, apply in writing with a s.a.e. to the Yeoman Clerk, H. M. Tower of London EC3. *Open Mar–Oct 09.30–17.00 Mon–Sat, 14.00–17.00 Sun; Nov –Feb 09.30–16.00 Mon–Sat, closed Sun.* Charge.
e Tower Hill
Docklands Railway: Tower Gateway
15, 42, 56, 78, 278

Tower Records   3N3
1 Piccadilly W1. 01-439 2500. Billed as the 'greatest record store in the world', this spanking new, prime site record shop on four floors offers the full spectrum of sounds from golden oldies to opera, trad jazz to hard rock. Exceptionally large selection of compact discs, videos and US imports too. Amazing opening hours should ensure high volume popularity. *Open all year (inc Xmas day) 09.00–24.00 Mon –Sat, 09.00–23.00 Sun.*
e Piccadilly Circus
3, 6, 9, 12, 13, 14, 14A, 15, 15A, 19, 22, 38, 53, 55, 88, 159

Town of Ramsgate Pub
62 Wapping High St E1. 01-488 2685. 17thC tavern with a glamorous, grisly past. Captain Blood was captured alongside and Judge Jeffries within; petty criminals were hanged in what is now the riverside garden; pirates were tied to a post in the river to be drowned by the incoming tide and secret tunnels are said to lead to the Tower of London. Bar snacks are available at most sessions. *Open Mon–Sun.*
e Wapping
22A

Tradescant Trust   3P5
St Mary at Lambeth, Lambeth Palace Rd SE1. 01-373 4030. The Trust has turned the pretty church into a museum of garden history in memory of the two John Tradescants, father and son, buried with grandfather in the churchyard, next to Captain Bligh of the Bounty. These two, gardeners to Charles I, travelled the world to introduce new plants to Britain – among them phlox and stocks and larch, plane trees and Tradescantia. They also collected rarities and curiosities which became the basis of the

Ashmolean Museum in Oxford. Fascinating exhibition within, relevant plants without. *Open 11.00 –15.00 Mon–Fri; 10.30–17.00 Sun.* Free but donation welcome.
e Victoria (then bus 10, 507)
3, 10, 44, 77, 159, 170, 507

Trafalgar Square   3N4
WC2. The whole square commemorates Admiral Lord Nelson's famous naval victory. His statue tops a 185-foot column in the centre. The pigeons and Landseer's lions are famous and provide a year-round attraction for visitors. Less well known are the Imperial Standards on the north wall and the minute police station inside a stone lamp on the east side. At Christmas, the annual gift from Norway of a giant spruce draws the crowds.
e Charing Cross
1, 3, 6, 9, 11, 12, 13, 15, 15A, 24, 29, 53, 77, 77A, 88, 109, 159, 170, 176, 199

Trafalgar Tavern
Park Row SE10. 01-858 2437. Pictures of Nelson and some early navigational instruments are on display in this large Thames-side tavern near Wren's imposing naval college. Snacks are served in the bars, with their large windows overlooking the river, and there are full lunches and dinners in the restaurant, for which it is wise to book. *Bars open normal licensing hours Mon–Sun. Restaurant open LD Tue–Fri, D Sat & L Sun; closed L Sat, D Sun & all Mon.*
e Surrey Docks (then bus 1, 188)
Docklands Railway: Island Gardens (then by foot tunnel)
1, 177, 180, 188, 286
≈ Greenwich

Trocadero   3N3
Piccadilly Circus W1. A large modern complex with entrances on Shaftesbury Avenue and Coventry Street. Shops, cafes, restaurants and wine bars are grouped around a huge central foyer with trees and a central fountain. A moving stairway leads up a floor to The Guinness Book of World Records Exhibition and The London Experience. *Open 09.00–24.00 (shops and exhibitions close 17.30).*
e Piccadilly Circus
3, 6, 9, 12, 13, 14, 14A, 15, 15A, 19, 22, 38, 53, 88, 159

U

Unicorn Theatre   3M4
Gt Newport St WC2. 01-836 3334.
Presents an extensive programme
of new and classic plays suited to
children within the four to 12 age
group. During term time there are
performances for school parties
every afternoon, Mon–Fri; and public matinees are held at weekends.
Puppet shows, mime shows, conjurors and concerts.
⊖ Leicester Square
🚌1, 24, 29, 176

United States Embassy   3N1
Grosvenor Sq W1. 01-499 9000.
The entire west side of London's
largest square is taken up by Eero
Saarinen's monumental building,
topped by a somewhat threatening
bald eagle with a 35-foot wing span.
In the six-acre square itself stands
W. Reid Dick's lifelike statue of
Franklin D. Roosevelt.
⊖ Bond Street
🚌2B, 16, 30, 36, 73, 74, 82, 137
(to Park Lane)

University Boat Race
Putney to Mortlake. This annual
contest between the universities of
Oxford (dark blue) and Cambridge
(light blue) can be viewed from the
banks of the Thames. *Sat afternoon
in Mar or Apr.*
Start of race:
⊖ Putney Bridge
🚌14, 22, 74, 220
Finish of race:
🚌9 (to Mortlake)
≽ Barnes Bridge

University College   1D5
Department of Egyptology
Museum
Gower St WC1. 01-387 7050. Includes the collections of Amelia Edwards, Sir Flinders Petrie and part
of Sir Henry Wellcome's collection.
*Open 10.00–12.00 & 13.15–17.00
Mon–Fri during university terms
only. Closed Nat Hols & university
hols.* Charge.
⊖ Euston Square
🚌14, 14A, 18, 24, 27, 29, 30, 73,
134, 137, 176, 253

University of London   1D6
Malet St WC1. Centred around the
Bloomsbury area, the University
was founded in 1826 (with University College in Gower St) by suppor-
ters of religious liberty to provide
higher education in literature,
science and art. It received its
charter in 1836 and in 1878 became
the first university in the UK to allow
women to sit for degrees. Now
incorporates many colleges and in-
stitutes of specialist studies spread
all over the capital. The monolithic
Senate House building (completed
1936) was rumoured to have been
considered by Hitler as a potential
HQ in the event of a British defeat in
World War II. Princess Anne is
Chancellor of the University.
⊖ Euston Square, Russell Square
🚌14, 14A, 24, 29, 68, 73, 77, 77A,
134, 168, 176, 188, 253

Up All Night   2K4
325 Fulham Rd SW10. 01-352
1996. An informal restaurant that
really stands by its name, serving
hamburgers, steaks and spaghetti
until 06.00 in the morning. *Open LD
Mon–Sun.*
⊖ Fulham Broadway (then bus 14)
🚌14, N14

Vanbrugh Castle
3 Westcombe Pk Rd, Maze Hill
SE3. Sir John Vanbrugh's own
house, built 1717–26. No admission, but it can be admired from
outside. The best view is from the
east side of Greenwich Park.
⊖ New Cross, New Cross Gate
(then bus 53)
▥ 53, 54, 75, 108, 286
≠ Maze Hill

Vanbrugh Theatre   1D5
Malet St WC1. 01-580 7982. A
theatre club in which students of
the Royal Academy of Dramatic Art
present a complete range of classic
and contemporary drama. Members bar. Membership details from
RADA, 62 Gower St WC1.
⊖ Euston Square
▥ 14, 14A, 18, 24, 27, 29, 30, 73,
134, 137, 176, 253

Vaudeville Theatre   3N5
Strand WC2. 01-836 9987. A listed
building which originally ran farce
and burlesque – vaudeville, in short
– and then went 'straight', which for
the most part it still is.
⊖ Charing Cross
▥ 1, 6, 9, 11, 13, 15, 15A, 77, 77A,
170, 176, 199

Victoria and Albert   2J5
Museum
Cromwell Rd SW7. 01-589 6371.
One of the most extravagant pieces
of Victorian architecture in London
and a wonderfully rich museum of
decorative art. Vast collections
from all categories, countries and
ages are displayed in more than 10
acres of museum, set around the
newly designed Italianate Pirelli
garden. There are extensive and
choice collections of paintings,
sculpture, graphics and typography,
armour and weapons, carpets,
ceramics, clocks, costume, fabrics,
furniture, jewellery, metalwork,
musical instruments, prints and
drawings. There are regular free
lectures and a pleasant cafeteria.
*Open 10.00–17.50 Mon–Thur &
Sat; 14.30–17.50 Sun. Closed Fri &*
some Nat Hols. Voluntary contribu-
tion.
⊖ South Kensington
▥ 14, 30, 74, C1

Victoria Palace   3P3
Victoria St SW1. 01-834 1317. Puts
on mostly musicals and variety
shows.
⊖ Victoria
▥ 2, 2B, 10, 11, 14A, 16, 24, 25,
29, 36, 36B, 38, 39, 52, 52A, 55,
70, 185, 500, 507, C1

Victoria Station   3P2
Terminus Pl, Victoria St SW1. Information on 01-928 5100. The
Brighton side of the station was
built in 1860 and the Dover side in
1862. The concourse and platforms
are currently being modernised but
trains still depart for the south and
south east London suburbs, Kent,
Sussex, East Surrey, Brighton, Gatwick Airport and the Continent.
⊖ Victoria
▥ 2, 2B, 10, 11, 14A, 16, 24, 25,
29, 36, 36B, 38, 39, 52, 52A, 55,
70, 185, 500, 507, C1
≠ Victoria

Victoria Coach Station   5W3
164 Buckingham Palace Rd SW1.
01-730 0202. The main provincial
coach companies operate from
here, sending coaches all over Britain and the Continent. Booking is
necessary.
⊖ Victoria
▥ 11, 39, C1
≠ Victoria

The Virgin Megastore   3M4
14–16 Oxford St W1. 01-631 1234.
A vast entertainment store selling
records, videos, hi-fis, compact
discs and players, music books and
tapes. Also resident DJs, live entertainment, a games centre, and a
large licensed upstairs cafe. A total
experience! *Store open 10.00–
21.00 Mon–Sat. Cafe open 09.30
–21.00 Mon–Sat. Closed Sun.*
⊖ Tottenham Court Road
▥ 1, 7, 8, 14, 14A, 19, 22, 24, 25,
29, 38, 55, 73, 134, 176

W

Wallace Collection   1E3
Hertford House, Manchester Sq
W1. 01-935 0687. This dignified
town house, with its small landscaped garden, contains an outstanding private collection of art
treasures amassed by two mar-
quesses of Hertford and Sir Richard
Wallace and bequeathed to the
nation by Lady Wallace in 1897. The
French 17thC and 18thC are especially well represented. There are
also Rembrandts, Titians, Rubens,
Canalettos, Bonnington oil and
water colours and Sèvres porcelain.
*Open   10.00–17.00   Mon–Sat;
14.00–17.00 Sun. Closed Nat Hols.*
Free.
⊖ Bond Street
🚍1, 2B, 13, 30, 74, 82, 113, 159

Warner West End Cinema   3N4
Leicester Sq WC2. 01-439 0791.
Five cinemas showing new Warner
general releases.
⊖ Leicester Square
🚍1, 24, 29, 176

The Water Rats   41Q
328 Gray's Inn Rd WC1. 01-837
7269. This 17thC refurbished inn is
now the home of the Abadaba
Music Hall which uses professional
actors to present lively, sometimes
bawdy, modern music hall, panto
and sing-songs. The rear bar has a
small stage and is licensed to *24.00.*
Enjoy a traditional English meal before the show; drinking and singing
during the performance. Booking
essential on 01-722 5395. *Open
Mon–Sun. Music Hall Thur–Sat.*
⊖ King's Cross St Pancras
🚍14A, 17, 18, 30, 45, 46, 63, 73,
77A, 214, 221, 259, C11

Waterloo Bridge   3N5
Designed by Sir Giles Gilbert Scott
and built in 1940–5 of concrete.
Connects Waterloo Station and the
South Bank Arts complex with the
Strand and Aldwych.
⊖ Temple (not Sun, north side),
Waterloo (south side)
🚍1, 4, 5, 68, 168, 171, 171A, 176,
188, 199
⇌ Waterloo

Waterloo Station   4U2
York Rd SE1. Information on 01-928
5100. Originally built in 1848, it was
modernised in the 1920s and again
in the 1980s but still retains its
grand Edwardian entrance in
Mepham Street with sweeping
steps and guardian statues. Trains
go to the south-west London suburbs, west Surrey, Hampshire,
Dorset, with fast trains to Portsmouth, Southampton and Bourne-
mouth. The adjoining Waterloo East
station sends trains to the south-
east London suburbs and Kent.
⊖ Waterloo
🚍1, 4, 5, 68, 70, 76, 149, 168,
171, 171A, 176, 177, 188, 199,
501, 502, 507
⇌ Waterloo

Watermen's Hall   4T5
18 St Mary at Hill EC3. The guildhall
of the Thames ferrymen, a beautiful
building with an Adam-style frontage surviving from 1780. Visits
arranged in summer through City
Information Centre, St Paul's
Churchyard EC4. 01-606 3030 extn
2456.
⊖ Tower Hill
🚍15

Waterstone's Bookshop   *3M4*
121 Charing Cross Rd WC2. 01-434
4291. Relatively new and very en-
terprising general booksellers of
new and second-hand books, with
their own charge card system (enquiries on 01-603 1303). They will
undertake a free search for second-
hand books with no obligation. This
branch is particularly strong on
academic books. Other branches
are at Southampton Row, Regent
Street, High Street Kensington
(strong on art and antiquarian
books), and Old Brompton Road.
*This branch open 09.30–19.30
Mon–Fri; 11.00–19.30 Sat; closed
Sun.*
⊖ Tottenham Court Road
🚌 1, 14, 14A, 19, 22, 24, 29, 38,
55, 176

Wellington Arch   *3O1*
Hyde Park Corner W2. By Decimus
Burton who also designed the nearby screen opening on to Hyde Park.
It has a tiny police station concealed
in one massive leg. The surmoun-
ting bronze of peace, her quadriga
drawn by vigorously lifelike horses,
is by Adrian Jones, a cavalry officer
and vet who entertained seven
friends within the structure before
it was erected.
⊖ Hyde Park Corner
🚌 2B, 9, 14, 14A, 16, 19, 22, 25,
30, 36, 38, 52, 52A, 55, 73, 74, 82,
137, 500

Wembley Stadium Complex
Wembley, Middx. 01-902 1234.
The complex incorporates the Sta-
dium, which holds 100,000 people
under cover, the Arena, the Conference Centre and the International
Squash Centre (the courts are open
to the public, book on 01-902 9230).
Perhaps most famous as the venue
for the FA Cup Final, but the Horse
of the Year Show happens here,
too, and also ice shows, pop concerts and a variety of important
sporting events.
⊖ Wembley Park
🚌 18, 83, 92, 182, 297
🚉 Wembley Complex, Wembley
Central

Wesley's House and Chapel   *4R5*
47 City Rd EC1. 01-253 2262. The
chapel, built in 1777, has a statue of
John Wesley in front of it, his pulpit
inside it and his grave behind it. In

the crypt below the chapel, there is
a well-presented museum about
Methodism, and some fascinating
items of Wesleyan memorabilia.
The house has simple relics – his
bed, his umbrella, some letters, the
electrical machine he used in the
treatment of melancholia. Opposite
the house is the Nonconformist
Burial Ground, Bunhill Fields, where
Daniel Defoe and William Blake lie.
Open   10.00–16.00   Mon–Sat;
12.00 (after service) Sun. Charge
(free on Sun).
⊖ Old Street
🚌 43, 76, 141, 214, 271, or 5 and
55 (to Old Street)

Westminster Abbey   *3P4*
(The Collegiate Church of St Peter
in Westminster), Broad Sanctuary
SW1. 01-222 5152. Magnificent repository of much of the royal history
of Britain. The original church by
Edward the Confessor, 1065, was
rebuilt by Henry III, completed in
1376–1506, with the towers
finished by Hawksmoor in 1734. In
fine Perpendicular style with a
mighty and soaring Gothic nave,
lavish and beautiful side chapels,
elaborate tombs and prestigious
monuments. The Abbey has been
the scene for the coronation of England's sovereigns since the time of
William the Conqueror. Most recently in July 1986, Prince Andrew
and Sarah Ferguson, Duke and
Duchess of York, were married
here with full pomp and pageantry.
*Open 09.00–16.00 Mon–Fri; 09.00
–14.00 & 15.45–17.00 Sat; services only Sun.* Free. (Small entry
charge for Royal Chapels and
Museum of Plates and Effigies.)
⊖ Westminster
🚌 3, 11, 12, 24, 29, 53, 70, 77,
77A, 88, 109, 159, 170

Westminster Bridge   *3O5*
SW1. Here, in September 1803,
Wordsworth observed of the view,
in his sonnet 'Upon Westminster
Bridge', "Earth has not anything to
show more fair" . . . The view is still
fair, though both it and the bridge
have changed considerably since
his day. The present flat stone
structure, by Thomas Page, was
erected in 1862.
⊖ Westminster
🚌 3, 11, 12, 24, 29, 53, 70, 77,
77A, 88, 109, 159, 170, C1

Westminster Cathedral 3P3
Ashley Pl SW1. 01-834 7452. This most important of England's Roman Catholic churches has a striking exterior of red brick with pale stone stripes and a tall slim campanile with magnificent views (a lift operates daily, for a small charge). The unfinished interior, its exquisite marble facings and darkly gleaming mosaics fading into the plain dark brick of the domed ceiling, has a true atmosphere of sanctity. Amidst the Byzantine beauty, by John Francis Bentley, 1895–1903, don't miss Eric Gill's stone reliefs of the Stations of the Cross. *Open 06.45–20.00 Mon–Sun; to 18.00 Nat Hols; to 16.00 Xmas day.*
⊖ Victoria
🚌 10, 11, 24, 29, 70, 507

Westminster Pier 3O5
Victoria Embankment SW1. 01-839 2349/01-930 4097. The main starting point for boat trips along the Thames. Some go east through the City and docks calling at The Tower of London and Greenwich; others go west to the exotic greenery of Kew Gardens and the Palace at Hampton Court. The River Boat Information Service (01-730 4812) has full details.
⊖ Westminster
🚌 3, 11, 12, 24, 29, 53, 70, 77, 77A, 88, 109, 159, 170, C1

Whitehall 3N4
SW1. Impressive, governmental and sometimes imperialist architecture fronts on to this wide processional way leading to the Houses of Parliament. The principal buildings are:
The Old Admiralty by T. Ripley, 1725–8, with a fine Adam columnar screen of 1760. The new Admiralty of 1887 lies behind.
The Horse Guards by William Kent, 1750–60. The Horse Guards Parade behind is the scene of the ceremony of Trooping the Colour *every Jun.*
The Old War Office by William Young, 1898–1907.
The Ministry of Defence, designed by Vincent Harris in 1913 and finished in 1959, incorporating Henry VIII's wine cellar.
The Banqueting House by Inigo Jones.
Dover House (The Scottish Office) by Paine in 1755–8, the entrance screen and rotunda by Henry Holland in 1787.
The Treasury by Sir Charles Barry, 1846.
The Foreign Office and The Home Office, mostly by Gilbert Scott in mid-Victorian palazzo style.
The New Government Offices, late Victorian, by J. M. Brydon.
The Cabinet War Rooms, Churchill's secret wartime HQ, now a museum.
In the centre stands The Cenotaph, memorial to the dead of two world wars, and the most notable side road is Downing Street.
⊖ Charing Cross (north end), Westminster (south end)
🚌 3, 11, 12, 24, 29, 53, 77, 77A, 88, 109, 159, 170, C1

Whittington Stone
Highgate Hill N6, near junction with Dartmouth Park Hill. In theory this is the stone on which Dick Whittington rested on his way home from London, and where he heard Bow Bells apparently ringing out 'Turn again Whittington . . .' In fact this is about the third replacement stone, set up in 1821, with the famous cat added in 1964. The stone may not be genuine, but man and cat were, and the former was Lord Mayor of London four times.

⊖ Archway
🚌 4, 17, 27, 41, 43, 134, 137, 143, 210, 263, 271, C11, Sun only 263A

Whitechapel Art Gallery   **4S6**
80 Whitechapel High St E1. 01-377 0107. Exciting and sometimes controversial exhibitions of contemporary art – painting, sculpture, photography. Also houses an audio-visual show, a good bookshop, a lecture theatre, educational workshops and a cafeteria serving the home-made snacks and sticky cakes that seem to go with the London arts scene. *Open 11.00–17.00 Tue–Sun, to 20.00 Wed. Closed Mon.* Charge.
⊖ Aldgate East
🚌 5, 10, 15, 15A, 22A, 25, 40, 67, 225, 253

Whitechapel Market   **4S6**
Whitechapel E1. Famous East End high street market with an immense array of stalls selling fruit, veg, foodstuffs, household goods, gifts and knick-knacks. *Open 08.00 –17.00 Mon–Sat. Closed Sun.*
⊖ Whitechapel
🚌 10, 25, 225, 253

Wigmore Hall   **3M2**
36 Wigmore St W1. 01-935 2141. An intimate atmosphere in which to hear chamber music, orchestral recitals, solo singers and instrumentalists. By tradition, international musicians make their London debut here. Also welcomes the lesser known and more unusual – medieval music and poetry readings for example.
⊖ Bond Street
🚌 6, 7, 8, 12, 13, 15, 15A, 16A, 25, 73, 88, 113, 159, 500

William Morris Gallery
Lloyd Park, Forest Rd E17. 01-527 5544 extn 4390. William Morris, designer, socialist, poet, craftsman and towering figure in the 19thC Arts and Crafts Movement lived here from 1848, when he was 14, until 1856. An excellent exhibition of his life and work and that of a few of his contemporaries. There is also a gallery of pre-Raphaelite paintings and sketches. *Open 10.00–13.00 & 14.00–17.00 Tue–Sat; 10.00–12.00 & 14.00–17.00 on first Sun of each month. Closed Sun, Mon & Nat Hols.* Free.

⊖ Blackhorse Road (then bus 123)
🚌 34, 69, 97, 97A, 123, 212, 275

Williamson's Tavern   **4T4**
1–3 Grovelands Ct, Bow La EC4. 01-248 6280. Reputedly the oldest tavern in the City and said to mark its exact centre. The wine bar in the basement serves food at lunchtimes but, in common with most City pubs, there is no food in the evening and the doors close early when the City workers wend their way home. *Open Mon–Fri. Closes 21.00 & all Sat & Sun.*
⊖ Mansion House
🚌 6, 8, 9, 11, 15, 15A, 17, 22, 25, 76, 149

Wimbledon Common
SW19. 01-788 7655. 1,100 acres of wild woodland, open heath and ponds protected by an Act of 1871 as a 'wild area' for perpetuity. There are Bronze Age remains here, abundant bird life and the wildflowers include some rare specimens. There are also 16 miles of horse rides, a famous old 19thC windmill, a golf course, playing fields, commonside pubs and nude bathing in Queensmere (traditional since Victorian times – it's historic so it must be OK). *Open 24 hours.* Cars not admitted after dusk.
⊖ Putney Bridge (then bus 80, 93)
🚌 80, 93
🚃 Wimbledon then bus 80, 93

Wimbledon Windmill
Wimbledon Common SW19. A hollow post mill, built in 1817, now housing a museum with models and photographs which explain how windmills work. *Open 14.00 –17.00 Sat, Sun & Nat Hols, Apr –Oct.* Charge.
⊖ Putney Bridge (then bus 80, 93)
🚌 80, 93
🚃 Wimbledon then bus 80, 93

Wimbledon Lawn Tennis Association Museum
Church Rd SW19. 01-946 6131. The history of lawn tennis from its origins to the latest championships – including dioramas, audio-visual shows and a popular quiz entitled 'So You Think You Know About Wimbledon'. Excellent shop. *Open 11.00–17.00 Tue–Sat; 14.00–17.00 Sun. Closed Mon. Opening*

times vary during Championships, enquire. Charge.
⊖ Southfields (then walk), Putney Bridge (then bus 80, 93)
🚌 80, 93 (to Wimbledon High Street then walk via Church Rd)

Winkworth Arboretum
Hascombe Rd, Godalming, Surrey. 048 632 336. 95 acres of steep hillside planted with trees and flowering shrubs, many rare species and many modern introductions. There are two lakes, plentiful wild birds, a small National Trust shop and tea-room and fine views of the North Downs from many of the footpaths. *Grounds open dawn to dusk all year Mon–Sun. Shop & tearoom open Apr–Oct 14.00–18.00 Tue–Thur, Sat & Sun, & Nat Hols; Mar & Nov Sat & Sun only.*
Green Line 741
🚂 Godalming

Windsor Castle
Windsor, Berks. 0753 868286. An imposing medieval fortress raised on a mound in the centre of town. The Round Tower is 12thC, built by Henry II, and St George's Chapel is fine 16thC Perpendicular. Very much a royal residence, with magnificent State Apartments which are still used for royal functions. Within the castle complex there are countless treasures to be seen: Gobelin tapestries; paintings and drawings by Van Dyck, Canaletto, Rubens, Reynolds, Leonardo da Vinci and Holbein; superb furniture, glass and porcelain; coaches and carriages; and Queen Mary's dolls' house, designed by Lutyens, is not to be missed. *Castle precinct open Jan –end Mar & end Oct–end Dec 10.00–6.15 Mon–Sun; May–end Aug 10.00–19.15 Mon–Sun; Apr, Sep & Oct 10.00–17.15 Mon–Sun. State Apartments open Jan–end Mar & end Oct–end Dec 10.30–15.00 Mon–Sat; Apr–end Oct 10.30–17.00 Mon–Sat; open Sun 13.30–17.00 May–Oct only. State Apartments closed when Queen in official residence – usually 6 weeks at Easter, 3 weeks in Jun and 3 weeks at Xmas.* Charge.
Green Line 700, 701, 702, 718
🚂 Windsor & Eton Riverside, Windsor & Eton Central

Windsor Safari Park
Winkfield Rd, Windsor, Berks. 0753 869841. Lions, tigers, llamas, zebras, camels, deer, giraffe, baboons and other monkeys are all in residence here and there is much excitement to be had from driving round those areas of the park where the animals roam free. Bear in mind that windows must be fully wound up at all times and also that there may be long queues. The Dolphinarium features killer-whale, dolphin and sea-lion shows; there's a new chimpanzee enclosure, a new bear reserve and a new children's zoo. Other attractions include walks through the tropical plants and butterfly house, and the adventure play centre. *Open 10.00–one hour before dusk Mon–Sun all year. Closed Xmas day.* Charge.
Green Line 700
🚂 Windsor & Eton Riverside, Windsor & Eton Central

Wisley Horticultural Gardens
Wisley, Surrey. 0483 224163. A 200-acre botanic garden which was acquired by the Royal Horticultural Society in 1904 and is now used for trials and improvements of new varieties. It is also worth visiting for its small exhibition gardens – a perfumed garden for the blind, a raised garden for the disabled and so on. There are greenhouses and a pinetum and a magnificent collection of roses, rhododendrons, camellias, heathers and rock garden plants. *Open 10.00–19.00 Mon–Sun in summer. 10.00–dusk Mon–Sun in winter.* Charge.
Green Line 715, 740

Woolwich Arsenal
Woolwich SE18. A fine example of early 18thC ordnance architecture by Sir John Vanbrugh. Open by appointment only.
🚌 51, 53, 54, 75, 96, 99, 122, 122A, 161, 177, 178, 180, 198A, 244, 269, 269A, 272, 291
🚂 Woolwich Arsenal

Wyndham's Theatre   *3N4*
Charing Cross Rd WC2. 01-836 3028. Small, pretty and successful theatre founded by Sir Charles Wyndham, the famous actor-manager. Straight plays, comedies and musicals are presented here.
⊖ Leicester Square
🚌 1, 24, 29, 176

Y

YMCA & Y Hotel *1E5*
112 Gt Russell St WC1. 01-637
1333. Large, modern building
(opened in 1976) incorporating a
hotel and extensive sporting and
leisure facilities. It has a heated
swimming pool, gymnasium, sauna
and squash courts. Wide range of
activities – weight training, aero-
bics, dance, sub-aqua, badminton,
chess, bridge, photography, tram-
poline, basketball, keep fit, pottery,
drama. Cafeteria and bar. Apply for
membership by 1st Thur in month.
*Open 08.00–22.00 Mon–Fri; 10.00
–21.30 Sat & Sun.* Charge.
⊖ Tottenham Court Road
🚌 1, 7, 8, 14, 14A, 19, 22, 24, 25,
29, 38, 55, 73, 134, 153, 176

York Watergate *3N5*
Watergate Walk, off Villiers St
WC2. When it was built in 1626, the
gate stood on the bank of the
Thames at the river entrance to the
Duke of Buckingham's York House.
It hasn't moved – the Embankment
Gardens have been reclaimed from
the river. The sadly eroded lions
support the Villiers' family arms.
⊖ Embankment, Charing Cross
🚌 1, 6, 9, 11, 13, 15, 15A, 77, 77A,
170, 176, 199

Young Vic *3O6*
66 The Cut SE1. 01 928 6363.
Established as a young people's
repertory theatre with the emphasis on the classics and established

modern plays. When the Young Vic
Company is touring the Royal
Shakespeare Company and the Ballet Rambert visit. Licensed vege-
tarian cafeteria.
⊖ Waterloo
🚌 1, 4, 5, 68, 70, 76, 149, 168,
171, 171A, 176, 177, 188, 199,
501, 502, 507

Z

Zamana Gallery   *2J5*
1 Cromwell Gdns SW7. 01-584 6612. A new gallery, in the basement of the architecturally interesting Ismaili Centre, but administered separately from it. The gallery is dedicated to the display of the art, crafts and architecture of the Third World in a series of changing exhibitions. Interesting bookstall. *Open 10.00–17.30 Tue–Sat; 12.00–17.30 Sun. Closed Mon.* Charge sometimes.
⊖ South Kensington
▦ 14, 30, 74, C1

The Zoo   *1B2*
Regent's Park NW1. 01-722 3333. Variously known as London Zoo, Regent's Park Zoo or, more properly, The Zoological Gardens. First laid out by Decimus Burton in 1827, with imaginative new animal houses added in recent years, of which the most famous is probably still the pointed structure of Lord Snowdon's aviary. One of the largest collections of creatures in the world saunters in the enclosures, swims or shambles in the Marine and Tropical Aquarium or obligingly reverses its nocturnal habits in the eerie light of the Moonlight Hall. Worthy of a very full day out and with a good restaurant-cum-cafeteria to make this possible. *Open 09.00–18.00 Mon–Sat;*

09.00–19.00 Sun & Nat Hols. Closed Xmas day. Charge.
⊖ Camden Town (then bus 74)
▦ 74 (also T1 summer service)

Ten Days Out in London

Here are suggestions for ten days of sightseeing in London, using London Transport, running from a Tuesday to the following Thursday week. For further details on all the places mentioned, check the A–Z gazetteer section of this guide.

The specific times of departure and arrival are offered as a guide only – keep to them and it will be possible to fit in all the recommended ports of call, but if the pace of any one day seems too much, simply spend longer in one place, miss out the next, and use the gazetteer to check transport information.

In almost every case, buses have been recommended rather than the Underground, because the bus traveller has the added pleasure of sightseeing en route. However, it is always quicker by tube, so if running late check with the gazetteer and take a quick Underground trip.

The diagrams on the following pages have been designed only to give an overall impression of the routes recommended. To pinpoint the exact geographical location of individual places on the suggested itineraries, it is essential to use a Nicholson *London Streetfinder* or a detailed street map.

The following symbols have been used in this section:

▄▄▄	Bus journey	🍺	Pub
⊖	Nearest Underground station	♀	Wine bar
⇌	Nearest British Rail station	●	Parks and green spaces
✕	Restaurant meal	▮	Shops
⊐	Tea/coffee/snacks		

A day out in the oldest part of London, its business centre, a place of medieval alleys, huge modern office blocks, Wren churches and ancient taverns is exciting on any weekday. At weekends the quiet streets make sightseeing easier, but everywhere, apart from the churches and the Barbican Arts Centre, is closed.

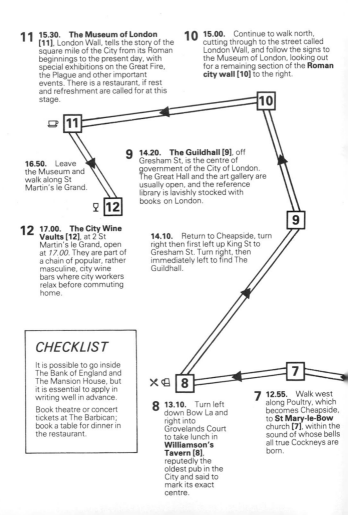

11 15.30. The Museum of London [11], London Wall, tells the story of the square mile of the City from its Roman beginnings to the present day, with special exhibitions on the Great Fire, the Plague and other important events. There is a restaurant, if rest and refreshment are called for at this stage.

10 15.00. Continue to walk north, cutting through to the street called London Wall, and follow the signs to the Museum of London, looking out for a remaining section of the **Roman city wall** [10] to the right.

16.50. Leave the Museum and walk along St Martin's le Grand.

9 14.20. The Guildhall [9], off Gresham St, is the centre of government of the City of London. The Great Hall and the art gallery are usually open, and the reference library is lavishly stocked with books on London.

12 17.00. The City Wine Vaults [12], at 2 St Martin's le Grand, open at *17.00*. They are part of a chain of popular, rather masculine, city wine bars where city workers relax before commuting home.

14.10. Return to Cheapside, turn right then first left up King St to Gresham St. Turn right, then immediately left to find The Guildhall.

CHECKLIST

It is possible to go inside The Bank of England and The Mansion House, but it is essential to apply in writing well in advance.

Book theatre or concert tickets at The Barbican; book a table for dinner in the restaurant.

8 13.10. Turn left down Bow La and right into Grovelands Court to take lunch in **Williamson's Tavern** [8], reputedly the oldest pub in the City and said to mark its exact centre.

7 12.55. Walk west along Poultry, which becomes Cheapside, to **St Mary-le-Bow** church [7], within the sound of whose bells all true Cockneys are born.

THE EVENING

Try a night out at the **Barbican Arts Centre** (the country's largest arts centre) which has bars, a restaurant, a main theatre housing the Royal Shakespeare Company, a small fringe theatre, a concert hall where the London Symphony Orchestra plays, and a cinema.

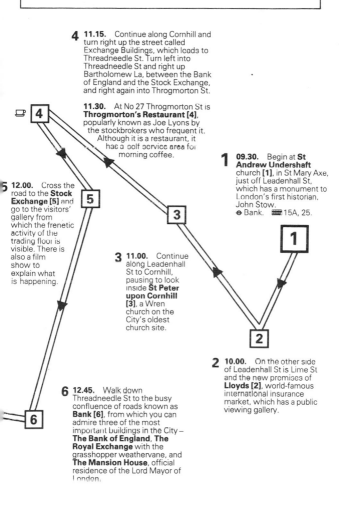

4 11.15. Continue along Cornhill and turn right up the street called Exchange Buildings, which leads to Threadneedle St. Turn left into Threadneedle St and right up Bartholomew La, between the Bank of England and the Stock Exchange, and right again into Throgmorton St.

11.30. At No 27 Throgmorton St is **Throgmorton's Restaurant [4]**, popularly known as Joe Lyons by the stockbrokers who frequent it. Although it is a restaurant, it has a self-service area for morning coffee.

1 09.30. Begin at **St Andrew Undershaft** church **[1]**, in St Mary Axe, just off Leadenhall St, which has a monument to London's first historian, John Stow.
⊖ Bank. 🚌 15A, 25.

5 12.00. Cross the road to the **Stock Exchange [5]** and go to the visitors' gallery from which the frenetic activity of the trading floor is visible. There is also a film show to explain what is happening.

3 11.00. Continue along Leadenhall St to Cornhill, pausing to look inside **St Peter upon Cornhill [3]**, a Wren church on the City's oldest church site.

2 10.00. On the other side of Leadenhall St is Lime St and the new premises of **Lloyds [2]**, world-famous international insurance market, which has a public viewing gallery.

6 12.45. Walk down Threadneedle St to the busy confluence of roads known as **Bank [6]**, from which you can admire three of the most important buildings in the City – **The Bank of England**, **The Royal Exchange** with the grasshopper weathervane, and **The Mansion House**, official residence of the Lord Mayor of London.

London abounds in royal landmarks from the Queen's residence at Buckingham Palace to the Tower of London, where royals lived from the time of William the Conqueror to King James I and where some died on the executioner's block. For centuries and to this day, London has been the scene of royal parades, processions and weddings – here is a suggested itinerary designed to give the visitor a glimpse of London's royal associations both past and present.

(Note: you can also do this day on a Thursday; but on Sunday & Monday the Queen's Gallery is closed; on Monday, Tuesday & Friday to Sunday the Royal Mews is closed; on Sunday the Horse Guards change at 10.00.)

11 **15.15.** Walk up Broad Walk to **Kensington Palace [11]**, Kensington Gardens W8. Here is where Queen Victoria was born and received the news of her accession, and where the Prince and Princess of Wales, Princess Margaret, Prince Michael of Kent and the Duke and Duchess of Gloucester still have apartments.

14.45. Catch a No 52 or 52A bus to Palace Gate.

12 **16.45.** Having viewed the public rooms which close at 17.00, walk along Palace Avenue to the **Royal Garden Hotel [12]**, Kensington High St W8, and have afternoon tea in The Garden Room. Bear in mind that tea is 'off' by 17.30.

ALTERNATIVE AFTERNOON

You may decide that an afternoon at **The Tower of London** to gaze at the Crown Jewels and other more gruesome sights is preferable to the suggested itinerary. If so, after lunch at The Albert, walk down Palmer St (alongside the pub) to St James's Park Station and take the District or Circle line direct to Tower Hill. For full details on The Tower and travel information, refer to the gazetteer entry on p.94.

10 **14.30.** Walk along Buckingham Palace Rd to **Victoria Bus Station [10]** to arrive by 14.45.
Or spend longer in the pub and walk right along Victoria St to Victoria Bus Station to arrive by 14.45.

9 **13.50.** A choice.
Either take Minibus C1 or walk along Victoria St, past the Army & Navy Store, turn right up Palace Street, turn left into Buckingham Palace Rd and cross the road to **The Royal Mews [9]**, Buckingham Palace Rd SW1, which opens at 14.00, where you can admire the Queen's horses and carriages.

8 **12.50.** Walk through Buckingham Gate to Victoria St and on the corner find **The Albert [8]**, 52 Victoria St SW1. Only the name has royal connections (Prince Albert was married to Queen Victoria), but this is an excellent Victorian pub with good bar snacks and an upstairs restaurant serving English roast beef. (You would be wise to reserve a table in the restaurant, telephone 01-222 5577.)

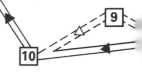

7 **12.00.** Return to Buckingham Palace and slip round the side to the **Queen's Gallery [7]**, Buckingham Palace Rd SW1, to view the selection of paintings from the Royal Collection currently on show. Admission charge.

THE EVENING

There are two 'royal' options for the evening.
Either return to base, put the children (if any) to bed, change and go to **The Royal Opera House**, Bow St WC2, 01-240 1066, where the Royal Ballet and Royal Opera Companies perform. (Advance booking is essential.)
Or return to base, change, and take children (if any) to **The Theatre Royal**, Drury La, Catherine St WC2, 01-836 8108. The Royal Box has accommodated every monarch since Charles II and the theatre is justly famous for its lavish musical productions. (Advance booking is essential.)

CHECKLIST

Book a table for lunch in the restaurant at The Albert (no need to book for a bar snack).
Book tickets for The Royal Opera House or The Theatre Royal, Drury Lane.

2 **10.30.** Walk along Storey's Gate to **Horse Guards Parade [2]**, Whitehall SW1.
3 Here you watch the **Changing of the Queen's Life Guard** on their magnificent black mounts, at *11.00*, come rain or shine. Virtually opposite Horse Guards Parade in Whitehall is the **Banqueting House [3]** where King Charles I went to the scaffold on 30 January 1649. There is a fine bronze statue of the King seated on his mount at the top of Whitehall, south side of Trafalgar Square.

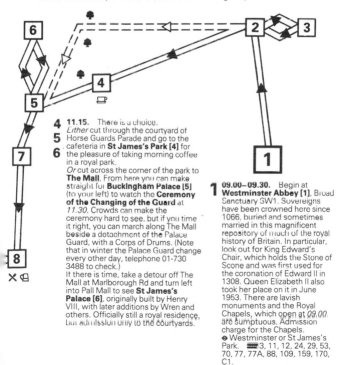

4 **11.15.** There is a choice.
5 *Either* cut through the courtyard of Horse Guards Parade and go to the cafeteria in **St James's Park [4]** for the pleasure of taking morning coffee in a royal park.
6 *Or* cut across the corner of the park to **The Mall**. From here you can make straight for **Buckingham Palace [5]** (to your left) to watch the **Ceremony of the Changing of the Guard** at *11.30*. Crowds can make the ceremony hard to see, but if you time it right, you can march along The Mall beside a detachment of the Palace Guard, with a Corps of Drums. (Note that in winter the Palace Guard change every other day, telephone 01-730 3488 to check.)
If there is time, take a detour off The Mall at Marlborough Rd and turn left into Pall Mall to see **St James's Palace [6]**, originally built by Henry VIII, with later additions by Wren and others. Officially still a royal residence, but admission only to the courtyards.

1 **09.00–09.30.** Begin at **Westminster Abbey [1]**, Broad Sanctuary SW1. Sovereigns have been crowned here since 1066, buried and sometimes married in this magnificent repository of much of the royal history of Britain. In particular, look out for King Edward's Chair, which holds the Stone of Scone and was first used for the coronation of Edward II in 1308. Queen Elizabeth II also took her place on it in June 1953. There are lavish monuments and the Royal Chapels, which open at *09.00* and are sumptuous. Admission charge for the Chapels.
⊖ Westminster or St James's Park. 🚌 3, 11, 12, 24, 29, 53, 70, 77, 77A, 88, 109, 159, 170, C1.

London's principal shopping areas are: Oxford St for mass-market purchases; Regent St for quality clothes, department stores, toys, china and glassware; Bond St for designer clothes, smart shoes, jewellery and Persian rugs; Covent Garden and the King's Rd for fashionable and trendy clothes and paraphernalia; Tottenham Court Rd for electronics, cameras, stereos and furniture; Knightsbridge for all-purpose luxury shopping. In fact, the quantity and variety of shops in London is huge. This suggested shopping trip takes in just a few of the most famous and popular. It can be enjoyed on any day of the week except Sunday – although on a Saturday in high season the shops and all facilities will be very crowded.

1 **09.30.** Begin at the Marble Arch branch of **Marks & Spencer [1]**, **Oxford St** W1. This is one of the largest shops in the internationally-famous high street chain which sells men's, women's and children's clothes, lingerie, food, home furnishings, books and gifts.
⊖ Marble Arch. 🚌 2B, 6, 7, 8, 12, 15, 15A, 16, 16A, 30, 36, 73, 74, 82, 88, 137, 500.

2 **10.30.** Walk east along Oxford St, crossing Orchard St, to **Selfridges [2]** department store (about 2 mins). In the course of exploring the store's many departments you will encounter a ground floor coffee shop and a first floor cafeteria, both of which serve coffee and rolls or cakes.

CHECKLIST

There is no need to book anything in advance.

14.45. Catch a 9, 14, 19, or 22 to **Harrods [8]**, in Brompton Rd SW1.

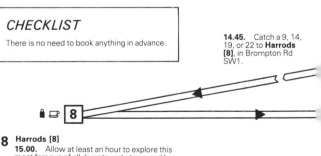

8 **Harrods [8]**
15.00. Allow at least an hour to explore this most famous of all department stores and be sure not to miss the magnificent, marbled Edwardian food halls.

16.00. Shopping is tiring and by now the idea of sitting down will probably be very attractive – try full afternoon tea in Harrods Restaurant or something lesser in one of the snack bars.

THE EVENING

Spend it enjoying the pubs, cafes and restaurants of Covent Garden – or, for a really suitable conclusion to a shopping day, browse in **Covent Garden General Store**, Long Acre WC2, open until *24.00 Mon–Sat*, which has a popular salad bar, open until *23.00*.

4
5
12.00. *Either* turn right in to Charing Cross Rd and walk down until you find, on your right, two bookshops – **Waterstones [4]**, relatively new and very enthusiastic general booksellers, and **Foyles [4]**, London's largest bookshop which aims to stock every British title currently in print.
Or, walk back a short distance along Oxford St to **The Virgin Megastore [5]**, 14–16 Oxford St W1, where you can browse or buy in a vast entertainment store selling records, tapes, videos, hifis, compact discs, music books and games. Also has a licensed cafe.

🚌 7, 8, 25 or 73

3 **11.50.** Catch bus 7, 8, 25 or 73 travelling east along Oxford St to **Tottenham Court Road Underground Station [3]** – about 10 mins.

🚌 9, 14, 19 or 22

🚌 9

16.30. Catch a 9 to **Covent Garden [9]**.

6
7
12.45. Catch a 14, 14A, 19, 22, 38 or 55 to **Fortnum and Mason [6]** in Piccadilly. Take an elegant continental or English lunch in The Patio or The Soda Fountain.
14.00. Browse around the old-established store with its smart floor-walkers, exotic foods and luxury goods. If there's time, wander along exclusive and expensive **Jermyn St [7]** to window-shop.

9 **Covent Garden [9]**
16.50. Covent Garden, once the site of the famous fruit and vegetable market, is now an exciting area to explore. There are arts and crafts stalls, books, herbs, soaps, chocolates and the latest fashions in small, if pricey shops, many of which stay open until *18.00, 19.00* or even *20.00* in season. It is also an area rich in pubs, cafes, wine bars and restaurants so, rather than look further afield for the evening's entertainment, remain in the area to sample them at leisure.

The River Boat Information Service, see *Checklist*, has details of the great variety of river trips which run each day, weather and tides permitting. Here are suggestions for two outings, using other forms of transport as well.

These days out can be enjoyed on any day of the week, but services are limited between October and Easter and to Hampton Court cease altogether.

HAMPTON COURT DAY

(Note: this river trip can only be done between Easter and the end of October.)

2 **14.30–17.30.** Allow two or three hours to explore the huge riverside palace of **Hampton Court [2]** in its beautiful formal gardens. Interior treasures include paintings by Titian and Tintoretto and ceiling paintings by Thornhill and Verrio. There is a cafe for afternoon tea between the palace and the famous maze.

3 **17.30–18.00.** Walk to the bridge and take an evening drink at **The Mitre [3]** with its large riverside garden.

1 **10.30.** Begin at **Westminster Pier [1]** and take a boat trip to Hampton Court (check times of departure). The journey takes from 4 to 5 hours, depending on tides, and passes right out of London through a delightful variety of scenery. There are always refreshments on board.

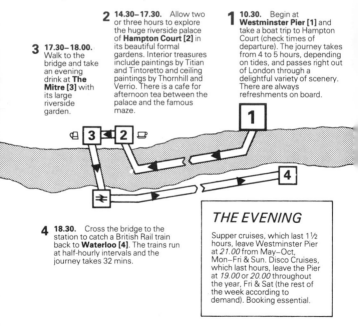

4 **18.30.** Cross the bridge to the station to catch a British Rail train back to **Waterloo [4]**. The trains run at half-hourly intervals and the journey takes 32 mins.

THE EVENING

Supper cruises, which last 1½ hours, leave Westminster Pier at *21.00* from May–Oct, Mon–Fri & Sun. Disco Cruises, which last hours, leave the Pier at *19.00* or *20.00* throughout the year, Fri & Sat (the rest of the week according to demand). Booking essential.

LANDMARKS TO HAMPTON COURT

North Bank: Houses of Parliament, Westminster Abbey, Millbank Tower, Tate Gallery, Cheyne Walk, Hurlingham House, Strand on the Green pubs, Syon House, London Apprentice pub, Marble Hill Park, Strawberry Hill, Thames TV Studios, Hampton Court Park.

South Bank: Battersea Power Station, St Mary's Church Battersea, Harrods Depository, Kew Gardens, Richmond Hill, Ham House, Kingston upon Thames.

Bridges (upriver): Westminster Bridge, Lambeth Bridge, Vauxhall Bridge, Chelsea Bridge, Albert Bridge, Battersea Bridge, Wandsworth Bridge, Putney Bridge, Hammersmith Bridge, Chiswick Bridge, Kew Bridge, Richmond Bridge, Kingston Bridge.

GREENWICH DAY

LANDMARKS FROM GREENWICH

North Bank: Isle of Dogs dockland development, Town of Ramsgate pub, St Katherine's Dock, Tower of London, Custom House, Fishmongers Hall, St Paul's Cathedral, The Temple, Somerset House, Savoy Hotel, Cleopatra's Needle.
South Bank: Old Royal Observatory, Royal Naval College, Cutty Sark, Mayflower pub, HMS Belfast, Southwark Cathedral, Bankside Power Station, South Bank Arts Centre, Royal Festival Hall, Shell Building.
Bridges (upriver): Tower Bridge, London Bridge, Southwark Bridge, Blackfriars Bridge, Waterloo Bridge.

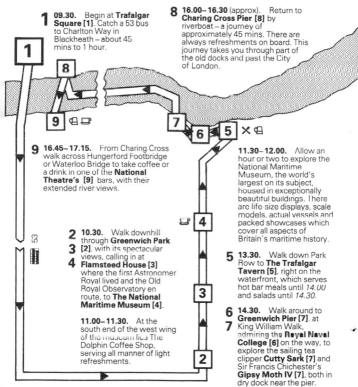

1 **09.30.** Begin at **Trafalgar Square [1]**. Catch a 53 bus to Charlton Way in Blackheath – about 45 mins to 1 hour.

8 **16.00–16.30** (approx.). Return to **Charing Cross Pier [8]** by riverboat – a journey of approximately 45 mins. There are always refreshments on board. This journey takes you through part of the old docks and past the City of London.

9 **16.45–17.15.** From Charing Cross walk across Hungerford Footbridge or Waterloo Bridge to take coffee or a drink in one of the **National Theatre's [9]** bars, with their extended river views.

11.30–12.00. Allow an hour or two to explore the National Maritime Museum, the world's largest on its subject, housed in exceptionally beautiful buildings. There are life-size displays, scale models, actual vessels and packed showcases which cover all aspects of Britain's maritime history.

2 **10.30.** Walk downhill through **Greenwich Park**
3 **[2]**, with its spectacular views, calling in at
4 **Flamsteed House [3]** where the first Astronomer Royal lived and the Old Royal Observatory en route, to **The National Maritime Museum [4]**.

11.00–11.30. At the south end of the west wing of the museum lies The Dolphin Coffee Shop, serving all manner of light refreshments.

5 **13.30.** Walk down Park Row to **The Trafalgar Tavern [5]**, right on the waterfront, which serves hot bar meals until *14.00* and salads until *14.30*.

6 **14.30.** Walk around to
7 **Greenwich Pier [7]**, at King William Walk, admiring the **Royal Naval College [6]** on the way, to explore the sailing tea clipper **Cutty Sark [7]** and Sir Francis Chichester's **Gipsy Moth IV [7]**, both in dry dock near the pier.

This day out can also be enjoyed on other days of the week, but not on Sunday when opening times are limited. For alternative places to take the children – see *FAMILY DAY OUT* on p. 000.

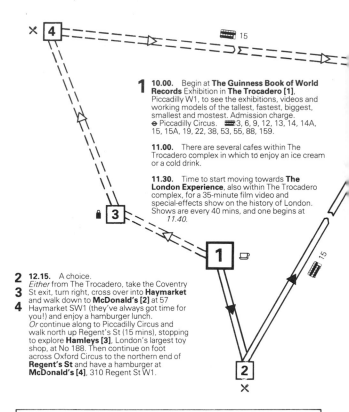

1 **10.00.** Begin at **The Guinness Book of World Records** Exhibition in **The Trocadero [1]**, Piccadilly W1, to see the exhibitions, videos and working models of the tallest, fastest, biggest, smallest and mostest. Admission charge.
⊖ Piccadilly Circus. 🚌 3, 6, 9, 12, 13, 14, 14A, 15, 15A, 19, 22, 38, 53, 55, 88, 159.

11.00. There are several cafes within The Trocadero complex in which to enjoy an ice cream or a cold drink.

11.30. Time to start moving towards **The London Experience**, also within The Trocadero complex, for a 35-minute film video and special-effects show on the history of London. Shows are every 40 mins, and one begins at *11.40.*

2
3
4

12.15. A choice.
Either from The Trocadero, take the Coventry St exit, turn right, cross over into **Haymarket** and walk down to **McDonald's [2]** at 57 Haymarket SW1 (they've always got time for you!) and enjoy a hamburger lunch.
Or continue along to Piccadilly Circus and walk north up Regent's St (15 mins), stopping to explore **Hamleys [3]**, London's largest toy shop, at No 188. Then continue on foot across Oxford Circus to the northern end of **Regent's St** and have a hamburger at **McDonald's [4]**, 310 Regent St W1.

CHECKLIST

Apply well in advance, by post, for admission to The Ceremony of the Keys at The Tower of London. If tickets are not available for the appropriate night, lock in 'Time Out', 'City Limits' or the 'London Standard' for a suitable film and, if necessary, book seats in the cinema.

6 14.45. Walk up Fish St and turn right into **Eastcheap** to catch a No 15 bus for the short distance to The Tower of London. If you look up at the wall of the building on the corner of Philpot Lane – the first turning left off Eastcheap – you will see two tiny plaster mice [6], carved there by the builders who had shared their lunchtime sandwiches with the local mice.

7 15.00. The Tower of London [7] – fortress, arsenal, prison and palace – has ravens and Beefeaters, armour and instruments of torture, the executioner's block, London's oldest church and, of course, the Crown Jewels. Admission charge.

5 13.30. From the Haymarket or from Oxford Circus, catch a No 15 bus to **The Monument** [5] (about 30 mins).

14.00–14.15. The Monument, which marks the point at which London's Great Fire began in 1666, is a tall column with 311 steps going up inside it. Those who climb to the top get a breathtaking view of London – if they have any breath left to be taken.

8 17.00. When The Tower closes walk round to **The Tower Hotel** [8] in St Katherine's Way. The hotel coffee shop, called **The Picnic Basket**, has a special children's menu of snacks, high teas and ice creams in summer. (The adults in the party may be glad to know it is licensed.)

THE EVENING

Attend **The Ceremony of the Keys** at The Tower of London, at *21.40*, one of the oldest military ceremonies in the world and much the most impressive and exciting, as the great fortress is formally locked for the night.

9 18.30. Take a trip on the new **Docklands Light Railway** [9] (opens summer 1987) from Tower Gateway to see the re-vitalisation of London's Docklands. The London Explorer pass is valid for the journey which will take approximately 45 mins there and back.

A Sunday in London does not have to be a lazy morning in bed, followed by the newspapers, a few pints down the pub, a late lunch and an evening in front of the television. Here are some suggestions which will give you a Sunday as activity-filled as the rest of the week.

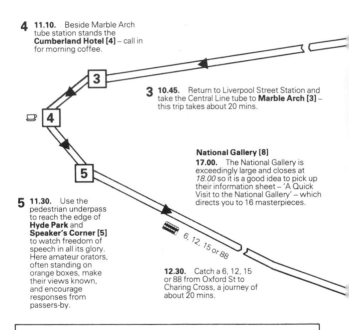

4   11.10.   Beside Marble Arch tube station stands the **Cumberland Hotel [4]** – call in for morning coffee.

3   10.45.   Return to Liverpool Street Station and take the Central Line tube to **Marble Arch [3]** – this trip takes about 20 mins.

National Gallery [8]
17.00.   The National Gallery is exceedingly large and closes at *18.00* so it is a good idea to pick up their information sheet – 'A Quick Visit to the National Gallery' – which directs you to 16 masterpieces.

5   11.30.   Use the pedestrian underpass to reach the edge of **Hyde Park** and **Speaker's Corner [5]** to watch freedom of speech in all its glory. Here amateur orators, often standing on orange boxes, make their views known, and encourage responses from passers-by.

6, 12, 15 or 88

12.30.   Catch a 6, 12, 15 or 88 from Oxford St to Charing Cross, a journey of about 20 mins.

CHECKLIST

It is wise to book a table for lunch at The Carvery at the Charing Cross Hotel, and also to book tickets for the evening concert.

THE EVENING

London is one of the world's most exciting music centres. Perhaps the most suitable venue for a Sunday concert is **St John's, Smith Square**, but if there is no concert scheduled for any given Sunday, there is certain to be something on at **The Royal Festival Hall**. Both places have their own restaurants to supply sustenance before the performance.

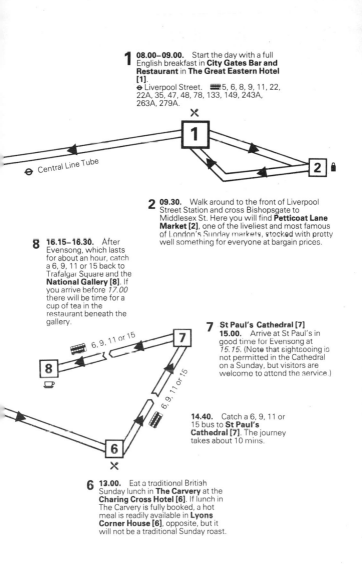

1 **08.00–09.00.** Start the day with a full English breakfast in **City Gates Bar and Restaurant** in **The Great Eastern Hotel [1].**
⊖ Liverpool Street. 🚌 5, 6, 8, 9, 11, 22, 22A, 35, 47, 48, 78, 133, 149, 243A, 263A, 279A.

⊖ Central Line Tube

2 **09.30.** Walk around to the front of Liverpool Street Station and cross Bishopsgate to Middlesex St. Here you will find **Petticoat Lane Market [2]**, one of the liveliest and most famous of London's Sunday markets, stocked with pretty well something for everyone at bargain prices.

8 **16.15–16.30.** After Evensong, which lasts for about an hour, catch a 6, 9, 11 or 15 back to Trafalgar Square and the **National Gallery [8]**. If you arrive before *17.00* there will be time for a cup of tea in the restaurant beneath the gallery.

🚌 6, 9, 11 or 15

7 **St Paul's Cathedral [7]**
15.00. Arrive at St Paul's in good time for Evensong at *15.15*. (Note that sightseeing is not permitted in the Cathedral on a Sunday, but visitors are welcome to attend the service.)

🚌 6, 9, 11 or 15

14.40. Catch a 6, 9, 11 or 15 bus to **St Paul's Cathedral [7]**. The journey takes about 10 mins.

6 **13.00.** Eat a traditional British Sunday lunch in **The Carvery** at the **Charing Cross Hotel [6]**. If lunch in The Carvery is fully booked, a hot meal is readily available in **Lyons Corner House [6]**, opposite, but it will not be a traditional Sunday roast.

This day out can be enjoyed from Monday to Saturday; but on Sunday the shops are shut, the museums don't open until *14.00*, and the Zoo doesn't open until *10.00*, although it remains open until *19.00*.

5 **14.50.** Those who have followed Morning A and Morning B should all arrive at about the same time at **The Planetarium [5]** and **Madame Tussaud's [5]** in Marylebone Rd. Buy a Royal Ticket which gives admission to both places.

15.00. There are 30-minute shows in The Planetarium on the hour and the half-hour. If there is a queue, which there usually is in high season, and you miss the *15.00* show, try for the *15.30*.

15.35–16.05. To Madame Tussaud's next door. There is a cafeteria for those who need refreshment, but there is a lot to see – tableaux of waxworks (royalty, pop stars, sporting champions, statesmen and film stars), the Chamber of Horrors, a reconstruction of The Battle of Trafalgar – and the exhibition closes at *17.30* so it might be wise to keep going.

3 **12.00.** **The Science Museum [3]** is one of the most exciting in London with real locomotives and aircraft, a space capsule and numerous working models. It would be easy to spend the rest of the day here, but those who hope to include the other ports of call should leave by *13.30*.

6 **17.30.** Madame Tussaud's closes. Stroll down Baker St to **Flanagan's Fish Parlour [6]**, which opens at *18.00* for fish and chips, tripe and onions etc. For those still in place at *20.00*, a pianist plays cockney songs.

14.30. For the sake of speed, catch the tube from South Kensington to Baker Street (change at Green Park, 20 mins). Alternatively, if there is time to spare take bus 30 direct to Baker Street Underground Station.

4 **13.30.** Cross over to Pelham St, at the side of South Kensington tube station, and take lunch in **Dino's [4]** – large, friendly, serving Italian food, licensed and welcoming to children.

A choice.

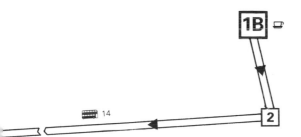

1A Morning A
09.30. Begin at **London Zoo [1A]**, Regent's Park W1, which has one of the largest and best-displayed collections of animals in the world. There is also a cafeteria for refreshments and lunch. Allow until about *14.00* to enjoy it all and then stroll south through Regent's Park (or take bus 74 or T1) to **The Planetarium [5]** and **Madame Tussaud's [5]** in Marylebone Rd.
⊖ Baker Street, Marylebone or Camden Town, then bus 74. 🚌 74, T1.

1B Morning B
10.00. Begin at the **British Museum [1B]**, Gt Russell St WC1, which has something for everyone in its vast halls – don't miss the Egyptian mummies and the Rosetta stone.
⊖ Tottenham Court Road, Russell Square. 🚌 1, 7, 8, 14, 19, 22, 24, 25, 29, 38, 55, 68, 73, 77, 77A, 134, 168, 176, 188.

11.00. For those who can tear themselves away from the exhibits, there is a large cafeteria in the British Museum for morning coffee.

2 11.30. Davenport's Joke Shop [2]
is immediately opposite the Museum and is worth a quick look. Then catch a 14 bus in Bloomsbury St to the Victoria and Albert Museum (20 mins) and walk up Exhibition Rd at the side of the V & A to the Science Museum.

CHECKLIST

Essential to book tickets for the London Palladium. Wise to book a table at Flanagan's Fish Parlour.

THE EVENING

Choose between an early 'cockney' evening meal at Flanagan's Fish Parlour, 100 Baker St W1. Or return to base to change and rest and take in a show at the **London Palladium**, which specialises in family entertainment.

LAW AND WAR DAY   Tuesday (8)

This day out can also be enjoyed on a Wednesday, Thursday or Friday but not on Monday, when the Imperial War Museum is closed, or on Saturday and Sunday when the Law Courts are closed.
(Note: the Law Morning is unsuitable for children because no-one below the age of 16 is admitted to the Law Courts, and at the Old Bailey, the minimum age for admission is 14 although an adult must accompany anyone under the age of 16. After lunch at The Magpie and Stump, the afternoon is accessible to the whole family.)

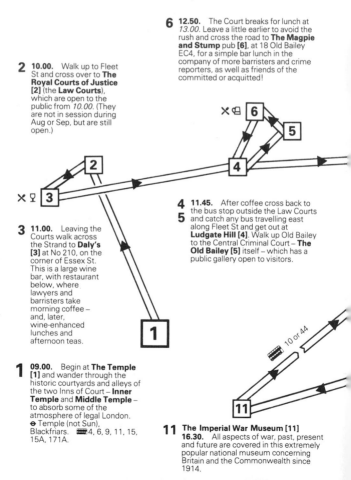

6 **12.50.**   The Court breaks for lunch at *13.00*. Leave a little earlier to avoid the rush and cross the road to **The Magpie and Stump** pub **[6]**, at 18 Old Bailey EC4, for a simple bar lunch in the company of more barristers and crime reporters, as well as friends of the committed or acquitted!

2 **10.00.**   Walk up to Fleet St and cross over to **The Royal Courts of Justice [2]** (the **Law Courts**), which are open to the public from *10.00*. (They are not in session during Aug or Sep, but are still open.)

4 **11.45.**   After coffee cross back to
5 the bus stop outside the Law Courts and catch any bus travelling east along Fleet St and get out at **Ludgate Hill [4]**. Walk up Old Bailey to the Central Criminal Court – **The Old Bailey [5]** itself – which has a public gallery open to visitors.

3 **11.00.**   Leaving the Courts walk across the Strand to **Daly's [3]** at No 210, on the corner of Essex St. This is a large wine bar, with restaurant below, where lawyers and barristers take morning coffee – and, later, wine-enhanced lunches and afternoon teas.

1 **09.00.**   Begin at **The Temple [1]** and wander through the historic courtyards and alleys of the two Inns of Court – **Inner Temple** and **Middle Temple** – to absorb some of the atmosphere of legal London. ⊖ Temple (not Sun), Blackfriars. 🚌 4, 6, 9, 11, 15, 15A, 171A.

11 **The Imperial War Museum [11]
16.30.**   All aspects of war, past, present and future are covered in this extremely popular national museum concerning Britain and the Commonwealth since 1914.

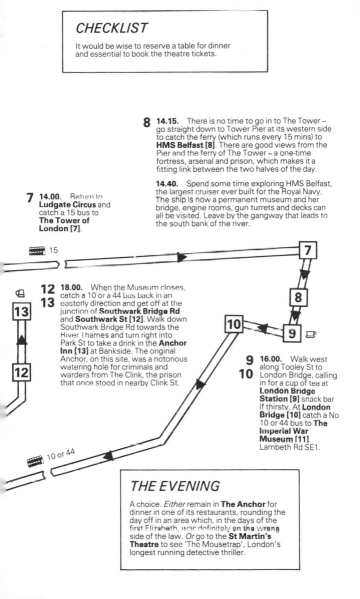

CHECKLIST

It would be wise to reserve a table for dinner and essential to book the theatre tickets.

8 14.15. There is no time to go in to The Tower – go straight down to Tower Pier at its western side to catch the ferry (which runs every 15 mins) to **HMS Belfast [8]**. There are good views from the Pier and the ferry of The Tower – a one-time fortress, arsenal and prison, which makes it a fitting link between the two halves of the day.

14.40. Spend some time exploring HMS Belfast, the largest cruiser ever built for the Royal Navy. The ship is now a permanent museum and her bridge, engine rooms, gun turrets and decks can all be visited. Leave by the gangway that leads to the south bank of the river.

7 14.00. Return to **Ludgate Circus** and catch a 15 bus to **The Tower of London [7]**.

15

7

12 **18.00.** When the Museum closes, catch a 10 or a 44 bus back in an **13** easterly direction and get off at the junction of **Southwark Bridge Rd** and **Southwark St [12]**. Walk down Southwark Bridge Rd towards the River Thames and turn right into Park St to take a drink in the **Anchor Inn [13]** at Bankside. The original Anchor, on this site, was a notorious watering hole for criminals and warders from The Clink, the prison that once stood in nearby Clink St.

8

10

9

13

12

9 **16.00.** Walk west **10** along Tooley St to London Bridge, calling in for a cup of tea at **London Bridge Station [9]** snack bar if thirsty. At **London Bridge [10]** catch a No 10 or 44 bus to **The Imperial War Museum [11]**. Lambeth Rd SE1.

10 or 44

THE EVENING

A choice. *Either* remain in **The Anchor** for dinner in one of its restaurants, rounding the day off in an area which, in the days of the first Elizabeth, was definitely on the wrong side of the law. *Or* go to the **St Martin's Theatre** to see 'The Mousetrap', London's longest running detective thriller.

THE DAY

Planning a day out of doors in London is rather like a game of chance because the weather, even at the height of summer, is so unpredictable. But on a fine, dry day all of London's parks repay exploration. Hyde Park and Kensington Gardens are the most central and cover, between them, the largest area. This day out may be enjoyed on any weekday, but park facilities are very limited between October and May.

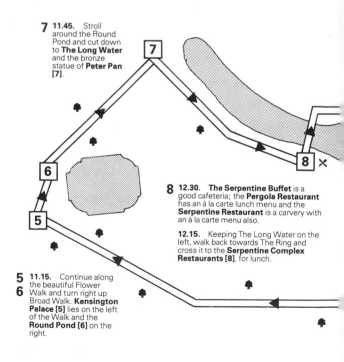

7 **11.45.** Stroll around the Round Pond and cut down to **The Long Water** and the bronze statue of **Peter Pan [7]**.

8 **12.30.** **The Serpentine Buffet** is a good cafeteria; the **Pergola Restaurant** has an à la carte lunch menu and the **Serpentine Restaurant** is a carvery with an à la carte menu also.

12.15. Keeping The Long Water on the left, walk back towards The Ring and cross it to the **Serpentine Complex Restaurants [8]**, for lunch.

5
6 **11.15.** Continue along the beautiful Flower Walk and turn right up Broad Walk. **Kensington Palace [5]** lies on the left of the Walk and the **Round Pond [6]** on the right.

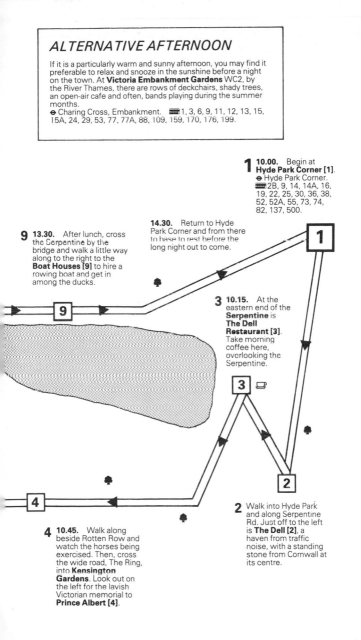

ALTERNATIVE AFTERNOON

If it is a particularly warm and sunny afternoon, you may find it preferable to relax and snooze in the sunshine before a night on the town. At **Victoria Embankment Gardens** WC2, by the River Thames, there are rows of deckchairs, shady trees, an open-air cafe and often, bands playing during the summer months.

⊖ Charing Cross, Embankment. 🚌 1, 3, 6, 9, 11, 12, 13, 15, 15A, 24, 29, 53, 77, 77A, 88, 109, 159, 170, 176, 199.

1 **10.00.** Begin at
Hyde Park Corner [1].
⊖ Hyde Park Corner.
🚌 2B, 9, 14, 14A, 16,
19, 22, 25, 30, 36, 38,
52, 52A, 55, 73, 74,
82, 137, 500.

9 **13.30.** After lunch, cross
the Serpentine by the
bridge and walk a little way
along to the right to the
Boat Houses [9] to hire a
rowing boat and get in
among the ducks.

14.30. Return to Hyde
Park Corner and from there
to base to rest before the
long night out to come.

3 **10.15.** At the
eastern end of the
Serpentine is
**The Dell
Restaurant [3]**.
Take morning
coffee here,
overlooking the
Serpentine.

2 Walk into Hyde Park
and along Serpentine
Rd. Just off to the left
is **The Dell [2]**, a
haven from traffic
noise, with a standing
stone from Cornwall at
its centre.

4 **10.45.** Walk along
beside Rotten Row and
watch the horses being
exercised. Then, cross
the wide road, The Ring,
into **Kensington
Gardens**. Look out on
the left for the lavish
Victorian memorial to
Prince Albert [4].

THE EVENING

London Transport's night buses link key points in London. They take over from daytime transport between *23.00* and *24.00* and run through the night.

Like all big cities, London should be treated with caution and respect at night. It's not sin city, but late-night revellers using public transport should try to keep their eyes open and their valuables out of sight.

(Note: this evening out can be enjoyed on other nights of the week, but London's theatres are closed on Sunday evenings and neither Spitalfields Market nor the nearby pub are open on a Sunday morning.)

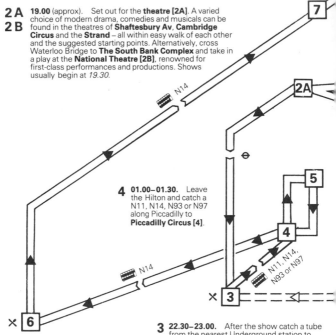

2 A
2 B **19.00** (approx).   Set out for the **theatre [2A]**. A varied choice of modern drama, comedies and musicals can be found in the theatres of **Shaftesbury Av**, **Cambridge Circus** and the **Strand** – all within easy walk of each other and the suggested starting points. Alternatively, cross Waterloo Bridge to **The South Bank Complex** and take in a play at the **National Theatre [2B]**, renowned for first-class performances and productions. Shows usually begin at *19.30*.

4 **01.00–01.30.**   Leave the Hilton and catch a N11, N14, N93 or N97 along Piccadilly to **Piccadilly Circus [4]**.

6 **03.00.**   The Hippodrome closes. Walk back to Piccadilly Circus and catch the N14 direct to the **Fulham Rd** and an informal restaurant called **Up All Night [6]** at No 225 for a plateful of spaghetti and a cup of coffee to restore energy.

3 **22.30–23.00.**   After the show catch a tube from the nearest Underground station to Hyde Park Corner, walk up Park Lane to the **Hilton Hotel [3]** and ascend to the **Roof Restaurant**. By now the special 'after theatre' menu will be on, and there is dancing to a live band.

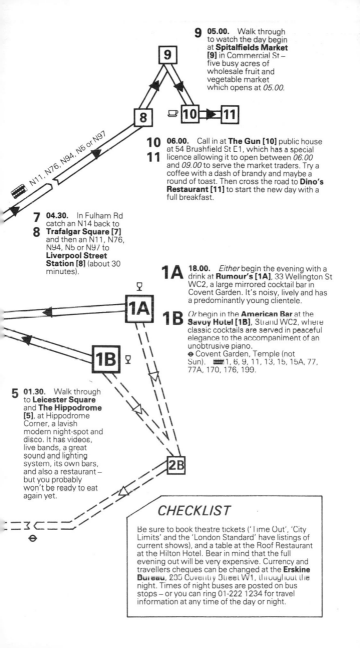

9 **05.00.** Walk through to watch the day begin at **Spitalfields Market [9]** in Commercial St – five busy acres of wholesale fruit and vegetable market which opens at *05.00.*

10 **06.00.** Call in at **The Gun [10]** public house at 54 Brushfield St E1, which has a special licence allowing it to open between *06.00* and *09.00* to serve the market traders. Try a coffee with a dash of brandy and maybe a round of toast. Then cross the road to **Dino's Restaurant [11]** to start the new day with a full breakfast.

11

7 **04.30.** In Fulham Rd catch an N14 back to **Trafalgar Square [7]** and then an N11, N76, N94, N5 or N9/ to **Liverpool Street Station [8]** (about 30 minutes).

8

N11, N76, N94, N5 or N97

1A **18.00.** *Either* begin the evening with a drink at **Rumour's [1A]**, 33 Wellington St WC2, a large mirrored cocktail bar in Covent Garden. It's noisy, lively and has a predominantly young clientele.

1B *Or* begin in the **American Bar** at the **Savoy Hotel [1B]**, Strand WC2, where classic cocktails are served in peaceful elegance to the accompaniment of an unobtrusive piano.
⊖ Covent Garden, Temple (not Sun). 🚌 1, 6, 9, 11, 13, 15, 15A, 77, 77A, 170, 176, 199.

5 **01.30.** Walk through to **Leicester Square** and **The Hippodrome [5]**, at Hippodrome Corner, a lavish modern night-spot and disco. It has videos, live bands, a great sound and lighting system, its own bars, and also a restaurant – but you probably won't be ready to eat again yet.

2B

CHECKLIST

Be sure to book theatre tickets ('Time Out', 'City Limits' and the 'London Standard' have listings of current shows), and a table at the Roof Restaurant at the Hilton Hotel. Bear in mind that the full evening out will be very expensive. Currency and travellers cheques can be changed at the **Erskine Bureau**, 205 Coventry Street W1, throughout the night. Times of night buses are posted on bus stops – or you can ring 01-222 1234 for travel information at any time of the day or night.

(Note: You can also do this 'day' on a Wednesday or Friday; but on Monday & Tuesday Carlyle's House is closed; on Saturday & Sunday Ye Olde Cheshire Cheese is closed; and on Sunday the houses are only open in the afternoon.)

CHECKLIST

Book lunch at Ye Olde Cheshire Cheese (telephone 01-353 6170). Book tickets for the evening at the Canal Cafe Theatre (telephone 01-289 6054), or the King's Head (telephone 01-226 1916). At the Players Theatre Club (telephone 01-839 1134), temporary membership can be obtained on the spot at the door, but a full membership must be taken out in person 48 hours before the show. It is also wise to reserve a table for a proper supper in advance.

10 **17.30.** It is opening time, and time to have a drink in the **Queens Elm** pub **[10]**, 241 Fulham Rd SW3, which has numbered many writers among its clientele, including Laurie Lee.

[10]

7 **14.45.** Walk back through to Fleet St to catch a 6, 9, 15 or 15A bus to **Piccadilly Circus [7]** (about 20 mins) and turn left into Piccadilly.

17.00. Stroll back up through literary and artistic Chelsea, and across the King's Rd, to arrive where Old Church St joins Fulham Rd at about *17.30*.

[8]

[7]

6, 9, 15 or 15A

8 **15.15.** Browse around **Hatchards [8]**, 187 Piccadilly W1, an old-established bookshop with an excellent stock of literature, both classical and modern, in hard and paper covers.

22 or 19

15.40. Catch the 22 bus to King's Rd, Bramerton St (about 30 mins) or the 19 bus to Cheyne Walk (about 30 mins), and walk (5 mins from Cheyne Walk, 10 mins from King's Rd) to Cheyne Row.

[9]

9 **16.15. Carlyle's House [9]**, 24 Cheyne Row SW3, remains much as it was when the author of 'The French Revolution' lived in it and worked in the sky-lit attic study. Note that the house closes at *17.00*.

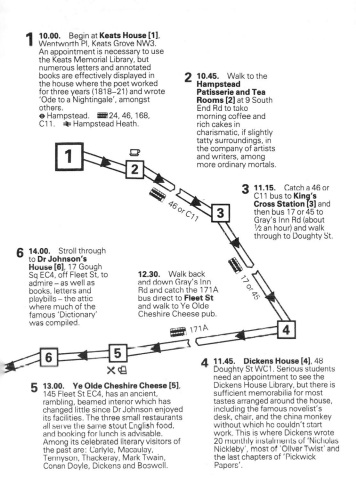

1 **10.00.** Begin at **Keats House [1]**, Wentworth Pl, Keats Grove NW3. An appointment is necessary to use the Keats Memorial Library, but numerous letters and annotated books are effectively displayed in the house where the poet worked for three years (1818–21) and wrote 'Ode to a Nightingale', amongst others.
⊖ Hampstead. 🚌 24, 46, 168, C11. ⇌ Hampstead Heath.

2 **10.45.** Walk to the **Hampstead Patisserie and Tea Rooms [2]** at 9 South End Rd to take morning coffee and rich cakes in charismatic, if slightly tatty surroundings, in the company of artists and writers, among more ordinary mortals.

3 **11.15.** Catch a 46 or C11 bus to **King's Cross Station [3]** and then bus 17 or 45 to Gray's Inn Rd (about ½ an hour) and walk through to Doughty St.

46 or C11

17 or 45

6 **14.00.** Stroll through to **Dr Johnson's House [6]**, 17 Gough Sq EC4, off Fleet St, to admire – as well as books, letters and playbills – the attic where much of the famous 'Dictionary' was compiled.

12.30. Walk back and down Gray's Inn Rd and catch the 171A bus direct to **Fleet St** and walk to Ye Olde Cheshire Cheese pub.

171A

5 **13.00.** **Ye Olde Cheshire Cheese [5]**, 145 Fleet St EC4, has an ancient, rambling, beamed interior which has changed little since Dr Johnson enjoyed its facilities. The three small restaurants all serve the same stout English food, and booking for lunch is advisable. Among its celebrated literary visitors of the past are: Carlyle, Macaulay, Tennyson, Thackeray, Mark Twain, Conan Doyle, Dickens and Boswell.

4 **11.45.** **Dickens House [4]**, 48 Doughty St WC1. Serious students need an appointment to see the Dickens House Library, but there is sufficient memorabilia for most tastes arranged around the house, including the famous novelist's desk, chair, and the china monkey without which he couldn't start work. This is where Dickens wrote 20 monthly instalments of 'Nicholas Nickleby', most of 'Oliver Twist' and the last chapters of 'Pickwick Papers'.

THE EVENING

After all that high-minded literariness, try an evening of fringe theatre followed by late-night cabaret at the **Canal Cafe Theatre**, Delamere Terrace W2. Home-cooked food is available and there's an all-inclusive price for both shows and dinner (or separate dinner, and either show). Alternatively, try dinner and a play at the **King's Head**, 115 Upper St, Islington N1, one of London's best-known theatre pubs, which again sells tickets for dinner-and-show, or just for the show. And for an evening of rollicking, frolicsome good fun, try the **Players Theatre Club**, Villiers St WC2, where Queen Victoria and music-hall are alive and well. There are two bars, a supper room, and drinks and sandwiches are served during the performance.

Index

Central London Maps

Key

16	Regular Daily Service	● ● ●	Main Shopping Street
176	Certain Days of the week only, or part-day only (Details shown at bus stops)	M	Street Market
	Night Bus Services are shown on a separate map on page 143 of this book		Monument or Statue
★ 31	Terminus of Route		Children's Playground
☆	Other Terminal Points		Children's Zoo
i	London Transport Travel Information Centre		Refreshments
⊖	Underground Station		Boating Lake
⇌	British Rail Station		River Trip
	Main Line Terminal		Canal Trip
✈	Air Terminal	▲	Entrance to Towing Path Walk
	Coach Terminal	♫	Open Air Music (Summer)
	Places of Interest		University or College
i	Information Centre - London Visitor and Convention Bureau / City Information		Hospital
SAVOY	Theatres and Cinemas	△	Embassy
		⊖	Starting point for the Original London Transport Sightseeing Tour

Scale 0   ¼   ½   ¾ Mile

Index

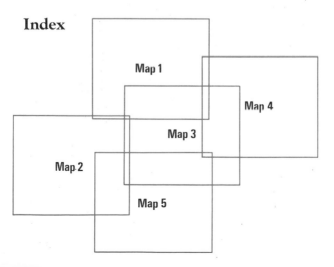

Map 1

Map 4

Map 3

Map 2

Map 5

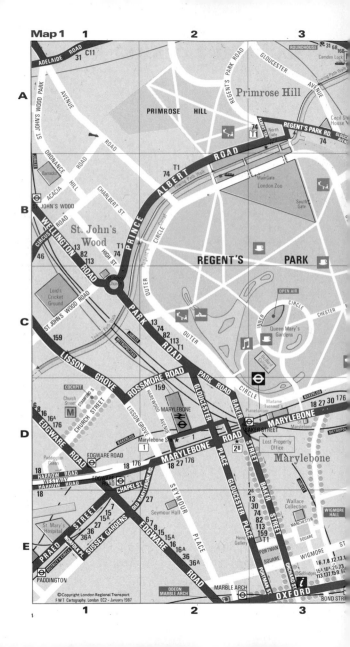

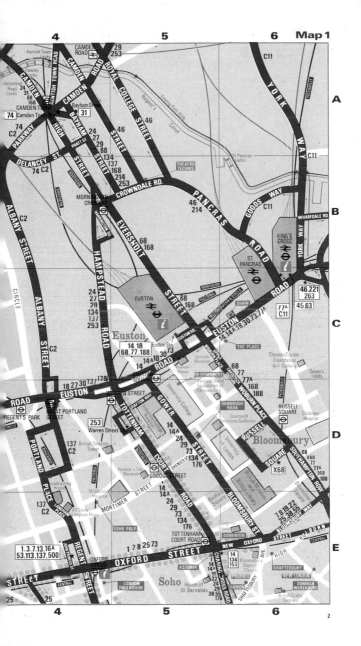

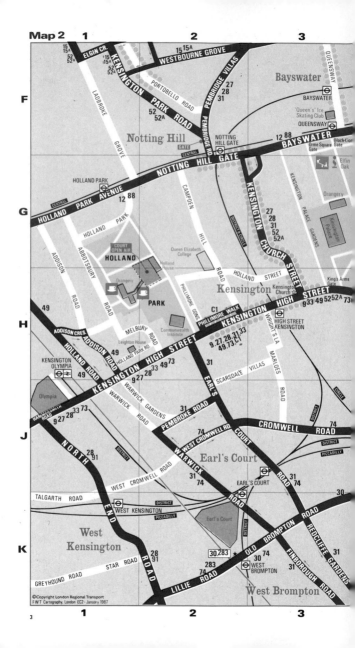

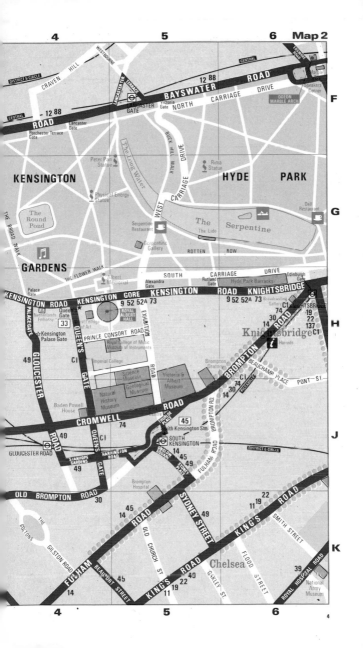

Map 2

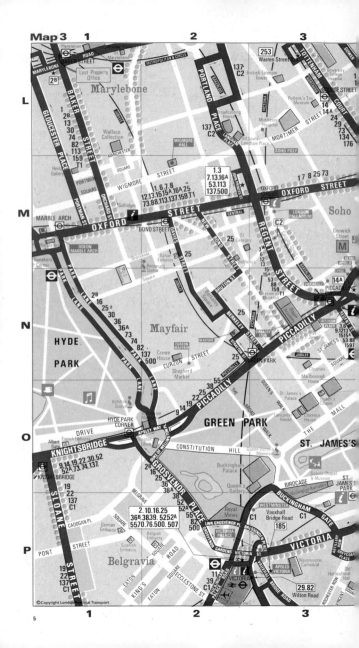

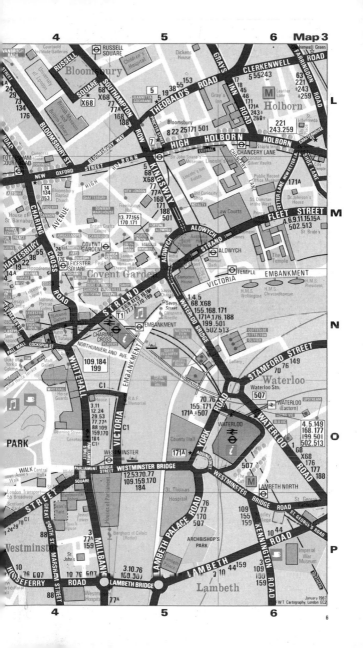

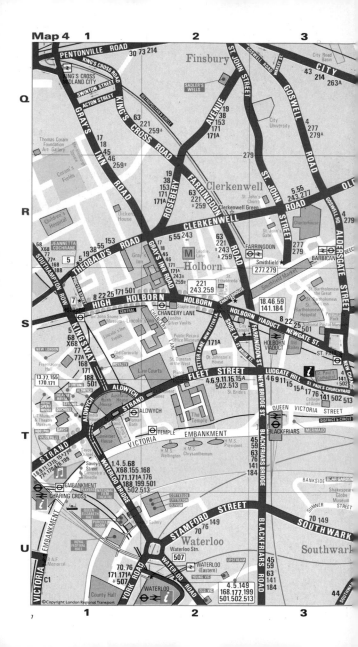

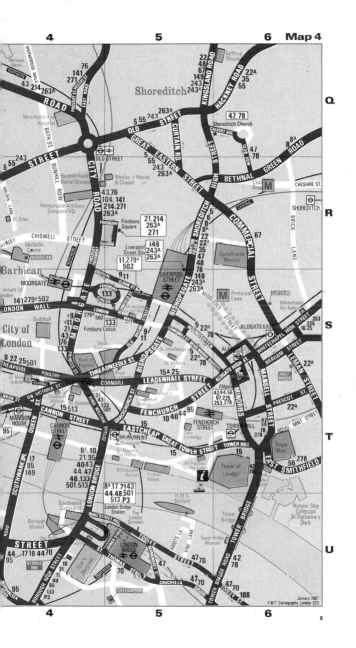

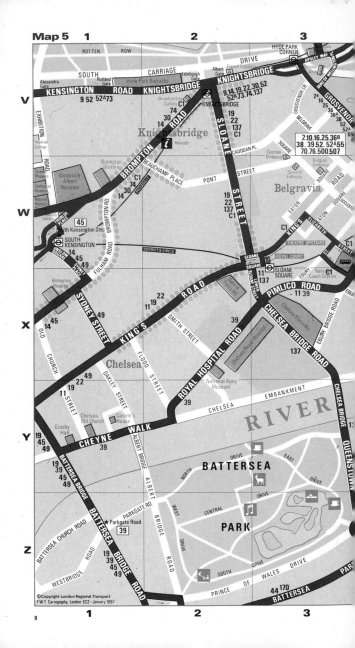

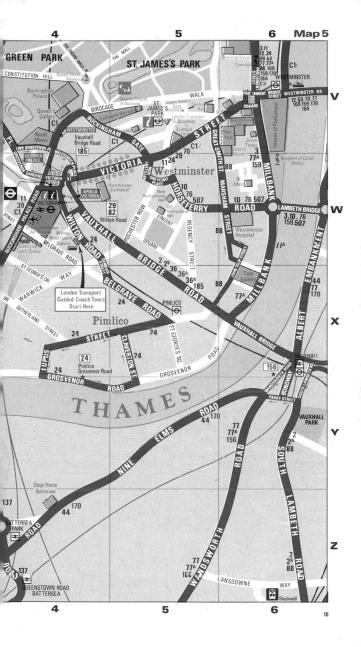

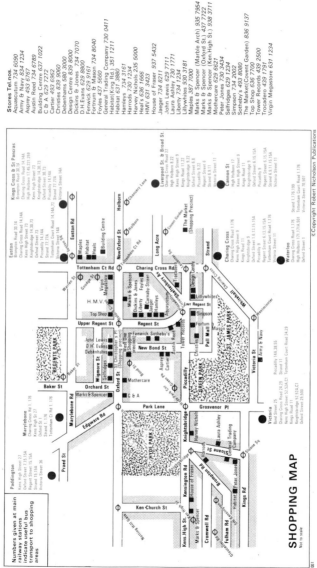

SHOPPING MAP
Not to scale

Numbers given at main railway stations indicate useful bus transport to shopping areas

Stores Tel nos.
Aquascutum 734 6090
Army & Navy 834 1234
Asprey 493 6767
Austin Reed 734 6789
Building Centre 637 1022
C & A 629 7272
Cartier 493 6962
Christies 839 9060
Debenhams 580 3000
Design Centre 839 8000
Dickins & Jones 734 7070
D.H.Evans 629 8800
Fenwick 629 9161
Fortnum & Mason 734 8040
Foyles 437 5660
General Trading Company 730 0411
Habitat(King Rd.) 351 1211
Habitat 631 3880
Hamleys 734 3161
Harrods 730 1234
Harvey Nichols 235 5000
Heal's 636 1666
HMV 631 3423
House of Fraser 937 5432
Jaeger 734 8211
John Lewis 629 7711
Laura Ashley 730 1771
Liberty 734 1234
Lillywhites 930 3181
Maples 387 7000
Marks & Spencer (Marble Arch) 935 7954
Marks & Spencer (Oxford St.) 437 7722
Marks & Spencer (Ken High St.) 938 3711
Mothercare 629 6621
Peter Jones 730 3434
Selfridges 629 1234
Simpson 734 2002
Sotheby's 493 8080
The Market(Covent Garden) 836 9137
Top Shop 636 7700
Tower Records 439 2500
Trocadero 439 7791
Virgin Megastore 631 1234

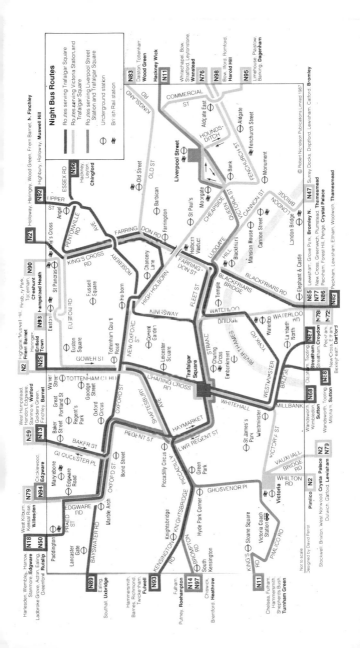

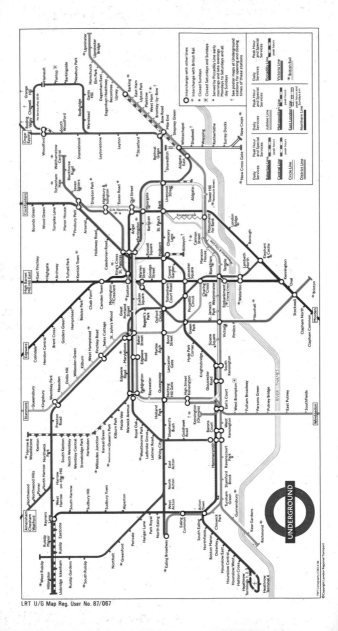

LRT U/G Map Reg. User No. 87/067

The traditional Red London Bus is the Routemaster. It's unique to London Transport, having been in service for over 25 years, and London Coaches operates a fleet of 50, in original livery, for sightseeing, enabling visitors to take in the most famous sights in the most authentic way possible. On sunnier days, open-top Routemasters give an even better view.

A classic sight...

...for some classic sights

Join our 'Original London Transport Sightseeing Tour.' It's the essential introduction to London — the Houses of Parliament, St Paul's, the Tower of London and much more. Frequent daily departures from Piccadilly Circus, Marble Arch, Baker Street and Victoria Street last about 1½ hours and include the services of an experienced Tourist Board-registered guide. Tickets are available from selected travel agents, London Transport & LVCB Information Centres, or at the departure point. Come to Wilton Road Coach Station, Victoria, for your ticket, and you can use this £1 voucher towards your adult fare (adults £5, under-16s £3).

LONDON COACHES

The **Original** London Transport Sightseeing Tour
01-227 3456

Exchange this voucher for

valid until end 1987

£1

THE 1

Off your fare (one voucher per person) when you buy your "Original London Transport Sightseeing Tour" ticket at Wilton Road Coach Station, Victoria.

Sit back and enjoy our experience.

SEE MORE FOR LESS.

A look at Britain with an approved guide

There are many ways to see the sights of London and other interesting parts of the United Kingdom. When you use London Transport Tours, you get the best—with decades of experience, ultra-modern coaches and classic London Buses, plus a warm, friendly service. Our guides are all Tourist Board registered, and they'll make your tour really informative, as well as enjoyable...

LONDON TRANSPORT TOURS

01-227 3456

Sit back and enjoy our experience.